And God Was Our Witness

By

Alicja R. Edwards

1stBooks - rev. 2/7/02

ACKNOWLEDGEMENTS

My special thanks with love and gratitude to my daughter, Tina Zagone; who worked so hard and selfless, giving of her time and patience to help me bring my memoirs to the public. To my son, Chris Edwards, for his steady words of support that kept me going even when it seemed useless at time. To my grandson, Stone, who became my tutor, helping me decode the mysteries of the computer. To my niece, Mary Schumacher whose enthusiasm kept me hopeful; producing and sending me the first disc of my story. To my brother, Jerzy for his continuous moral support and his help to recollect events I had almost forgotten in my story. To Rick Zagone, my son-in-law, for his quiet encouragement.

I would like to thank a great person and my special friend, Janet LaValle, for the countless days spent helping me with matters concerning my book and lifting my spirits during some dark hours.

To Henry Forget of Florida for giving me faith in my own writing and a signal to go forward while he was editing the manuscript; leaving the story in my own style.

To Kathy Zavada, Patty Burczyk, Rudy Sarna, Barbie Whitney Cathy and Dr. O'Donnell for reading the manuscript in its' early stages and loving it. Also Kay and Neal Miller who kept daily vigilance by e-mails filled with analysis and reminders of how interesting it is.

And to my new friend, Sandy Tooley, a mystery writer from Highland, Indiana, aka Lee Driver of the Sam Casey series, who bombarded me with information and advice on how to publish my story.

Lastly, to my recently departed friend, Helen Sarna.

DEDICATION

The written memoirs, I dedicate to my deceased grandmother and parents and to a countless number of forgotten victims who had suffered and perished through the slaved labor in Kazakhstan, Siberia and other regions of Asiatic Russia, during World War II by the rules of the bloody tyrant–Joseph Stalin.

To this day, history keeps silent on the horrible injustice inflicted on Eastern European nations, reminding the world only of the Holocaust and the Nazis; but others suffered also.

"And God Was Our Witness" is meant to bring to light to the rest of the world the events unknown to post–World War II generations; to pay homage to the memory of those valiant and silent victims whose fate became a slow death.

Today, I am free, as are many others who escaped Communist Russia, but that kind of endurance will not be erased from my mind or the minds of others that witnessed the degradation and cruel oppression.

My recollections remain vivid as if it had happened only month's ago—some of a despicable nature, some of a humor with which we tried to live to ensure our survival. The events described in the book are true with names, sequences and locations changed to protect the living, God willing.

FOREWARD

Look down where eternal fog darkens the surface
Of Sluggishness and Chaos
That's earth!

(Adam Mickiewicz)

The moving finger writes; and having writ
Moves on
Nor all your Piety not Wit
Shall lure it back to cancel half a line,
Nor all thy Tears wash out a Word of it.

(Omar Khayyam)

Priceless Freedom has never been perceived or truly understood by anyone, till it
was lost or forcibly taken away.
Only then, one becomes aware of the magnitude of its potency and power in
directing one's life and fate.
Only then, one becomes a survivor or…nothing.

(Alicja R. Edwards—from memoirs of Iran)

"REST IN PEACE—JAN ZABLOCKI—1914-1939"

Read the sign above, inscribed with huge letters into the brass plate, whose fellow mate, a sturdy oak cross glistening with sharp splinters where it cracked in the middle, lay helplessly over the grass covered hill, as if to offer itself in a final gesture of protection to the one who, ironically, could no longer rest in peace.

The bomb did not spare the cemetery. The raid was over, for hours maybe. I kept reading the sign over and over again, the letters staring at me with their black engraving— "rest in peace" —the significance of it seemed a ridiculous contradiction to the violence around us. From now on, there would be no more rest or peace–for either the dead or living.

September 1939—unforgettable! Under the blue skies death ran hand in hand with fear and destruction–bombs, machine guns, explosions–the endless nightmare that tormented our country from the first day of war, seemed to hang on like a prolonged and painful illness to the very end, so incongruous with the azure sky and golden autumn. The nightmare persisted while the sun shone on, shamelessly, watching the end of a tragic drama–the death of Poland. History was repeating itself and I, who, just a few months ago, had studied the subject in a classroom, became an eyewitness to a new chapter. This phase, I thought, would remain in my mind like an etched plaque in remembrance of the past and oncoming cataclysms in thousands of tomorrows. Yet, in the years to come, the detailed reports would be reduced to the essential facts only.

The screams of horror will be expressed only in novels and movie scripts for a second-grade imitation of a true-life tragedy. The painful memories will be recalled in poems and plays with well-suited words and phrases, but as for the naked truth of the feelings, you could not recapture it and associated events you would not dare to recreate. Thus, the human Gahenna of the 1939 war will fade into a legend, except for short paragraphs and brutally official and cold statements; history will move on, patiently recording events—a loyal secretary to God.

Someday seemed like another planet. Yesterday meant everything because it happened already and you were a part of it, living through each moment, cherishing it as some secretly stolen prize. Now though the passing time left the imprints of rapid events like a bloody tattoo, hurting deeply, it was the sign that you were still alive and that was of the most importance.

If only one could shut off the past, yet strange, how the fall of a first bomb carved the moat around the bygone days of the past month and lifted them high as in a dream, where I could look upon and long for them, but never reach and touch them again.

Somehow I knew there would never be another year or day like those that remained behind me. The remembered peace and secure life made them seem like an imaginary fairyland I once walked through—the carefree moments stood out in memory like dimensional pictures, inspiring the yearning for them to come back and creating a Shangri-La out of something that was the happy days of my childhood.

Though the war didn't actually speed my age, I realized slowly that my thoughts and feelings became progressively different. There were new elements emerging from hiding, unknown to me a few weeks ago. The uncertainty of wartime, brought puzzle-like problems of a difficult nature, leaving us to cope with one then another, until the pieces fitted together, but the picture somehow always appeared dark, gloomy, devoid of any hope, for the near future.

In those oppressive moments, I tried to escape reality by seeking refuge in my memory. I would sit for hours sometimes, perfectly still, recalling silly incidents, or not thinking at all, not realizing that my spiritual escapades were changing me into a lazy and listless individual. At home, I was no help at all; instead, with various problems arising I became an additional one. Places not frequented by people I welcomed as my sanctuaries, away from the faces of even my very close friends, for it seemed that all of a sudden the world became so cold and everyone was an enemy. I played games each day, cheating myself, pretending to see and hear only what I wanted to, shrinking from the responsibilities and tasks laid upon me by my family and simply refused to participate in living, at least for the time being.

I might have gone on my solitary way, but for a small incident. One morning I was going through the drawers (just any drawers) looking for remnants of yesterday, for usually the things I came upon were connected with the past. However, that day was not a day for the serious analysis of a safety pin, which kept my high-school beret in the latest style. I opened the lower drawer of our armoire, which was stuck as usual from a load of shoes it carried, most of them from the summer. I pulled harder and became curious when noticing the folds of white tissue paper around something unshapely looking. I tore the delicate paper away and a lump came to my throat. It was a pair of silver sandals purchased for my first dance, a sweet sixteen birthday to be exact. What a debut I would have made!

The entwined leather straps lay in the nest of white tissue, giving off a soft metallic luster and exposing the surface of the pinkish soles, without a smudge of wear, so dainty and virginal–still awaiting the ball that never came, the first waltz and bashful smile…oh the anticipation of it, but it all went to rest in the corner of the armoire drawer as I folded the thin paper over the silver slippers.

Thus, without tears and bitter regrets, I took my first step away from my imaginary Shangri-La of the past and rejoined the present at its pace. The changeover was harsh, but it held a promise of better grades for a graduation into a maturity and understanding of my own psyche to guide me through a severe crisis that I was faced with now.

How well I remember those first steps as a premature adult, painful and uncertain, like a little girl playing in her mama's high-heeled shoes. With a mouth as dry as cotton, I tried to scorn the sharp whistling sound cutting the air, a prelude to a bomb explosion and pretended to mock the danger with clumsily disguised nonchalance of heroines I remembered reading about in novels. I tried, but instead, my insides quivered violently, my knees knocked disobediently and I had a sudden stupid desire to be a freak with six hands in order to hold my ears, head and stomach at the same time.

Now the bombing had ceased and as I looked over the cemetery, a strange stillness hung over it like an invisible protective cloak. It penetrated the air and reached into my soul, pouring in peace and calm resignation. My glance halted at the enormous pits along the graves, rasped by the fallen bomb. All of a sudden this place, claimed as my retreat many times in recent days, now frightened me. With a shock, I thought, what am I doing amongst the dead? I turned and wanted to run with fear as though the ghosts might begin attacking me for trespassing in their own grief over the raids, disturbing their eternal rest. Without looking back, I started toward my home.

Half of September had gone by. Gradually it became quiet, very quiet. The skies weren't shadowed anymore with silver sentinels of death and destruction, as echoes of machine guns and cannons faded. The atmosphere was suffocating with silence as before a storm. The seventeenth day had answered the question weighing on the minds of millions of people. From the eastern borders, the hammer and sickle marched into Poland, shouting to Poles the promises of liberation (we didn't know from what) and everlasting protection. Our fears had materialized, we were trapped from both sides and though Poles remained Poles with their heart and soul, Poland, the country, on the map, existed no more.

****

So it all began in 1939, but it really happened in 1940; April 13, Friday, 2:30a.m.; two knocks on the door–then silence. I knew it was "them."

I was dreaming an awful dream and while part of my mind subconsciously was wading in the hazy world of the unknown, I could faintly hear the low voices beyond my window. Once I even caught the sound of clinking metal. My heart beat slowly, but it seemed to me, louder than the large clock in my bedroom. I knew now, as I was fully awake, my dream had gone and a great tension was arising in me, gripping my inner being, choking the air.

I looked at the yellowed face of the clock and saw how late it was–2:30am– the thieves hour, the time when crimes are committed. There was another knock, followed by a loud but rather muffled shout: "Open up the door!" (Odkryvaitie dvieri). Then silence again. I assumed my mother was awake, keeping the habitual vigil at the dark windows as she had done for the past few months since

3

the arrest of our father. Through the long hours of the night, her motionless silhouette could be seen sometimes till dawn, forever, waiting. Now, there would be no more waiting. How strange...the house remained quiet, without any sounds of approaching steps or opening of the door. The clock kept ticking, with each musical tick of a second bringing us closer to our fate. Only the oak doors and stucco walls kept us separated from it, but I knew it was there outside in the darkness of the night, waiting for us.

A prayer came to my lips but the words, whispered automatically, lost their meaning. My mind was empty of any thoughts except trying to guess how many seconds were left to the zero hour. My instinct told me it was very close and, by now, I was certain my mother was aware of what was happening, but more likely, wasn't going to open the door. Her refusal was an open challenge and common by now for all condemned Poles, a defiant attitude and "come and get me" routine. And come and get us they did. As a rule, the members of the NKVD were patient, but also as a rule, wasting time wasn't one of their habits. Thus, in order to retain their prestige, they followed the normal procedure. I was still counting the seconds and before I arrived at the zero hour, there was a thunderous crash coming down like an avalanche on our heavy door and over the threshold poured the invasion of darkly clad figures. I couldn't quite distinguish who they were, militia or soldiers, because the house was still dark. My ears caught the words spoken in Russian first, rather quietly, then as if out of the blue, a violent curse ripped through the air. Evidently the light switch couldn't be found. Then a click. Our grandmother came to the rescue. Any foul language always got the best of her. She could never understand why people had to swear. My bedroom door was slightly ajar, which allowed me to get a first glance at "them." From the noises of moving feet and voices carrying different dialects of Polish, Ukrainian and dominating Russian language, there appeared to be quite a number of persons. Someone pushed the door wide open to my room and what a sight appeared in front of my eyes! Our kitchen was flooded with uniforms of all sorts. At first, I thought half of the Russian police had paid us this nocturnal visit, but then I noticed the cocoa-colored coats of the Red Army and local militia, all mixed with now well known blue caps of the mighty NKVD.

To think that all this was done in our honor: two women, a young boy, my brother, and me. I suppose we should have been flattered.

The rising hum of the voices was interrupted by the angry shout: "Why didn't you opened up?" There was no answer, but I assumed it was mother the NKVD member was unleashing his wreath on. The words in Russian kept flowing faster and louder, not exactly as in a conversation, and to put it plainly, the tovarish was sending all of us to hell. Mother kept quiet, lucky for us, for the way things were shaping up, we were heading there fast enough without mother irritating them further with her anger. I strained my ears to hear more, but my attention was diverted by the sound of heavy footsteps coming toward my bedroom. On an impulse, I dived under the pile of goose feathers (generally known in my country as a "pierzyna"). Heaven knows why I did that. Now it seems so childish and stupid, but at that time I was filled with fear and cowardice. No power on earth could have made me face this situation with at least a little gumption or spunk; instead, for at least five full minutes in the dark tunnel of soft feathers, I knew the comfort of warmth and peace I wouldn't know again for the next three years. Only five precious minutes, then I realized the "hide and seek" game was over, when a stream of light sneaked in under the covers and somewhere above my head, my eyes glimpsed the beam reflected in something long, pointed and shining. I blinked my eyes, staring at the object, which I thought resembled a knife, perhaps, a bit larger then my mother's kitchen bread knife. I blinked again, but the strange article looked dangerously the same!

The third time I closed my eyes, praying for it to be just a nasty illusion, but when I opened them again, I knew this wasn't a hallucination or table cutlery! The point of a flickering bayonet, holding up one corner of the pierzyna, was silently commanding me to get out of the bed, or else! Imagining what else could be, I panicked again and dived under the covers once more and came out to the light at the foot of the bed, which put me at a fair distance from the ugly blade and the rest of the part that it was attached to.

I was kneeling in my long flannel nightgown, I still remember its peach color, speckled with a confetti-like dots design, holding on to a bed rail, trying to collect my wits, when I noticed the soldier who held the carbine. Without thinking, I blessed myself hurriedly and a cold sweat broke out all over me. If the sight of a rifle with the shinny steel attached to it left me horrified, the glance at his face was worse still. I swallowed hard, as my slowly returning wits had vanished again, for I was facing a person whose looks we were not accustomed to seeing frequently or none if at all, (except maybe a last cinema series of Fu-Manchu. I was staring fully at a face of a man from the Far East, Mongolia maybe, I was guessing. His features were so different, the ochre-color face had protruding wide-set cheekbones and eyes slanted with inky dark pupils, now glaring at me at this moment: "davai davai, skoro-podnimaisia" (come on quick, get up)he was saying. He looked like a picture out of my geography book. I am sure under different circumstances I would have been somewhat fascinated, imagining him in his national ensemble, a true figure from the far away steppes we had learned about from history class. But now, as a plainly speaking Russian soldier, it seemed the devil himself had arrived to claim me and my soul.

"Davai, davai"...brought me back to reality and I tried to reason that actually seeing his unique features wasn't the first time for me. There were quite a few of them, members of the Red Army, occupying our town. We saw them occasionally riding in madly speeding, rickety trucks, while circling the area many times around, the old soviet trick, of trying to impress our people with their force and might in number.

5

But it was the strange eventuality of our arrest, I believe, bringing this man of a different race so close, face to face, the effect of the horrid night, the nearness of the guns, all magnifying the incident into a fantasy of terror, making this soldier look as if the ghost of Ghengis Khan had broken out of his tomb and was on the loose in this part of Poland. Though his manner and appearance seemed unfriendly, he meant no harm, at least he gave no sign of it. With jerky gestures and repetition of the same "davai, davai"…he insisted I get ready, which wasn't very easy, because the uniformed mob was everywhere, and my hands were clumsier than ever and my stomach behaved like the time when the first bombs were falling.

My grandmother was busy in the kitchen, packing. The sight of her cheered me up. She was all dressed (very warmly it appeared) for the hems of her skirts and sleeves were showing three different colors and she looked quite chubby, which she wasn't.

Grandma was the only person in our family who, without wasting any time on arguing, talking or dreaming, had faced the facts and assumed the responsibilities with the ancient stoicism. The swiftness, with which she kept stuffing our huge vacation wicker basket with victuals, amazed me. After all, she was nearing her eighty-sixth birthday, but just the same, I didn't lift a finger to help. Like the soldiers guarding each door, I also stood and watched her until loud noises in another room aroused my curiosity. I hesitated before the door, listening to the fragments of the shrill conversation, guessing the NKVD was there talking to our mama. Well, not exactly talking! Good God, mother, not being of a complacent nature, was making things quite difficult.

I suspected from the very beginning she wasn't going to give in so easily this time–still having fresh in mind the trauma of our father's being arrested last October. This being a second battle, she knew a defeat was inevitable, but as long as she was breathing, she would give them hell. Sometimes, to this day, I keep wondering who actually was the victim of that night?

"Idie k tchortu," meaning go to hell or the devil kept repeating itself constantly, more often than any other words. I peeked from behind the heavy door drapery and saw our eloquent mama, standing in the middle of the room, dumping the bedding into the old tapestry bedspread lying on the floor. Each time she threw an article on the top, I heard her blasting loudly "zaraza"(a plaque), "svolotch" (a scum), "psia krew" (no translation), a very uncomplimentary selection of words released while her temper reached its worst.

One of the big square pillows landed on its corner and sat on top of the feathered pyramid like Napoleon's hat; another smaller version called "jasiek," was thrown carelessly, missed the pile and fell by the officer's feet. There was a small rip on the side of it, letting some feathers out. The officer kicked the little "jasiek," filling the room with white floaters, then started to sneeze and swear to beat hell! Quickly, I bent down and tried to pick up the pillow, but mother almost stepped on my hand with a glare: "Go pack your own things," she yelled.

The situation began to look very serious to me and I finally realized we were being sent away! I had to pack. I felt like a whipped puppy and without a further word retreated to my room. Passing through the kitchen, I noticed the basket was almost full to the top. Where did all that food come from? It was strange to think that for two months, we were mostly content with barley and potato soups—our only main course, without other courses or desserts. Our huge appetites didn't require any provocations and anything edible in sight was devoured with great speed. Even the substitute for an afternoon tea, which at first we spat out with disgust, was welcomed later and greatly enjoyed.

The wartime tea was brewed from our own dried strawberry roots and judging by its color, it gave an illusion of once-remembered tea, but the flavor? Well, even our imagination couldn't stretch that far, but mixed with mother's jams put up during the summer and supported with a dried chunk of bread, it always passed as a great filler until that supply had diminished and mother, without reluctance, traded her best clothes in the nearby villages for anything related to food, to stop the never ending refrain: "What's there to eat?"

Now looking at the various sacks, the colorful pre-war tin boxes and glass jars with conserves, I could hardly believe my eyes. Grandma was pulling a rabbit out of a hat! I kept looking at the cupboards and the kitchen "credenza," which one of them was a hat? It always remained a mystery, for as far as I recalled, my brother and I explored every inch of them thoroughly many times before, without much success, but here in front of my eyes, the huge basket, the size of a sea trunk, undoubtedly was filled with food. It looked like a horn of plenty, mysteriously stored away for what we called "a black hour," and tonight, this being April 13, 1940, was the darkest of hours.

It didn't seem important any more trying to find out where the accumulated stash was hidden, as I soon discovered, I wasn't welcome in the kitchen, either. Like my mother, grandma didn't approve of my puttering about the rooms, her weary eyes were scolding and she seemed out of breath, angrily telling me to hurry up and pack. That was it! The awful truth was hovering about but still didn't quite penetrate my mind, which refused to accept it, although the indications were everywhere for me to realize that we were to leave.

When I entered the bedroom, the incarnation of Ghengis Khan was in a trance, studying the big wall clock, his eyes twitching to the right and left with the movement of the shiny pendulum. There was a trace of a childish smile around his mouth. He turned his head when I walked in, resuming the authority of a guard. "Come on, quick"(davai, skoro), he kept urging. The tension and fear were slowly wearing off and repeated orders of haste didn't have any effect on me any more as I turned my attention to packing. With a vicious tug, I pulled my suitcase from the shelf of the old wardrobe. It fell with a loud clatter and a cloud of dust. I felt sorry for mistreating my old companion of school days and train rides. I opened the lid gently and winced at the sight of a small brown ticket to my high-school town of Stryj, lying on the bottom of it. I left it there and with a rage, began to throw my clothes into the valise.

My heavy ski shoes landed on top of my uniform, with small chunks of dirt settling into the folds of the navy blue, light wool material and silver buttons still shiny over the blue edging of the collar and cuffs. My favorite skating set of Himalayan wool sweater lay squashed in the corner with suede gloves and unfolded taffeta ribbons for my hair. As the shelves and drawers kept getting empty, my suitcase resembled more of an untidy laundry basket than a traveling bag…and I didn't care. With a last item sitting safely on top of a messy pile, I finally managed to close the lid with the help of my behind and heaved a sigh. The mission accomplished, I wondered what to do next, without being reminded how useless I was at my age. Then I decided, for the next few minutes or more, I would be just that –useless. Sitting on my valise, I looked over the room, taking into my mind every detail–the way the furniture was arranged, the patterns on the stucco painted wall, the picture of the daffodils between the willow branches hanging aside my bed, the soft light seeping through a green lamp shade with a bronze ballerina sitting in a restful pose, underneath–the shiny parquet floor now soiled with muddy footprints, but all the same, the room remained somehow peaceful and serene. It still appeared untouched but for the crumpled covers on my bed and the soldier standing in front of the wall clock.

When will I see it again? Will I ever see it again? The questions seemed to unfold and twist to serpentine doubts, without any immediate answers. Everything looked so hopeless, as if the end of the world! I kept gazing at the familiar walls and corners of the room, trying to capture the image of every feature to carry with me as a silent souvenir.

Above the headboard of my bed, I caught a soft shimmer, walked over and reached for a small picture of the Black Madonna. The thin silver thread glittered, although the brocade material was getting old now, yet the dark face of Madonna with a scar across her cheek projected the strength and faith. "Matko Boska Czestohowska," (pray for us), I kept whispering, believing it was our only salvation, for the rest of the world wasn't aware of our afflictions or simply didn't give a damn! The picture of Madonna was quite small and I managed easily to slip it between my "packed" clothes, noticing at the same time, that the soldier was watching me, intently. I thought he would interfere any minute, but he left me alone.

Somehow it seemed strange for us to be allowed to take so many of our possessions. Whatever lay within the reach and sight got crammed into the baskets, sacks and luggage, practically everything in larger items, except the furniture and the house itself. How considerate this seemed, at least then, at the beginning, but later we learned, we under estimated the twisted thinking of the

Soviet rulers, whose speculations always had deep-seated causes lying underneath.

Right now, the house resembled a beehive. The NKVD was becoming very impatient, stating we have detained long enough. "Davai and skoro" was the motto of this night. The harsh voices were urging us to make haste, —like vampires they were in a hurry, before dawn would arrive and catch them in their morbid ritual of wrong. My brother's blond head appeared in a doorway: "Better come quick," he said, "they want all of us, in there." He pointed to the other room and disappeared. I felt a cold twist and a harder thumping in my chest, but I followed my brother. The room where all were gathered seemed hazy from the blue veils of smoke from the strong Russian cigarettes. Four members of our family looked a lonely and pitiful group among the uniforms and rifles. The climax of the ghastly night was drawing near. The officer sitting by the table was shuffling papers in front of him. To this day I am amazed at the amount of records they gathered on us, useless at this point, for we were of no importance or danger to them, but as in the rest of the world, so were they also wrapped in the "red tape," giving our eviction or disposal of us some official basis. Now the officer picked up one of the documents and stood up "Listen" (svushitie)- he cleared his throat and began to read.

We didn't quite understand much of it, but from recognizable words, we had assumed this was an expulsion act with an explanation of the reasons why we couldn't live in Poland any more, why we had to start a new life in the Soviet Union. One of the reasons was a horrifying disclosure, a shock in learning for the first time that our father had been executed as an enemy of the USSR.

The reading became monotonous. We had already absorbed the essence, the verdict—we were to leave our country of Poland, forever.

Mother tried hard not to cry, but her eyes were getting helplessly red. Quietly she said, "We are ready," then turning slowly, she slipped her heavy black coat on. I never realized how much she had aged recently. There were deep lines set in her forehead and her face, always so smooth, had lost its roundness and color. Strange, how looking at her each day, we missed the changes in her features, but now the crushing truths of her aging as well as our capture would emerge. I felt sadness and pity for her especially.

Outside was still semidark. The wind whipped the black contours of trees in the orchard and unfriendly clouds were pushing across the already graying sky. Somewhere the rooster began to crow, nature's alarm clock for those more fortunate who could open their eyes to the familiar walls and curtained windows, the familiar faces around, then sigh in gladness and thank God for the new day.

All of us were ready to depart, still dry eyed, waiting impatiently for mother, who still seemed to linger at the house for a reason, so I thought. Minutes raced by, but mama was not coming out. Being both curious and worried, I decided to check and see what was delaying her exit. I went back to the house and my sagging spirit was uplifted. As sad as it was, it became amusing. Mother was turning the house upside down, pushing everything standing in her way to the side, her cheeks wet from tears were glowing pink from the excitement and anger in searching for a small case containing the family papers and jewelry. As she propelled herself around the rooms, she was repeating that she wasn't going anywhere till she found it! I couldn't believe my eyes, she was actually giving the ultimatum to this pack of Huns!

One of the officers of the NKVD tried to steer her through the door leading outside, but she slapped his hands down viciously: "Keep your bony fingers away from me," she shouted and elbowed her way past the guards standing by the door leading to a room occupied by a Soviet major and his pregnant wife. The Russian couple had lived with us for over three months now, both of them being rather quiet and pleasant and although a little elusive, were likable as two human beings. Tonight, throughout the whole ordeal of our arrest, their door remained mysteriously closed, though I was sure they were not sleeping besides, our mother's soprano would have wakened anybody and if the major didn't hear her before, he surely heard her now.

The door had opened and out came the major, dressed in a full uniform. "What is going on?" he asked, as if he didn't know. He looked at the group, as if waiting for an explanation and while the soldiers were snapping to attention, the head NKVD was trying to relate the cause of trouble, which in this case happened to be our mama. During the exchange of the Red Army military protocols, mother decided to act on her own. She sprang like a weasel, past the major standing in the doorway and disappeared inside their room. Within seconds we heard the major's wife scream! Mother came rushing out, clutching a small case tightly against her chest and a pleading voice trailing behind her in Russian: "It's my phonograph"-(et moi patiaphon)! Major stopped my mother in her tracks, released the grip on the case and opened the lid, gently. It was a phonograph, with a crank handle and a record I listened to so often, a song by a then popular singer named Kozin, a Gypsy baritone. In desperation to get us out of the house, everyone helped to search for our family heirlooms and soon the case was found. Finally the door of our porch had slammed shut behind us and the NKVD officer wiped his forehead, muttering to himself: "the devil" and "family"—I guess he meant us.

The blurry shadows of the night were now visible shapes of the neighboring homes and trees. The horses stood motionless, only the steam from their nostrils gave a sign of life in them. I felt a few drops of rain on my cheek. Good God, of all things, we certainly didn't need any rain. One by one, we climbed aboard the cart and tried to settle on top of our belongings, which wasn't an easy task, making me wish I was half of my pint size and had feet shorter for the limited space I had to accommodate them. My brother curled up somewhere in the middle and all I could see of him, was the blond top.

Why weren't we leaving? It was pure torture to linger looking at the house and our orchard still slumbered as in a deep sleep. To break the agony of waiting, I began to count...one, two, three...got past ten, when I saw the major coming out of the house, carrying something large in front of him which I recognized to be a sack of potatoes, he meant for us to have.

"Take them with you, you will use them," he said quietly. Mother's face had darkened; angrily she kicked the sack and tried to push it off the cart: "Get them out of here, half of them are rotten" —then she turned away, disgusted, but the Russian was not giving up: "take them, you will thank me for it!" Mother leaned out of the cart with a wicked grin: "Yes, I have a lot to thank you for—my husband, my home, my family...surely you're joking, major!" —and then she kept on, "remember, we are going to the Soviet Union, your red paradise, the land of the most and the best, why should I worry about a sack of rotten potatoes?" Finally she just couldn't resist the last mouthful, while she snickered: "I just can't wait to taste the oranges, grown using your grand tractors!" then she cackled like an old shrew.

That used to be a standard joke on Soviet bragging about the mighty power of outdated Russian machinery, the legendary tractors that were supposed to make everyone's life easy, a sort of magical "red genie." As a defeated nation, being under their occupation, we used the insulting jokes as a small weapon to needle their haughty egos. The frustrated and idle minds of Poles were busy, keeping up the morale and our national spirit in laughing at the conquerors, the Soviets, who I am sure didn't like being the butts of our jokes. Yet thinking was still free and there was hardly a power to stop your mind from expressing personal beliefs and ideas. Almost each day, new and fresh quips would surface, bringing a smile and a chuckle during the hard and dark months of occupation.

The major didn't flinch at mother's sarcasm; he paled a bit, but still tried with both hands to hold up the dirty sack to keep it from slipping off the cart. Mother didn't help, but the potatoes made their way with us to Russia. He saluted us in a farewell: "Do svidania," he said, and wished us good luck. There was something in his expression, halting a build up of bitter hate in me for every Russian in sight, perhaps it was the sincere sympathy expressed in his eyes somehow held back with a self control of the emotions, making him appear as any of us, except for a discipline and obedience to the country he was part of.

"Go!" came the signal from the NKVD, one slap of the whip and the horses moved. Our long journey had begun.

*****

Thus, we staggered through our first turning point, on our way to "the red paradise" and though decisions on our uncertain fate belonged to the bloody Soviet leaders, we sensed that each step was camouflaging a deep purpose beneath. The ensuing years would reveal their corrupt plans, but as of today, this deplorable act meant to us the imprisonment and punishment for the wrong we hadn't done or weren't told.

The streets were still empty and very quiet, not a soul in sight. I closed my eyes and buried my head between the sack of potatoes and hastily thrown bed covers. I wasn't sure, but I thought mama was sobbing quietly. I put my hands over my ears. It helped. I could only hear the staccato of horses' hooves on the unevenly paved streets. Then the rain came. At first the fat drops fell slowly, and then faster and faster until it seemed that the skies opened up and the water was everywhere. Our cart absorbed a lot of it and the only waterproof apparel I had on, was my brown rubber boots, now being buried under the sack of smelly potatoes. Grandma threw a heavy quilt over my brother and I and told us to pray. I realized how calm she was throughout this difficult ordeal, without a word of complaint or disgust on her part, while being old and uncomfortable, undoubtedly suffering in silence. It didn't cross my or my brother's mind what turmoil she was going through by the uprooting of the family, leaving the home she lived in all of her married life—her children, the friends and the surroundings she loved so much. Being young and selfish, we only thought how miserable it was for us, but as usual, she was more concerned with my brother and I. "Cover up and try to stay dry," she said, "there is nothing we can do but take care of ourselves to keep well. You are young and strong and must train your mind and body to cope with future hardships—this is only the beginning." She sighed deeply and kept on: "I know everything seems so harsh, unbearable, -the whole night like a bad dream -leaving everything and now this rain, not exactly the cheerful sight, but you can begin telling yourself—it's nothing."

I realized quite well what she was talking about, but aside from that I also knew, with her being old and I so young, both of us were very wet and miserable. The water kept seeping through the sack of potatoes and I felt mud drying on my cheek. I wiped it off though it was supposed to be good for your complexion. The rain didn't stop–so cold, ugly, penetrating deep into our bones. Funny, how many times before we had gone in the early spring and loved being soaked with the first April showers, changing by the tall stoves, leaning against the warm, shiny tiles, drinking cocoa or tea with honey, and contemplating going out to get wet all over again. This was the right time, April, and we were getting soaked, but the joy and excitement were gone–there was nothing left even to our wild imagination, not one prop to change those drops into something else but cold and stinging.

LEAVING HOME

Everything around was hostile and gloomy. When the sun finally came out from behind the dark clouds, we realized, looking over the countryside, that we were traveling in a quite different direction we had expected to. We passed the village we used to hike to during the summer for fresh dark bread and sour milk with thick cream settled on top of it. The vision of small, shiny, tan and brown pottery jars kept appearing in front of my eyes over the plowed fields. Although we were far past the village, I had quite a time brushing the picture away, knowing my ever-hungry stomach would catch up with a bad idea, and start the nagging for food. I tried to absorb grandma's advice, repeating "that's nothing," but the common sense of this attitude didn't quite agree with a feeling of hunger.

Two hours had passed and we were still in the middle of nowhere. The small farms we went by began to come to life. Peasants doing their morning chores, didn't turn around to look at the creeping cart, although I imagined their hearts must have been beating faster and hands perhaps trembled, envisioning themselves and the families atop a cart like ours, sometime in the future.

I saw terror flashing through a woman's face as she was standing in the doorway of a dwelling. She blessed herself and quickly disappeared inside. It seemed as we were already marked and condemned even to our own people. The last few hours had put us into an inferior status, separating us from the others, branding us as prisoners, "outlaws," - it just wasn't clear, whose laws we had transgressed…

It didn't matter what we were called, it wouldn't have changed anything. Grandma was right. We had to learn to draw strength out of anguish and heartaches to handle each crisis and be prepared. We were chosen, although unfortunately, out of many in our large population and while the world wasn't aware of this terrible injustice being inflicted upon the innocent people, we knew that only God was our witness and as long as there was God, crimes such as this one must be paid for by those who committed them.

Hours had passed of our bouncing up and down, and by now it occurred to us that this ride was stretching too long. Our speculation was, we were being herded into a larger unknown-to-us town, with a concentration of "special" trains.

This so-called "special" train, which included the ordinary cargo boxcars used for transporting cattle, was waiting for us. What made them so special was a symbolic feature attached to each boxcar, an insignificant long and narrow chimney, the sight of which made the blood curdle, for whenever it appeared at the railway tracks, it silently foretold doom and the long journey east. By noon, our cart was approaching a town larger than the one we lived in. One would have thought it was a market day; with the multitude of people, wagons and horses, but no products for sale.

TRAINS

We saw familiar faces of our friends, their tears, red eyes. Someone yelled: "Jak sie masz?" (How are you?), not quite an appropriate question, but it was a greeting.

Our burden seemed to lessen, for we were sharing it with old friends and many others. The carts, one by one, were driven alongside the long line of empty boxcars and slowly the process of unloading and loading had begun–like cattle!

Realization descended on those in the first group entering the black entrance of the sliding doors. Women clung to their belongings, still lying in the wagons, until they had to be dragged away and helped into the boxcars. A gray-haired old man gripped the sides of the heavy steel frame of the door as if to gain more strength, then looking skyward, in a loud voice called on God's help then cursed Soviet Russia and bloody Stalin, disappearing inside. The small boxcar seemed like a hungry dragon, swallowing families one by one, the jaws opened, till you couldn't quite believe the capacity for containing so many persons.

We were still sitting, waiting our turn, and watching the cars being filled. Even today, I can still hear the sound of the slowly turning wheels of the heavy sliding doors, low and threatening, like the growling of a mad dog, followed by a short slam. The doors were shut. The heavy iron bar had slid into the loops and people inside were demoted, pushed down, below their status. Civilization was taking a step backward, giving a seat to an old, primitive law, the law of the mighty and the power of a fist.

It was April 13, the longest day in my life. The sun shone brightly, unconcerned. It sneaked its curious rays behind the bars of the first boxcar, where a face of a young girl appeared, a girl perhaps my age, with light hair, untidily framing the tear-stained red cheeks. So young, innocent... a prisoner, condemned without cause, doomed, because God only knew why! Was there any law written against such acts of injustice and tyranny? Where the hell was the rest of the world? Where was the League of Nations? The Geneva Convention? To hell with treaties, non-aggression pacts. To hell with diplomats, glib and slippery, full of eloquent nonsense and their clumsy documents! What power did they possess stored safely away behind a glass in musty museums like fragile souvenirs!

YOUNG PRISONER

The swastika, the red sickle had laws of their own, curse them all! The war was their ally!

"Inter arma, leges silens" - Cicero once said, "Laws are silent during a war," and we were the living proof of this deafening silence. Time had elapsed since ancient Rome and Cicero, the planet Earth had changed its surface and nature, allowing us slowly out of the wilderness of habits and concepts, yet how far had we distanced ourselves from skins and stone hammers? At times it seems that we only exchanged them, improved the shapes, concealing the intent under the modern weaponry...a high-tech deceit.

Our emotions, although tamed by civilized upbringing, tend so easily to revert to the primitive instincts of our Neanderthal fathers, betraying the progress of the 20th century.

In the times when the world has striven to aid humanity, some nations traded noble causes for false convictions of their own beliefs, throwing half of our sphere into a turmoil and bringing so much suffering to countless people.

I began to count the boxcars, wondering which one would swallow us into its darkness, not that it made any difference, they were all the same, faded red, hiding behind the door a space we would be confined within for uncertain numbers of days. Just the thought of being enclosed, without moving freely, took my breath away and I shivered. We had escaped the bombs, then you could run or die, but here it was so hopeless, no way out! Each moment a confusion of guesses and thoughts scurrying around like frightened birds tired in flight but too scared to rest.

The empty carts began to pull away in front of us and I almost wished we were already inside. Only ten hours had gone by, yet the short time had been filled with crises, imbedded in the memory, etching the pictures we were not likely to forget.

Suddenly our cart was at the dark cavity of a boxcar, our belongings were flung on the wooden floor and we were in. The red soldiers helped us over the narrow threshold, still chanting the repetitious "skoro, skoro" then we found ourselves the first occupants in the then empty car, giving us first choice of electing a space, of upper or lower berth. Naturally we chose to go up toward the light, fresh air and the bars. We settled in the corner, by the window, watching our space shrinking as the families kept coming in. From five wide planks of the upper shelf, we found ourselves squeezed into half of them, discovering the strange positions the body can twist itself into, out of necessity. In a very short time, our car was full, crammed I would say! As seen by us, the upper shelves were abuzz with activity, each person trying to arrange as close to a comfortable position as the space allowed, which was for most the part, futile. God forbid Siberia to be our destination! No, it wasn't Siberia we were heading for, but the journey was just as long and harsh.

There was still one empty space below us we weren't aware of, but in no time we knew the bottom shelf was waiting as if reserved. The closed door was flung open again and as I looked through the bars of the window, I saw three carts creeping slowly, close to the car's opening, loaded with sacks, baskets and people, a lot of people. It was a large family from the village of all ages and character, as we learned in a short time. Their arrival dispersed the gloomy feeling of resignation everyone felt after settling and resettling quietly like "squatters" on the splintery wooden planks.

The solemn air disappeared, giving way to angry shouts and swearing from the members of the farmer's family. There were so many of them I lost count, for the militia men frantically tried to round them up, running wildly in circles, mainly the small boys who screamed and spat at the soldiers, kicking from behind, moving like lightening, while the older members, without any hurry, were gathering up the pierzynas and it seemed half of their property's personal possessions.

For a second, I thought we were watching a circus. As time had gone by and not a single member had entered the boxcar. I noticed a young girl with long braided hair reaching down to her waist, standing erect in the horse wagon, holding tightly a sack, which she swung like a propeller each time one of the soldiers came near her. There she stood, like wrath personified, glaring at everybody, daring the whole world to a challenge. What guts, I thought, but so useless. In minutes, she will also have to crawl into the dark and the stench of the crowded berths, -but her foolish action momentarily inspired awareness of the stirring spirit of defiance and will power to endure, whatever may happen in the time to come. The young farm girl with rosy cheeks, swinging the sack at the red soldier, threw a little spark of hope on this painful departure, even with doubts and misgivings we knew we would be confronted with on this difficult journey.

The belongings gathered from the three wagons came first and were thrown on the floor. One of the bundles began to move, —horrors! Were my eyes playing tricks on me? I don't recall crying; in fact, I couldn't shed one tear. But the "thing" was moving and then the cackling came out of it - what a relief! It's just that things were happening too fast and my tired mind had a tough time absorbing it all...

For the farmer's family, it must have been a general arrest and the whole stock came along, but I doubt for sentimental reasons. Finally, the light in the door was barred by a stout figure of a woman stepping over the steel threshold of the boxcar, pushing away the guards with her big elbows, swearing to high heaven: "suki syny—zaraza na was" (sons a bitches-plague on you), she raged. Then at once she was still, as if with entering through the door a curtain fell to hush up the cries, seeing other faces in the dark, hearing sobbing at a far corner. I watched her change rapidly from a brave feisty soul to a helpless creature-arms hanging loose at her sides, realizing the game was over and everything was lost.

But then, she turned around and blasted another ugly curse at Russia and the bloody leaders!

From then on, each member of the family repeated the same performance, with the exception of the two small boys, who, without a word, spat viciously at the guards and the whole clan was finally in.

Our car was the last one to be bolted from the outside, a sign of an imminent departure with most of us reconciled to the fact that nothing was going to change, no sudden rescues- no miracles!

However, the farmer's family members were not exactly settled or ready. We couldn't see exactly actions for they occupied the shelf below us, but from the squawking of still live poultry, we gathered there was murder in the air and we guessed right, for in no time at all the feathers started to float up to our level, while the kill took but few minutes. Thank God they were so skillful! Then they pounded the door and screamed for the water, which was rationed already for drinking only. They got the water and the cooking began. The huge pot was filled, boiling away on a little "primus", an alcohol stove, spreading a pleasant aroma of the fresh cooking fowl in the stagnant air and by the same, tickling our nostrils and empty stomachs. This is going to be some voyage, I thought, but the big family also turned out to be very goodhearted, treating everyone to a bowl of chicken broth and I must say, I have never tasted such a light soup, though that kind of consistency we credited to the amount of feathers floating in it, but aside from that it was quite delicious and nourishing, bringing first smiles and jokes to such distressed people, for we had learned already, that an empty stomach can become a menace, while a satisfied one puts the matter in a different light.

Around four o'clock in the afternoon, with a hard jolt of the clanking boxcars, we departed. Train rides, were always pleasant interludes to me before; I loved those first clickety-click sounds of the moving wheels, watching the scenery rush by, with never tiring moments, although I traveled by train to school each day during the spring and fall. This time, I had a strange feeling in the pit of my stomach... The old "clickety" had a different sound, like a hammer pounding deeper and deeper, and the scenery passing by fast, too fast...had colors I had never noticed before. I tried to remember each tree and wheat field we went by, but it seemed like one picture was sliced into several ones by the bars in the window I was looking out of...and through the blur of stinging tears, our country was slipping away from us with each second.

Before evening we arrived in Lwow, a city we had loved with a passion. I was relieved we didn't come through the main station but waited on the outskirts, where trains with cargo, such as ours, stood in lines, lingering. Here, the story and sights were repeated all over again. Tear-stained faces, red eyes, grave expressions. From some of the windows the sounds of the national songs floated freely, even the chords from guitars and mandolins were loud, proof that a spirit was there, for among the arrested families, there were so many young.

Our arrest and deportation seemed like pulling away roots of live nerves against our will, realizing we had to succumb to the persecution and decisions of the ones controlling our destiny. It was more than losing our home and material possessions. I loved Poland. I loved this land with its simple life, its history, tradition and people. At home there was always a strong feeling of patriotism, handed down through generations and more notably yet, from our father, who fought for Poland's independence since he was twelve years old. And of course our grandmother's numerous accounts of the family's heritage would never let us forget the ancestral deeds and services rendered to the country, stressing the fact that, somewhere in the past, our roots were of nobility, the feature never quite impressing the younger family members, getting at times, our grandma irritated at our disrespect, when we made fun of the titles and heraldic emblems awarded centuries ago. Even the symbols in our family crest, I don't quite remember, except the quarter moon, indicating it had something to do with the Turkish wars. True, we snickered at the old bloodline, but deep down, without outwardly showing it, we were quite proud of it.

And now it was all slipping away from us. Each mile gone carved a chasm between our past life and a sobering, mind-chilling presence of being forced to leave the country, without any hunch or notion as to our destination or the length of time.

When I looked to both sides of our train, I saw all of the tracks occupied by the human cargo of boxcars with barred windows, faces pressing against the vertical bars. We were not alone, we were in such large numbers.

Next to us the track was still empty and the locomotive was just pulling in. The passing trains by now had everybody shouting through the windows, identifying themselves, the towns they came from, shaking fists with death threats to Soviets and Stalin, the loud vows and battle cries of coming back to repay "the Commies" with a vengeance!

The brief encounters through the barred windows were establishing the camaraderie among the strangers, being born out of these tragic events, putting warm touches on the very troubled souls. I was hoping the incoming train would give me a chance for a little talk, but then something else had happened...

When the train stopped, the guards immediately began to pace back and forth, as they did with every other cargo car, from which came the most natural noises of people talking, children crying, strong swearing here and there, a normal display of human existence in an abnormal way of living.

I was hanging on to the window bars, with my face close, watching the window parallel to mine, across from me, when a woman's head appeared at a rather larger than other barred window. The bars seemed to be set very wide apart as I could see her leaning out of a frame. She looked quickly to both sides, as if watching for someone, but only the guardsman was approaching. For a second the window remained dark and empty, then the object came into sight; it was white and it seemed as if someone's hand carefully maneuvered it between the bars and held it there as if suspended in the air. I sat with a curious feeling, for I realized with a jolly shock, that the white object was a small chamber pot, evidently not empty, which hung in between the bars perfectly still. I was sure now the hand holding the pot belonged to the woman I saw looking out before. She planned it and her timing was good, for while the soldier was passing under the window, a cascade of yellow urine hit him right on the head. The comrade swore loud and ugly, the woman apologized with a bitchy grin with fast-invented excuses, but all I could see on her face was a deep satisfaction and pleasure. The soldier kept threatening her, cursing some more but finally departed, wiping himself off with a heavy uniform sleeve. And the woman? She didn't quit there. She stuck her head out again and clearly in Polish rattled out loudly: "Buster, I am sorry I had to do it with a piss pot, if my ass wasn't so wide, I would have pissed on you myself!" I guess some still had guts and spirit!

It was getting dark when we left Lwow. Time didn't matter any more. I tried to sleep, but the anxiety and tension kept me awake wondering what was ahead.

Sometime during the night, we crossed the Soviet border; behind us now, faraway, was Poland. The train was speeding across the vast territory of the Ukraine, with a short stop in Kiev, the old, historic city. From afar, we could see the outlines of churches and monuments, bringing back to my mind the stories from literature and poetry, the legends and tales told to us in the evenings by our maid Dorka, who came from the Ukraine. It was a desolate country. There seemed to be no limit to the horizon, the sky and the land were of equal size, wide and big, powerful but lonely… The collective fields lay like gigantic divans with a dark monotony of colors, patiently waiting for the green to show up. For miles and miles, the countryside hadn't changed. I had to tear myself away from this dismal landscape flashing now through the window. The gloomy atmosphere inside the car was enough to drive one to a melancholic state, without any help from moody Mother Nature.

Morning brought our train to a stop in the middle of nowhere, for it was feeding time or what we once called "breakfast." We never knew the hour or place for our daily repasts, guessing only by the sounds of unbolting doors and the impolite summons, "Get out!" The buckets were placed by the door and we were ordered to walk toward the locomotive, where others already stood in line, waiting for something being distributed with steam coming out of it. When I glanced quickly, I noticed a grayish liquid hiding behind the hot vapors and as this was our first meal on this journey, we were to get acquainted with a load of mysterious and unfamiliar nourishment, called by the Soviets, "lapsha." Even before tasting it, we made some bets as to the source, being close in calling it a soup, but actually it was a slop, consisting of a lot of hot water and the few long, gray noodles playing "peekaboo" with each other.

And so we were introduced to our first Russian dish, which would become from now on, a greeting in the morning and a filler for good night, giving us a long stretch of idle time in between as a rugged test in controlling our hunger. It wasn't easy. I remember trying to occupy myself by watching the rushing scenery or in my mind reciting poems by Mickiewicz, Slowacki, even turned to Latin, with Ovidius still fresh from my second year of high school, just to keep my thoughts away from my aching stomach. It helped sometimes, but mostly it was irritating and by the evening we were eager for the taste of "lapsha." The meals at dawn or other ungodly hours, were the cause of occasional stops at opened spaces for the benefit of the rest of the organs, to keep sanity in check, although it usually became embarrassing as hell, for we always had the guard at our heels, watching closely, an indescribable misery! Yet your health was placed above the shame and soon we had learnt to overcome many difficult obstacles, except when at times, things became unpredictable and couldn't be controlled. When those urges occurred and the train was moving, we had two young guys offering their services for providing a "powder room." The curtain from two blankets held up in a V shape, served as a divider to block off the sight of intensely personal activity. What a terrible humiliation in such an embarrassing exposure, especially for the young girls such as I, going through it, while we wished to crawl under the floorboards and die there from shame, but in the face of physical torment, the vanity had vanished somewhere and there we were as of in our childhood years, sitting on the potty, feeling the pain and anguish and, many times, also the splinters from the crudely constructed wooden "toilet" seat, while we tried to stand up in a hurry, to get out. To make the matters worse, the two clowns, the crap-can custodians, took advantage of this ungratifying job and turned it into a sideshow, pretending it to be a wartime air-raid, by imitating the radio forewarnings of the oncoming alarms before the bombs hit! However, this farce ran its course and ceased operation by the end of the first week of our journey, when the wooden plunger got stuck in the square opening of the toilet seat and broke sadly in half, without yielding to go in or out. That was another nightmare, indeed! But there were still train stops and guards, and other problems galore!

By the end of a second week, we crossed the Ural Mountains and realized it was a farewell not only to Poland but to Europe as well. Ahead of us lay Asia.

My thoughts went back to my second year of high school, the lessons of geography and the recollection of the excitement they created while traveling through the pages of the book, absorbing easily the statistics of the strange countries and their people. The acquired information of the last year's learning kept clicking slowly in my mind, creating rough sketches of this unknown continent.

How alien this land appeared, not because of its color or texture, but its breath of gloomy fascination and hidden mystery, for we could feel the strangeness in the air, the sky and the sandy terrain, visible for miles. Back in school, Asia was a subject, a distant territory, but now it was frightening, because we could touch it and feel its hostility. Along the tracks the scenery was changing and following the larger cities on the map, we tried guessing our destination, maybe Siberia, but a after few days, the path of the eastern direction had changed, pointing the course, due south.

Thus, we entered Kazakhstan, a land we hardly knew anything about, except for the sights now flashing in front of our eyes through the slats of the window. Some of us shuddered, some prayed silently. A stop at one of the stations brought a sad and tragic scene in a car behind us, where a woman became very ill and had to be taken to a local hospital. I shall never forget the cries of her two little girls, being left alone, the frightened little voices: "Mama, don't go, mama... mama..." And the whimpers... We were almost at the end of a second week, wondering how far yet before we reached our final destination, while the train was cutting deeper into the east of the unknown desert region. There were infrequent stops at small towns, where the curiosity overtook the troubled guessing as we stared with astonishment at the gathered crowds of, as we presumed, the sunburned faces of the natives, with features of true Asiatic inhabitants. The startling pictures produced some minor shocks and recognition of what was awaiting us, at the end of the line.

These strange individuals, staring back at us, appeared as if in a bad dream, not because of who they were, but what they represented to us at that time. At first glance, I would imagine them on a book cover of an Oriental mystery novel, but seeing them so close, so real— a grim thought crossed my mind: "The emissaries" of Scheherezade's tales, they were not! Their drab looking apparel was out of our class. In color and design, they reminded me of our "hippies" in the sixties, sporting a unisex garb. Men and women alike wore wrinkled, questionably white tunics and pants and some as it was an early spring, had thrown over their shoulders, the gray quilted and shapeless jackets, called, as we learned later - the" fufaikas."

The view overall, had a touch of the Orient, perhaps a little shabby and frayed at the edges, but nevertheless, it was beyond a doubt, the Orient.

As we were leaving one of the small stations, someone made a loud comment: "Look at them squinting devils, gawking at us, as if we were some circus animals"–now the laments were coming from all corners: "All saints preserve us, we may be living among them!" That was enough to inspire another call for help–"Matko Boska, pray for us." The noise associated with various opinions kept rising, though we could hardly see the speakers, except the farmer's family, who didn't mince words in their testy expressions and sentiments. During the long days of our journey, we hardly got to know everyone in this confined area, but now with many voices raised, it hinted there was life in the lower part of the dark quarters, in spite of a dim light, even more obscured by the thick bluish haze from the potent Turkish cigarettes. The arguments and cross words kept up the excitement of guessing our destination: "You can be sure they are not sending us on vacation," someone said and that stirred up another flurry of questions, even woke up an individual with a rather weird disposition, who occupied a bottom space corner of a berth. Many times during the trip, I had watched his feet clad, in a U-boat like foot-wear, always dangling over the end boards of the shelf when he was lying down, as he did mostly. His shaggy head looked as it hadn't seen a comb since we left Poland and was like a center point for collection of hay straws and tiny feathers from his neighbor's pierzynas. He was young, but there was a strange aura about him, giving an impression of advanced age.

Now he stuck his head out and gripped it with both hands in a desperate gesture: "What's the difference whose land we get off in –Kazakh, Turk's, Kyrgyz—it's all bloody Russia! Can't escape nowhere, we are all doomed!" He spoke slowly with a whining pitch, giving everyone a slight case of shivers. Others tried to hush him up: "What an awful attitude, young man, you sound like a crow in the cemetery; we are not dead yet, and as long as you keep breathing, there is always a chance and hope that some day we'll find our way back to Poland." The remark made an impression, and it became quiet. The mention of our country became painful and throbbing like an infected sore, bringing back the reminders of the last days and worries of everything we had left behind.

The train was picking up speed, leaving the station and its exotic crowd in a blur, now giving us a chance to observe the new to us Asiatic "fauna and flora." Flora would be too pompous of a word for describing the dull and earthy blending colors of the grasses and dry spears of brush growing close to the tracks. The first sighting of the camels stirred some excitement; being in their own habitat, they walked freely, not as we used to see them in a circus or a zoo. It seemed a reversal of roles; were we the sad circus now?

As I closed my eyes now, I could still see so clearly the caravan in numbers of them, moving slowly, swaying over the sandy trails, with a rider at the front and a couple of shadowed figures walking beside, with bulging sacks thrown over their shoulders. In minutes, the picture grew pale, as the distance had widened, and we were headed toward our unknown destination.

For as far as our eyes could see, we were surrounded by steppes—the yellow sand and skies the color of lapis, with hawks hanging high above the stillness of the barren plains, then disappearing over the wide horizon.

While crossing this vast territory, looking out both sides of the train at the forlorn spaces, I thought about God. Was he with us? I hadn't prayed for days, didn't forget, I just didn't pray. Up to the time we had reached the Ural Mountains, my head was still filled with delusions of instant miracles and a last-moment turn of events that would take us back to Poland, but when nothing had happened, it seemed as if Ural was the last gate closing on us, banishing all our hopes and dreams, for now…

******

By the end of a second week of our journey, the train stopped at dawn some distance past the station whose name I could barely read, mainly because it was spelled in Kazakh strange hieroglyphic script, resembling a flock of wriggly worms. Each door of the cargo cars was flung wide open. We had arrived at our destination, so we presumed, or why else would we be allowed so much daylight and oxygen at one given time? I sneaked a glance through the top of the opened door; the patch of gray sky began to look brighter, promising a nice day, possibly warm as the air was comparable more to summer's temperature.

Without fanfare or joyful shouts, people slowly began to climb down off the shelves, then cautiously jumping onto the gravel scattered along the train tracks. I felt glad, still being alive and at the amount of fresh air being pumped into my lungs, so I followed everybody else's example and jumped to the ground, then found myself on my knees. My legs were jelly, weak and light, and I saw others wobbling and groping for support, dispensing my fear of being paralyzed.

The temporary feebleness didn't last long; just feeling the good earth under our feet was reason enough to bring the strength back and put the body into motion to circulate the blood in our half-collapsed veins. The families sat in groups in front of each car, faces looking pale, some tear-stained, quietly glancing about, like convalescing invalids coming home from the wars, frightened and confused.

At least the first part of our journey was over and a fraction of our suspense had ended. Around us, the sights were familiar, a repeat of the ones we had viewed from the train while entering Kazakhstan: monotony of sand, desert grass, some low, mud-slapped dwellings scattered beyond the station, separated by large distance between them. There was no shortage of land.

The air was warm, hanging low like a heavy blanket, but in spite of it, a chill ran down my spine!

Somehow, without a formal introduction, I knew this was going to be part of our life, an immediate future. The surroundings, the people, the animals, we would have to blend with them, live like them, in order to survive.

Now, the recollection of our life in Soviet Russia comes back to me in jagged fragments, somehow torn and hazy, a little out of focus. But the essence is there, beneath the scramble of years after, like an old tintype photo, pale, yet with strong and visible traces of what was once life or, rather, shaky existence at that time in this new land. Had I recorded, earlier in my life, the accounts of our duration on the steppes in the span of the three years, perhaps I could have given in detail a journal of day-by-day events, but pity though, after being released and freed from the "red paradise," it would have been painful to record the memories, the nightmare we have tried so hard to forget and erase from our mind.

That first morning when we arrived, our belongings were tossed out of the "Orient Express" and four of us gathered them and sat closely, like watchdogs, guarding the last of our possessions. I lay down, stretching myself across a couple of the stuffed sacks and stared blankly at a pale sky. I tried praying... "Our father..." but before I came to "give us our daily bread..." there was a commotion. It startled me, for the food was brought in - the bread. Actually, it was dumped in a large burlap wrap and there was still steam coming out of it. I blessed myself hastily while a brief thought of an answered prayer crossed my mind, but I dismissed it as a coincidence. I looked at the fresh Russian bread, a first breakfast in the fresh air, on the Asiatic soil, in the beginning of our long exile. The slices were thick, chunky and dark like fudge cake, but the taste didn't match the appearance. Still we all sat and devoured the ration (there always was a ration) in silence. The warm chunks slid down to the stomach and lay there like pieces of lead, filling the cavity. Too weak to digest it, I was mainly trying to quiet down the loud growling, from hunger.

Alicja R. Edwards

DESTINATION KAZAKHSTAN

Time had elapsed as we sat waiting. People made small talk, some whispered, still in fear, while the hours seemed to drag in the anticipation of the next step. There was always the guessing, supposing, keeping the nerves on edge. The best we could hope was staying put, without any more traveling, even in this place we hadn't learned the name of yet, where we were unloaded.

The warm April day, and the dreary little town, was the very beginning in the first phase of the long three-year span in our exile in Soviet Russia.

If by some super clairvoyance, one would have taken a peek at the distant future and foreseen the number of years for us to serve in this ordeal, it might have been easier to gather up sufficient strength and distribute it wisely throughout the time. To help us endure the hardships that were to be inflicted upon us in such excess, so ruthlessly. But our crystal ball was cloudy and revealed nothing. The time moved slowly, stretching the waiting, the anxiety and speculations; nevertheless, it pressed on, with hours barely recognized, only by the position of the sun. And the sun was ablaze, raising the temperature to a very uncomfortable level, unknown to us before. It was hot, damn hot.

Suddenly, we saw carts pulled by oxen, being driven close to the railroad tracks and each family, one by one, got loaded up and left, silently waving good-bye.

After the last cart disappeared in the cloud of dust, we were told by authorities, the local militia, that for now, we were to stay in the village, the village named Gzaroon.

Before the evening, we were driven to our new living quarters, a hut constructed out of the mud blocks, sitting at the edge of the village, occupied by a Russian family. There must have been plans for the dispersion of our people and somewhere we fitted into them, but for now, at least we knew we had a place to live in Russia. The silence of the early dusk and softly howling wind touched us like a cold hand and from the other dwellings, sitting some distance away, we could feel the eyes watching us from every direction.

The hut was built low and at the moment semi-dark inside. We were given a smallcubby hole with enough space to stretch our legs at night and walk around the "pietchka," a burning stove. Two peepholes called windows, built into each side of the wall, presented a view out to the world of sand and emptiness. Besides us we had two families moving in with us, though the space didn't seem large enough for so many persons. With difficulty, we divided it fairly and finally settled down.

Four of our members were to occupy two corners of this Russian "adobe" type construction, with walls smelling strongly of lime painted in a blue-gray color and a few wooden planks for a floor, laid over the yellow clay foundation, where we stowed our belongings. The floor, despite its primitive appearance, looked clean enough to spread some bedding on and claim as a sleeping zone, but then only later I found out, the small stretch of two wooden planks contained brigades of nasty fleas. With all our earthly possessions piled in one corner, mother didn't seem to be quite ready to unpack. She kept fiddling around with her huge linen purse, opening the large wooden clasps, looking inside then closing it, as if undecided. Her lips clamped together, indicated there were heavy decisions being made and knowing her I also knew it wouldn't take longer but a minute, and I was right. She stood up, composed, and in a calm voice she said: "Don't unpack - I will be right back." She went out through the dark doorway. I watched through the small glass pane of a window, wondering where she was heading, this place being unknown to her, but I couldn't see her at all.

Time had elapsed, grandmother was praying, her mouth moving silently and fingers sliding over the dark rosary beads. There was a momentary comfort in this quiet waiting without clocks or watches in sight, it seemed as minutes extended into hours. Dusk was descending, the shadows of the squatty huts grew longer, stretching freely over the smooth sandy spaces. There were hardly any sounds coming from anywhere, there was no life, or so it appeared to me, that first evening in Soviet Kazakhstan. Soon though, we heard mother's voice and another woman speaking in Russian, who happened to be our "land-lady." Both of them were struggling with a brightly painted green piece of furniture—a bed. We were thrilled at mother's returning ingenuity and energy, boosting our sadly sagging spirits, even throwing a tiny spark of hope into this horrible change in our life.

A simple article such as a bed created an excitement and a great deliberation, where to place it. The bed was tall, with wide slats painted kelly green and could only fit in one corner, considering we had only two available to us and one too close to the door, so the fuss was short-lived. Finally the bed was put up, taking up most of our allowed footage, to serve us as a niche of our own little world, in which to sleep, to eat, read and write letters and cry at the beginning, though less as the time went by. We moved fast, unpacking. All the heavy excess clothing went into the making of a mattress then got covered on top with a thick linen-like material, serving as a sheet. Pierzynas went on the top of it, and *voila*-it promised to be a quite comfortable "lair."

"Three of us," mother said, meaning her, grandma and my brother, "will share the bed, and you, my dear, you will have to squeeze yourself on the wicker basket." It was fine with me, I told her, besides there was no other choice anyhow, so I turned my attention to "making" my bed. The basket was large. It usually sat in the kitchen in our house in Poland and served as a "catch-all" for useless things, except during the summer vacation it had a function as a trunk, when we spent the month of July in the Carpathian Mountains. The roomy basket held linens and all sorts of tins of tea, coffee, cocoa and a variety of non-perishable victuals. The squeaky noises it made, brought back the memories of mountain holidays, the leisure time of adventures and wishful thinking that it would never end. And now, no more.

The throbbing recollections came back to harass with a mockery, these moments of temporary adjustment, while the mind was lingering, going back to cool nights and soft breezes drifting out of the pine forests, the steady whisper of rushing water over the slippery, mossy stones, so clear and cold even in the heat of a summer. The early dawns when grandmother would wake us up, out of a deep, healthful sleep to view nature's wonders in the sky, a perfect sickle of a moon suspended between the two dark mountains and Venus hanging at its tip like a Christmas ornament, a sight so lovely, now only a brief memory, but here in Gzaroon, it was getting dark and the wicker "bed" was calling for attention.

The basket itself stood about two and half feet tall and three feet in length. Its width would comfortably fit my posterior. The only problem remaining was my legs, as short as they were, they would still dangle at any tried position, which at this funny angle, wasn't my idea of a relaxed night's rest. Surviving the long train ride, I dared to dream of the luxuries: sleeping like normal people. But I wasn't upset, I knew mother would improvise and come up with a solution. In the meantime, I threw on top of the basket my old "buddy" from high school, a uniform-type winter coat in order to serve as a referee between my ribs and the wicker, then signaled my brother to hand me a small "jasiek," the pillow. Things were falling into place and I fell onto my bed. The tension and anxiety had left us exhausted, yet sleep didn't come.

Mother was playing around with couple of small suitcases, taking some things out, then snapping them shut. In the darkness it was hard to see why she was so busy, but in a short while she was standing at my feet. "Put them up," she said. It may sound like a western joke, but at that time, she meant my feet not my hands. The stacked suitcases now served as an extension to my wicker bed and my spirited legs at last found their own lodging. What a relief it was! Soon after, I couldn't account for any hours or minutes, the sleep finally came.

I woke up, looking out of a small opening, the window, seeing the pale glow of dawn. With the heraldic morning sounds of a crowing rooster, I knew why I woke up. It was bad enough during the traveling, but now, we had to get accustomed again to unfamiliar patterns and habits, and I was getting restless. Mother should know, she always knew what to do, but I hated to wake her up. I knelt by the shiny green bed and looked at her face, not quite sure if I should disturb her sleep, the only restful oblivion and detachment from all the worries of the past few weeks. Then she stirred and I sensed she was half-awake, so I blurted hurriedly "Mama, I've got to go!" With her eyes still closed, she whispered, "Out back, there is "ubornaia." "Ubornaia?" I repeated, "what is that?"

"Go out and look, you will see for yourself," then she turned away and went back to sleep. For some reason, I found myself feeling rather cheerful; after all, four of our members of the family were so far in a good health, there didn't seem to be any threats of our being eliminated. We were guessing we were brought here into this part of Russia for some purpose (that made us a bit uneasy), still we had a roof over our heads, the mere basics of life.

Quietly, I went out of the room in search for the intriguing "ubornaia." My steps quickened in the narrow corridor, still dark and smelling musty from the damp clay floor. At the end, there was a streak of light trying to slip in between a heavy wooden door, being slightly ajar. I pushed it opened. It squeaked like my wicker bed. Standing on the high stoop and now being wide awake, I took a long look at the landscape around me. Straight ahead, at my eye level, there was nothing but grass and short growing scrub and as far as I could see, the endless steppes. Not a sign of my mother's ubornaia. At the moment I abandoned the idea to explore the Russian outhouse and looked for higher growing brush, feeling apprehensive of the strange surroundings. Out of my peripheral vision I spotted a half-finished structure, a cube built out of the mud bricks, about five stacks high. I changed my direction and walked toward it. The swarm of flies forewarned me that I found my mother's "ubornaia," a model I thought, an unfinished venture, standing only up to my knees, primitive and simple in its appearance but I discovered later it was typical for the area and meant to be airy, with all of the season's ventilation.

"Good morning, Russia," I said to myself as I stood in the free open space, feeling the warm breeze coming from the steppes and listening to the cheerful sounds of a rooster, far in a distance, crowing his head off, without pausing for a rest. The day was barely beginning, but the air was pulsating with life, emitting strange notes of high pitch–wailing donkeys and sorrowful bellowing of the camels. This dispersed the doubt about the land that we would have to get acquainted with, the land of contrasts, full of hidden and unknown-to-us traits and habits. As far as I could see, toward the horizon, a line was drawn between the now light blue sky and a destitute-looking terrain—empty, lifeless…so depressing, so sullen.

I turned to walk back and stopped to take a good look at the village of Gzaroon, spread out widely in every direction, highly concentrated along the railroad tracks. The monotony of the architectural mud didn't seem to raise any excitement; it seemed austere and drab, giving the overall impression of a "sand castle" city, built by adults to maintain life, according to their style. Now, it would also be our style.

The weather indicated a summer-like air, but it was still spring and it was also Russian Easter. Although the shadow of Stalin, the tyrant, lay dark, reaching far over the vast Soviet land, still in the hearts of the older people, the sparks of sentiment for the old religion, brought back the traditional, though secretive rituals of once-remembered lively and rich times.

On the second day of our arrival, later in a day, a woman of Polish origin brought to us some lovely colored eggs and Easter bread called "pashka." The gesture itself stirred the emotion among the homesick souls, but it also felt like a balm, easing the pain of the memories of the recent weeks, not to mention a delight in a taste of a great morsel of a sweet "babka-like" bread. We were grateful for the gifts but mainly touched by the warm feelings of friendship of a citizen whose government had brought us here into exile. She was an older woman, in her sixties, with an angelic-looking face and a beautiful smile. Her voice was soft, sometimes becoming a whisper, which she explained later, came as a habit because "the walls could hear."

At the first visit, she tried to give the facts and prepare us for the quality of life we would be faced with, in order to survive. We listened to every word she spoke, for she was the first person to befriend us and diminish our worst fears, speaking in our Polish language, broken at times, but it didn't matter, for we respected and admired her. Her name was Lena, and she had a large family and by the Soviet standards, they were very well off.

Because it was Easter, she talked of religion, now forbidden rites of the humble believers, of the sacred icons hidden in the bottoms of ornately carved, ancient hope chests, the churches now empty or shut, closed as if believing was a fatal disease. The Russian people were suffering and bewildered at the multitude of broken promises to improve their lives under the communist rule. They traded the oppression of the czars for a bloody tyranny whose leaders were determined to break unscrupulously the last links with the past, to subject their own people to pay at any price. We listened, terrified at times, for if they, the Russians, were victimized by their own government, what chances would we have for a fair treatment, we Poles, although their neighbors across the borders (not so any more, we were their property), even being of Slavic block as the half- brothers. It didn't matter, as long as the heads of state imposed the hostilities and instigated the hate, passing to people the violence and senseless distrust, without basis. To their people, we were guilty of once being free touched by the wrong culture and rich, far too rich. We were the capitalistic intelligentsia. We were the outcasts to the idealistic new breed of red Russians and now we were going to have a chance to learn their way to live, a right way, so they thought!

For now, we realized there was a small group of people left in this village called Gzaroon. Most of them were strangers, from different areas, except the three families from our own town and two already living with us, in the same dwelling. We were told there would be jobs found in the village later or even work on far away fields. Mother went at once into a collective shop and was put on a sewing machine, where a few other Polish women worked side by side with Russians, Kazakhs and Tartars, both men and women. My brother had to go to school without any protests or questions. At his age he was sensitive material for the making of a young communist. Our grandmother, the "babushka," as she was called, was left alone and as for me, at the moment, no job had materialized so being out of the group of a working class, I couldn't earn my rationed grams of bread. Without relying upon sucking my fat thumb, I learned to stand in bread lines, where occasionally you could get a slice of the gooey mess and slowly grasping the first ideas of what life in Russia was going to be. I had to learn to be patient, mostly when waiting in lines for anything related to food that was being given or other articles as important, such as soap and kerosene. Sometimes I went away empty handed, for I couldn't stomach the vicious brawls and assaults. Early on, I watched so many times entanglement of feet, hands and hair, enough to teach me to stay away from the "combat zones," even at the risk of hunger. In the days when I stood in lines, I began to listen and learn more of the Russian language and about the strange environment. It seemed important for us to get familiarized with this horrible way of living, but in order to survive, we had to adapt to the pattern of unknown and unusual conditions.

Mother worked long hours at the shop, earning the few grams of bread to be shared with us, leaving me up in the air, wondering what kind of work I would be burdened with, to earn my own grams. For a while we thrived on the half-rotten potatoes the major had shoved at us back home. His gesture wasn't one of exaggeration, he knew his country quite well and now we were learning what he didn't tell us in so many other words!

As the days were passing, we found ways to create a sort of "oriental" menu, a little lean on the side, but it aided our imbalanced meals with necessary vitamins of fresh, green variety. What we learned from the natives, was the fact that Mother Nature was kind enough to offer assistance in the form of edible plants such as garlic, onion, sorrel, berries and pinkish-looking mushrooms growing under the ground, and some of those combinations amounted to quite the meals.

How well I remember those walks into the steppes, that month of our arrival. The spring shed all of its glory on this dejected and forlorn piece of land and to compensate for its bareness and gloomy colors, the good earth opened its heart and gave all of her love to all living above her. I seem to recall my first shock upon seeing the most vivid carpet of colors spread before me, while walking out to search for the wild plant food. I stood in the middle of a sandy road, stunned at the magnificence and perfection of the picture, making me forget my task, my status, myself. Neither Van Gogh nor Monet could have chosen a more suitable pallet to bring this splendor of color onto the canvas. The rights to this creation, only Nature could claim herself. Beyond the splash of colors, the green and bluish hills rose on the horizon, with highlights on the slopes from a bright sun and in the stillness of the open spaces, I could hear the steppes breathing and pulsating with life... I didn't know how far I had gone, but when I turned around I couldn't see the muddy huts or the telegraph poles and I had an urge to keep walking, hoping this scenery would never end, and at the end of the line there would be another country and people to welcome me! The fragrance from the wild plants and flowers must have affected me in some way, for I kept dreaming and walking farther away. The mere idea of picking smelly garlic and onion made me feel depressed. I wandered off the road and came closer to take a look at the flowers creating such an impact in the otherwise lifeless desert. I bent down and to my great surprise, amazingly I was looking at tulips! Tulips, in this forsaken place called Kazakhstan? I was astonished at the immense variety and combination of colors in the flowers, growing quite close to the ground with stems short and thick, carrying large heads of ruffled petals variegated in many hues. I tried to pick each sample in combination of colors, actually hating to do it but eventually ended up with an armful. They were so lovely, the brilliant heads bursting with warmth, dazzling against the hot and intense blue sky. For a brief moment, the tulips made my spirits climb, for a moment I forgot my mission, the garlic and wild onion, I was in a wonderland of peace and tranquility where there were no wars and rations of bread.

The sun came up so high and the noon heat began to blast with a force. I Knew it was too late to search for the plants and time to turn back. I couldn't find the road I had walked on before! I started to sweat, trying to remember which direction I should take to locate the telegraph lines, the panic was making me dizzy! I closed my eyes, trying to calm down. The peace and serenity of the surroundings somehow lost their fascination in my hectic search for a way back to the village, back to the dreaded world, but a safe haven at the moment.

It was so hot! I could feel the sweat trickling on the sides of my forehead. Then suddenly I heard the bleating of a sheep. I walked over, closer to the approaching sounds and saw the familiar sandy road full of noisy sheep, the Kazakh shepherd walking on one side. I began to sweat again, furiously thinking, "What do I do now? Hide? Run?" I walked fast and as I passed him, the shepherd uttered a greeting in Russian, "zdrastvuitie," a sort of a hello. Not looking around, I returned a mumbling of something similar and was off in a hurry, leaving a sigh of relief and blowing a kiss at the site of the telegraph poles, running fast toward the squatty mud dwellings.

The incident was a small though frightening one, for our entire existence in Russia depended on walking, for food and other necessities of living, as we had no other ways, but using our feet. Our fears had diminished though, upon learning that punishment for crimes such as assaults on women was quite severe. It took time for us to slip into the lifestyle of the Soviet mainstream, their rules, habits, beliefs, and it all came with a day-by-day existence, without anyone's coaching or guidance. After all, who would listen to our complaints? It seemed there were two alternatives to contend with: feed your face and try to stay well, the rest was up to your fate and if you believed in God.

I approached our habitat with an armful of the vivid flowers, feeling a little guilty because I was sent out to collect edible greens. I didn't even try to explain or look for excuses; the annoyed look and frown on grandma's face, waiting for fresh produce, was enough of a scolding on wasted time, picking so frivolously the useless flowers. Food was a serious matter (as if I didn't know it), but I swallowed my bitter dose and promised to make up for this mistake. There were still some staples such as flour, barley, kasha and other mystery grains, all sitting on the bottom of my "bed," the invincible wicker basket. Grandma untied the string from one of the squat fat sacks and threw couple of handfuls into a large white pot. A healthful yet gassy dark kasha would be our supper, delayed now because of me. However I wound up on the trail again, this time running off to our friend Lena, to bring a splash of milk for which I paid dearly, as I found out later. My watch, the graduation gift, was traded off behind my back, without even giving me a chance to grieve for it. Everything was bartered for or traded off.

Rubles, the Soviet currency, were seldom used, only by our mother, for there was hardly anything to buy, except when we stood in lines for the government-dispensed product and had to shell out the legal money, normally in a small amount, for whatever was sold, never commanded a high price. The products offered were shoddy anyhow and given not often enough, without a concern for people's needs. The Soviet experiment with "piatiletka," the system running on the principles of production every five years (piat, meaning five), wasn't proving to be much of a success to aid the humble masses, making everyone aware that in supplying a certain article, it would only come every five years. Therefore, whatever appeared on sale, while we were standing in line for hours, we had to suspect that's the last we would see for the next five years. It seemed to be a continuous conflict of availability in necessary items for a simple living. By the time your clothes became somewhat presentable, the shoes were worn and out of style, though without a great loss, for there was no style to get excited about, only the sizes to cope with. Life ran its course in a vicious circle, with people waiting and hoping for better times. And now, we were waiting, feeling hungry and trying to help prepare a meal, this being quite a ritual, for our only means to improvise it, was a small three-legged device, called a "primus." The brassy bottom part served as a container where normally a pure methyl alcohol (denaturant) was poured in, however here in Russia we had to be content with kerosene, a very unfragrant fuel, giving out a dirty, burning flame. By the time the meal was done, there were blotches of soot floating around, coating the bottom of the pots with a thick layer of black grime, clinging to our hair and any exposed flesh.

At the beginning of our life in Russia, we were blessed with possession of the precious soap, also resting at the bottom of my "bed"(I seemed to be resting on a pile of treasures). Wrapped in a linen towel, sat the few elongated pieces, taffy colored with a jumping deer impressed on each cake and the letters of the maker, the Schifht Company. The jumping deer was a sad reminder of our shopping expeditions in Lwow and my great fascination with a huge electric sign of a dazzling blue jumping deer, above the tall (few stories high seemed so tall to me then) building, blinking silently. The ordinary efforts of boiling dark kasha involved a struggle before and after, mostly when cleaning up the sooty mess, from the primus. The simplest of daily chores became a string of irritating dilemmas, and there was no escape from it with grandma's reminders that it was wartime and in other places in the world, people were suffering in a worse way. Only then I thought, I would rather face the bombs than this kind of life, even being buried alive.

To think and look toward tomorrow, we had to care for the physical part of our being. The contemplation and meditating had to be put on hold, so as not to be crushed under the weight of awareness of the changes brought on since the beginning of the war and us, imprisoned here in Russia, a partial result of it.

It was so hard to absorb and recognize the reason for the harm and devastation that were done to each of our lives, but it happened and now we had to cope with, live with it, without any illusions of miracles. Our daily motto became clear— "Do your damnedest to survive today, so you could see tomorrow."

The soot and sweat didn't diminish our appetites. We ate in silence, savoring the dark, steaming, lumpy kasha flavored with valuable milk and swirls of the settled grime. It seemed like a feast, so satisfying, to the point where I was forgiven for my idle tulip gathering venture. The radiant bouquet became a conversational subject throughout the evening, keeping grandmother talking on her favorite topic, botanical science- the plant life and me contending with "dishes," the primus and the dirt. The first Russian influence began to show up in our dinnerware, - mother brought home a couple of wooden bowls, the well known Russian lacquerware, but it was new to us - made of light wood, very colorful and great for maintaining the even temperature of food. I loved them at first sight and sometimes when eating I would mercifully forget the taste of the meal while studying the intricate arabesques of bold colors in reds, orange, black and splashes of gold. I often marveled at their durability and quite often later, wished I'd brought them with me out of Russia.

******

During my free times of walking around the village or going into the steppes searching for greens, I met a Kazakh girl. Actually, she came to my rescue when I tried to cross the yard without realizing it belonged to a Kazakh family and was closely guarded by huge borzoi dogs. I didn't notice them at all until, in a flash, they were around me, baring their long teeth and snarling, ready to attack! I stood petrified, waiting for the worst, when at that instant I heard a call, a strange guttural command. At once, the dogs stopped growling and slowly walked away.

From behind a mud-bricked wall a young girl walked toward me speaking in Russian: "Are you hurt?" I shook my head. Still scared, "Niet." I said. She smiled and extended her hand. "Come sit down," she said simply. We sat on a wooden plank laid across two large stones, forming a bench. It was such a beautiful day, so warm and quiet, the breeze and blue sky pushing away disconcerting thoughts. I looked at the young girl next to me. Her face was deeply sunburned or it could have been a natural complexion, her eyes were jet black and round like plums. Her body frame was slender and I guessed her age was close to mine. She seemed very friendly and spoke rapidly, leaving me thinking it was her native Kazakh lingo, but then catching a few words I realized she was speaking Russian, which to me was still fuzzy and hard to understand. I shook my head, and then she began to speak slowly, emphasizing each word with a gesture. "What was my name? Do I have a family?" She knew we came from Poland. I was taken pleasantly by her friendliness and tried hard to concentrate on giving her the right answers and somehow with a hesitant exchange, we came to understand each other very well. The short time while we sat, trying to communicate was a bright spot in our first dreary months of adjusting to life in this land that belonged to her people, the people of Kazakhstan. Zoia was her name. She lived behind the mud-brick wall in a largely spread out dwelling. She had a large family: four brothers, three sisters, two grandmothers and grandfathers, a couple of uncles and naturally mother and father. I thought to myself, they better have a good-natured disposition to live together in such a close concentration, but in Russia it was nothing unusual for families to camp together, restricted to certain space and acoustics.

In their simple way of living, for every complaint and whining, the sober word followed, the word I had learnt to despise at the beginning: "pryvyknesh," meaning you will get used to it- it trailed us throughout our existence in Russia, like a shadow. You fought to lose it and sometimes, we gave in. Except for dying, their philosophy of living was based on this theory, meekly accepting the turns of fortune, without much complaining or useless screaming—a submission to a fate empty of beliefs, fearful of protests and its consequences, a secret disappearance, without an explanation.

Only once as I recall, I went inside Zoia's house. It was some weeks later and I don't exactly know what was the occasion, but was quite surprised at the neatness and a quiet splendor of the interior that met my eyes, mainly created by dazzling colors of the carpets strewn all over the spacious and clean area. The room itself was dark but in one corner, by the window where the sunlight entered through a small pane of glass, there was a stack of at least a dozen rugs, fashioned into a sort of a comfortable divan-like settee. I marveled at the astounding array of tones in the carpet spread on the top, before I slowly sat down. It seems the native weavers tried to fuse into this kilim, all the colors as symbols of their great land: the burnt orange and vermilion of the sunsets, the sienna of the deserts, burgundy and purples of the shadows. The warm tones seemed to radiate throughout a rather spartan but neat room. Some older family members sat cross-kneed on the floor, a steam drifting from their bowls of tea, I imagined. Women wore white tunics and pants in a simple cut, silk scarves tied low on the forehead with satin fringes falling over the shoulders. One elderly with a long braid of gray hair covered by a bright orange scarf smoked a pipe.

As I walked in, some nodded toward me, but otherwise there was complete silence. Zoia handed me a small "tcharka" with a liquid: "It's tea" (ato tchai), she said "strong, and good," she smiled. It was strong and flavorful, also very good. I sipped slowly for fear of burning my mouth, when one of the family called Zoia over and handed her something very small, which turned out to be a sugar cube. She dropped it into my bowl of tchai. "Your style," she said and winked.

A simple tea, a simple gesture, but how great it seemed to me at that time! Even today it remains a lovely recollection of an afternoon with a Kazakh family, drinking tea, like a page out of a travelogue, the nicest of memories from Russia, of so long ago, still bringing a smile and a lot of sentiment.

Zoia and her family were complete strangers, but they treated me with kindness and courtesy. A gesture with a hand, a nod of a head or a slip of a smile, let me know that these people of a different race and language were offering a friendship and understanding, without a trace of hostility.

******

Time was passing, uneventful and the end of spring, all of sudden was thrust upon us with enormous heat and dry sandstorms, producing new (to us) nature's phenomena, called "devil's dance." Sort of a miniature tornado, acting up as a whirl of sand being lifted high in the air and disappearing, a common occurrence, later becoming a normal sight during the summer.

Warm weather brought on problems associated with this new (to us) climate, unknown and intense heat, bringing sweat, dirt and not enough soap for normal washing. Nights were a hell to sleep, for that was a time when an army of bed bugs would come out in force and feast on our blood. The bright green bed, our mother acquired from the landlady, was loaded with them. For a while I was safe on my wicker, but they found me also and my strong resistance began to crumble when I developed a very uncomfortable and torturous itch, which being contagious, I passed on to the other members of my family. The itching drove us insane. It settled mostly between the fingers and until the skin broke and some yellow fluid started to ooze out, we could almost bite the finger off. There was no medicine and nowhere to turn to, nobody to complain to. Our friend Lena sent some orange- colored salve to ease the pain, which helped a bit with a combination of grandma's faithful "microcid," a medicine she used to obtain in

39

Poland through the mail. We knew it wasn't legally approved, yet in our home, it was believed in, like a Bible. On our own, we resorted to any means to hold on to health and sanity, but for few weeks the ugly itch was a messy nightmare.

When my hands were almost healed, I was called to work. I remember it was early June, because everything was dry and the heat was unbearable. The wind blew from the steppes and made your eyes crinkle and skin tingle from flying sand and particles of the tumbleweeds. I often wondered but finally understood why most of the native women wore heavy shawls wrapped around their heads and faces, exposing only the eyes and nose. But even that kind of protection didn't help completely from the multitude of forming wrinkles, created by the constant battles with sun and wind.

When I reported to work at a place, outside of the village, a hovel no different from the others, there were two older girls from our transport, from Poland, waiting. We sat quietly, until an official came out with a work order and showed us where to pick up the tools we would be working with, and those happened to be sharp-pointed shovels, foretelling the type of job that was ahead of us. We were to work on the outskirts of a village in certain designated areas, clearing the brush and growth of the scorched steppes.

My shovel was heavy, and each lift and hack at the scrub was an effort. Fine dust filled the eyes and there was no end to sweating, with my glands working overtime. The first hour seemed like half a day. Two other girls, Liska and Nina, were going at a fast pace but, all of sudden, I saw them throwing the shovels on the ground. I wondered why they stopped: "It's not dinnertime yet, we hardly started." I stated. "No, it's not that time," Lizka said, "but my head feels like it's going to explode, I have to find something to cover it." Her face was red and dirty from the trickling sweat and fine dust. Then suddenly she picked up her dress, took the underpants off and put them over her head with a nonchalant pose of a fashion model: "It may not be a lot of protection, but it will have to do!" We laughed. It wasn't a bad idea at that. The sun was beating on the already scorched earth and with each step we took, the dry brush cracked and fine dust rose in puffs. Our shovels scraped the dirt in silence and the scrub piles were growing bigger, but the sun was still hanging high as if not willing to move from the same spot. Something began to pound in my head, like small hammers and I thought about my underwear, but kept at the hot dust - shove, cut, scrape over and over until I began to feel blisters— ugh! My hands started to burn and by the end of the day, my palms were raw. I kept looking up, hoping for signs to end this labor, but hours went by, without any relief, while we worked silently, slower as the sun was finally descending. The heat didn't let up. The dusty gray steppes were like an open furnace and we still had a hell of a chore to do. Each time, when I straightened my back, I looked ahead of me and I saw the endless area of scrub and dust, all to be worked on with our three shovels and blistered hands, so frightening. But no matter what we endured, there were always so many grams of bread, envisioned as a payment.

For now, I didn't feel hungry, only thirsty. The brief contact with a bottle and by now, somewhat warm but still wet with each sip, water- brought a small relief, but the tension and stress created an anguish with questions, why this? Why such an injustice? What did we do to deserve a treatment equal to criminals? Were we being punished for being born to different style of living? What were they trying to prove in changing our destiny in such a ruthless manner! The suffering of old people and children was incomparable and with the younger generation, the added fear for the future spelled hopelessness, as if we were buried alive.

While the sweat ran down, all over my body, all I could think of was the choking heat and ache in my muscles and burning blisters from gripping hard the large shovel's handle. We tried to chase away the thoughts that made us bitter, taking the energy and hallucinating as if we were being crucified, while the rest of the world didn't care.

In a short time one can grow up so fast! Since the war began, the months had multiplied into years and I hoped, mine would have equaled nine, like a cat's.

The sun finally was sinking down, with a magnificent explosion of blazing fuchsia and I couldn't help but marvel at the colors, however the shouting of the girls caught my attention "We're done, let's get out of here," Nina said, then she smiled when looking at Lizka— "Hey, Lizka, your pants are still on your head; the Russkis will think you're crazy!"

"Who cares?" Lizka shrugged, "crazy or not, they need my working hands, not my head."

And so like little troopers, we walked away from the hot field, and headed for the village. Our tools were put back in the labor "office" and we were told to come back to continue our work as we did today, learning later we were clearing the area for a future airport— in this forsaken territory? Evidently their plans didn't have much scheduled for the near future, with only us working on it. For them it may have been the project of building—for us only few grams of bread, which we received after the work. The thick slices were still warm and gummy; I nibbled absently on a crust, while walking back to our dwelling.

The village actually was small, but it was spread out at a higher level, along the wide avenues, which were all sandy, deep, giving you the feeling of sinking or walking in the snow. The houses sat along the sides dividing the streets, their stature not very cheery looking, with long and squatty shapes and flat rooftops and monotone of blue, white and muddy tan, quite depressing.

The word "pryvyknesh" flashed for a moment in my mind and I couldn't help but smile. Before I reached our habitat, I faintly heard a melody, floating somewhere in the distance. Listening more intently, I realized it was music and knew definitely, without a question, we were in Russia. The sound was that of a

41

balalaika, the melody so melancholy and so lovely, reaching deep, engulfing listeners with sadness.

I walked slowly, so as not to lose the sounds, floating so freely into the hot and sultry air. In the distance I saw my brother, who came to meet me. I knew what his interest was, mainly the bread or rather the crust that I had eaten already. Mother was worried, he said—was my work hard? We have never known heat like this before—did I get very hot? My insides just quivered, remembering those last hours in the sun, but I managed to fake my misery with a calm: "Yes, it was hot and my hands are sore."

"Wow," he winced when he saw my blistered palms. "It will be the same tomorrow," I said, "might as well get accustomed to it."

"As they say here in Russia..." Jez started. I knew, pryvyknesh. Sometimes I thought it wouldn't be such a bad idea if we really valued life itself, providing we preserved our sanity, good health and a hopeful spirit that a course of world events may change and benefit us some day.

The sun disappeared over the horizon, but its leftover breath was still producing an incredible heat. As we approached our dwelling, we noticed people sitting along the walls, squatting or cross legged, men and women chatting, nodding their heads, most of them smoking those horrible, strong cigarettes and pipes. It seemed like a page out of the *National Geographic* magazine or a travel journal, a peaceful village of peaceful people, a story to read on the long winter evenings, imagining the strange way of life, but feeling safe, not participating in person. Yet, here we were, transported as if by a real nightmare, not quite believing but living through it!

We walked around the group of older persons and went back through the "squeaking" doors where sat another congregation of a younger variety, closer to our age, acting somewhat arrogant, for they wouldn't move to let us through, laughing and teasing, making us spell out the proper words in Russian(like the damn French waiters in Paris, trying to trip us on their French).

At this moment though, all I wanted was some cool water in which to soak my hands and to die quietly on my "bed." Grandma did wonders as a nurse with patience and her indispensable medication, the miraculous "microcid," a black thick, awful-smelling jelly matter, supposedly concocted from the end parts of the red ants. She made sure it came with us to Russia. Now, this legendary preparation was at work, grandma rubbing it gently into my hands with an assurance that "by tomorrow, your hands will be fine." I don't exactly know if it was the heat, the labor in the steppes or her remedy, but with the sounds of a balalaika still drifting in from a distance, I went out like a light, asleep and dead to the world.

Early the next day and day after, into the weeks, we worked like obedient animals, clearing the dusty areas, while the space we worked on previously was already sprouting new weeds and as far as I can recall, nothing had materialized there for a long time, except for the memory and the sweat of three young girls.

Before the end of this ordeal, Liza and her family were moved to a far away *sowchoz*, where a few Kazakh families were raising sheep and horses, a sad event for it was considered a punishment, a transfer that cut their ties with the rest of the world.

We thought ourselves to be lucky so far, staying in the grand village of Gzaroon, which in comparison to the wild steppes, seemed like a metropolis. Gzaroon had a post office, a place becoming familiar to us in a short time, where we would pick up our care packages, beginning to arrive from Poland, making it like a holiday to drag our feet through the hot sand, not paying any attention to discomfort but hurrying with an elated feeling of a knowledge that we were still remembered back in our country. Even the weight of the parcel didn't matter; in fact, the heavier they were the better the contents.

I remember, in seconds, after getting through the door, feverishly tearing at the wrapping, almost smothering with kisses the heavy burlap and the linen, the box was sewn into (the linen was saved for our future underwear). It was like touching a ghost of the past, a sacred possession, so priceless with its contents of food in cans, glass jars and some perishables, such as smoked bacon and skinny "kielbasa" called "kabanos," which believe me, had never reached the perishable stage. I remember the joy of opening the very first package, the loud shrieks and yelling at each article being pulled into the open. To this day I can taste the "goulash" with rice out of a fat glass jar, which I wouldn't relinquish, stuffing my cheeks with an enormous speed, until a jab with a fork into my knuckles forced me to give up the remains for the rest of the family to enjoy it. In wild moments of such frenzy a person really forgot civilized behavior, turning so selfish. During the summer months, we had made a number of trips to the post office and were thrilled and grateful to our relatives and friends back home.

Other important structures in the village were a large school sitting at the edge of town and most civilized looking of all the buildings, a railway station, a Victorian-looking structure, most likely erected before the revolution. This place was like a gathering point for all the natives, a social event for greeting incoming and departing trains— waving good-byes, visiting for no reason at all, just to keep contact with the world. We came to the station occasionally, watching wistfully the trains heading west, wishing we were on one, going back to Poland.

On the corner of the marketplace, known as a "bazaar," was a shop. A shop is not exactly the name it could be described as, rather a place where we could get certain articles and sometimes (not very often) we could risk a battle for soap or sugar, or something exotic in that category, whenever there was sudden distribution, without any announcement.

There didn't seem to be any regular Sundays, as we had known as the seventh day in a week; their resting day was the eighth day and was called "wychodneye," translated as "going out." We seldom knew when it was scheduled, but we took their word for it. Sometime later, the mixed up calendar was eliminated and Sunday was back on its seventh day!

My "wychodneye," I utilized for browsing in the only store, the one at the bazaar. It didn't take too long to nose through the place; after all, how much time did I need to examine the packs of safety pins (one size), some sets of water color paints in very small containers and matches, lots of matches, shelves full of them. I could also come across some bottles of cologne water with very impressive titles such as "golden autumn," but we never tried the strong scent, which we heard sometimes was used when there was a shortage of vodka, most of the time. There was a section for food, always idle in sales, for lack of merchandise, except for the large quantity of salt sitting forever on the shelves, for it was horrible looking in color and texture, moist and slightly brown, giving an appearance that it never was processed, however it had its function as a seasoning- it was salty.

One time when I was purchasing matches for lighting the primus(they were always breaking- weak product), I noticed some small rectangular containers with colorful pictures of fruits embellished on them. I didn't ask the fat sales woman what it was, I just bought it being curious, while simply watching the Soviets eat the dark chunks and spit a lot and it made me wonder if I was missing something. The woman behind the counter handed me a pack and said, "Good for you." I didn't argue the point of what they thought was good for us, but I was willing to try this Soviet product. What it really was, were compacted bricks of dried wild berries and fruits, with lots of pips and pits and as I recall one quarter of the container was all pips and pits. It served as a dessert as often as we could get it, mainly because it contained a fraction of something we could associate with a sweet taste. That's without a comparison to our rum-filled chocolates and "tutti-frutti" halvah—a pure torture to think about, but the Russian fruit brick tasted great at the time, except there was a setback, when we had to gather all of our patience, trying to pick the bothersome pips from between the teeth. Thank God for the endless amount of matches, handy as toothpicks. During many idle hours, we sat and wheedled the burnt-out matches, fashioning them into other uses. We were learning fast that in Russia, nothing was wasted, and one lived on the principle of conversions.

Some of the very sharp toothpicks I saved in case, one day meat would enter the picture, but so far that article was as elusive and forgotten as a Dobosh cake!

The small corner store saw a lot of action only when there was a shipment of certain merchandise. No one knew what was coming for distribution, except the people handling the sale, yet the lines were always long at the crack of dawn with a mob waiting patiently to find out exactly what was being sold and how long the supply would last. Depending on the item, some would go home or to work, some would just remain and gab a day away.

Necessities such as food, soap or clothing, sometimes would create a riot or fist fights, hair pulling and a lot of swearing. How they could swear! I have learned some ugly and forbidden words, standing in those long lines.

There never was a prediction or even a guess at the big sales, not to us anyway, but sometimes through a native grapevine or secret hints, we could get some useful information. The best place for gossip was on Saturday morning in the bazaar, where we mingled with Russians, Tartars, Kazakhs and occasional Poles, many of whom walked miles away from the "kolchozes," to be close again to news from the outer world and food, not available in the isolated places in the deep steppes. The bazaar was itself a happening on Saturday morning, a marketplace where owners of the small garden plots, sold vegetables in a small variety, some elusive dairy products, not seen too often, butter or pot cheese, thin, bluish looking buttermilk, and lots and lots of kefir, presently known to us as yogurt. Except the kefir in the black pottery jars we consumed at that time was thick and mighty sour and never, never, except for an occasional centipede, did I find any fruit on the bottom. The amounts we ingested, must have kept our health on the plus side; in fact, without realizing it, our entire diet then was very nutritious and would have been readily approved by today's dieticians and health nuts.

Nevertheless, our bellies cried constantly for other rich foods, such as those we were receiving in the care packages. The status of our teeth was poor because, although we had brushes the tooth powder wasn't obtainable and we used ashes instead, quite a mess. Sometimes it was hard to tell, unless we were in pain, if we really had a cavity or dirty ash in between our teeth.

Well, luckily for us, Mother Nature took care of our needs for those three long years, at least around the mouth cavity area, for unknowingly we had the best dental cleaner in the form of dark, coarse bread and raw vegetables, although some of them we worked with in the fields tasted mushy, being a little rotten, yet they satisfied the hunger and cleaned our choppers.

Another Russian specialty that kept our gums from deteriorating and became a "snack," were red and green tomatoes put up in large barrels, being prepared as sauerkraut, tasting as tart, maybe even more with other veggies thrown for variety, which I really loved. It was a wonderful source of vitamin C, although it puckered my mouth into a letter O and sometimes unnecessarily enhanced the appetite, which we could easily dispense with. On the surface, we fell into the mainstream of Soviet lifestyle, except we took it one day at the time, while at the end of it we gave thanks in the evening prayers and asked for another tomorrow, and the strength to get through it.

******

45

Toward the end of summer, we moved to a different place. Mother became very friendly with the two Polish women who also worked in the sewing shop and they all decided it would benefit them, if they lived together, sharing the quarters, food and multiplied misery, with so many creatures around. I didn't think it would work, but my opinion wasn't important. The two other women had large hordes of very young kids, who were constantly hungry and always fighting among themselves like a pack of wild animals.

My brother found companions and became somewhat rambunctious like the others, but I also found a soulmate in a sister of my mother's friend, two years older than myself, - her name was Baska. With all the screaming and complaining, we got along pretty well, sharing together the food, tears and work.

At this time, I was called to another job. I had a strange knack for being selected into the unusual tasks. This time I went for the production of "valenkys," the felt boots that every Russian foot was equipped with for the winter. I remember back in Poland, when we were small, our father brought for us two pairs from the east, the frontier line with Soviet Russia. They were nice and soft and so very warm. We had a grand time sliding in them on our shiny parquet floors, without being scolded by either mother or Dorka, for in a way, we were polishing the herring-bone inlaid strips of oak. The valenkys lasted a few winters then finally when we had outgrown them they got thrown into the old trunk sitting in the attic to keep company with dusty zithers and black taffeta frocks, the useless articles, presently viewed as sentimental antiques.

Now, I was going to discover the secret that went into making the warm footwear. I was naturally curious but scared, being told before how hard this job would be. The appearance of the building, from the outside, was no different from the other village hovels, maybe a bit larger, but when I walked inside, it was dark and hazy from the steam and my eyes had to adjust to see more clearly. There was a steady murmur of running machines. A supervisor woman with a big bosom and a bigger derriere, took me through two large rooms and had put me in front of a large vat, filled with brown, yucky hot water, which seemed to be in motion, as if something was getting washed and true, there were sheets of compacted sheep's wool, swirling around, then being lifted and fed through the huge turning rollers, squeezing the dirty brown liquid out of them. It was my task to fish them out of the vat and feed them through those hungry rollers.

Well, at least there was no sun, thirst or sweat. No, I am wrong about the sweat, it came later with a few accidents. At the beginning, in my first days of trying to grasp the idea and the stinky, slippery wool, I almost fell into the vat. My short torso didn't seem to stretch far enough over the whole contraption and many times I felt like Grimm's fairy tale witch, stirring the dark brew, peering through the vapors, devoid of evil thoughts, only scared.

Each time I managed to empty the tank of dirty wool, there was another mountain of it waiting, shipped from the adjoining room and I felt some bastard's hands were working overtime piling on me the reeking lint, possibly trying to earn the "stachanovka" title, a name bestowed on a member of the communist society with great honor only on the speedy individuals working for the glory of Mother Russia, the country, about whose welfare I didn't give a damn! All that mattered to me was handling the growing stacks of fleece and using all my muscles to avoid falling into the rust-colored "Jacuzzi." With the tension and a continuous alertness, the time moved fast. At noon, I had a moment of rest, just enough to gulp some cold drink and a bite of dark bread.

On hotter days, I would bring a jar of "borsht", or rather, beet extract, not made into the soup yet. The beets, purchased at the bazaar, were washed and sliced unpeeled (save the vitamins) and put into a crock, sprinkled with sour crystals, with hot water poured over it and a few lumps of bread thrown in for fermenting, then covered with a light cloth, to keep the bugs away. A quite futile effort, for they always found the way to get in and pointlessly drowned themselves in the purple liquid, sinking to the bottom, for us only to discover the gruesome sight, after we used up all of the juice. The first time, it gave me a sickly feeling, but later we learned to tolerate the bugs by erasing their grisly image for there was no change in taste, and wasting food was unheard of. Here again, the Soviet philosophy was staring us boldly in the face, "pryvyknesh."

It was etched in my mind while I drank the tart liquid in the hot summer days. At that time I didn't pay too much attention to my co-workers, as each had a different hour for "lunch," until later when the time of rest was established for everyone working and also the machines. I was the only "foreigner" among the few Russians, some Tartars and Kazakhs. At noontime, we all sat on a hard, cleanly swept clay sidewalk, with me listening to their conversation and language that was rapidly becoming familiar to my ear. Sometimes they tried to draw me into their idle chatter, being very polite, without the usual hostile stares or nasty remarks.

For once, I was seeing the other side of the Soviet coin, learning to evaluate the true Russian soul, basically a good human being, who often, at these times, concealed feelings but occasionally shed the hard shell to reveal a very humane part of their nature. With time, I got to know them better and began to understand the riddles of their existence, the heartaches and ills, the general human conditions called life. Some of the friendlier ones, instead of calling them "comrade," I called by their first name, learning how melodic some of the lengthy names sounded, especially the female names. The men's names, rang a funny bell, such as Grisha, Tola, Misha, which really sounded like girls names!

Well, who am I to question the centuries-long tradition of their appellative style? In fact it was charming and somehow soft about pronouncing the names, once I learned the sound of it. I loved to listen to a pair of the old Kazakh gents, listening to the verbal exchange in their native tongue, which I couldn't understand a word of but enjoyed the gesticulations and expressions. It was like watching a foreign movie with strange characters, except the sad part was that I was a part of it, also.

On days when the machines were being repaired or something else was out of order (it happened quite often), while waiting I would wander around the empty bazaar or the stalls where occasionally the line would form, without asking what was being offered, I would stand behind the last person, to pass the time.

On one of those awkward days, I met a great person, a gentleman and later a lady, whose faces I can see clearly at the present time. I remember the day was unusually hot and the winds blew from all directions, spinning the sand into a dozen funnels, then spewing it out in a flurry under the dense blue skies. The natives were saying the devil was getting married. I watched the phenomena, fascinated, thinking only a devil could settle down in this place, because, after all, it was hell.

I was lost completely in my dark brooding, when out of the blue I heard someone speaking English. I wasn't quite sure if the person was addressing me, but I knew it was English, and a person standing next to me was speaking correctly: "And how are you today?"

The question was directed at me. I followed the sound and looked up, way up there where it came from, at a tall and older gentleman, with gray bushy hair, a pale face lacking the darker tones of a sunburn, indicating he was not a steppe original, rather a city dweller. His blue eyes sparkled mischievously and he seemed to be waiting for an answer, apparently taking for granted that I spoke English. I did, but barely enough to hold a simple conversation.

Back in Poland, my brother and I had an English tutor, giving us private lessons during the summer vacation. Shana, the teacher, like my piano instructor, came from the city of Stryj, twice a week, to torment our tired minds, which we tried to unloosen and relax after the hard, yearly cramming of school studies, and twice a week, I would try to run into the orchard to find the shadiest of trees to hide under, however unsuccessfully, for I don't recall ever missing a single lesson. Though rebelling at the time, later in life I felt grateful to my parents and Shana the teacher, whose unlimited patience carried us through the summer's ordeal, implanting into our unwilling minds the grammar of the language, sounding like a croaking frog or someone trying to speak with a mouthful of hot boiled potatoes. With Shana's help and time, my understanding of the gurgling sounds improved and we began to comprehend the language we thought we could never learn.

Now, with slight confidence I turned and replied, "I am fine, and how are you?" The words came out all right, but the accent, well, it has shadowed me throughout all my English-speaking life and up to this day, I cannot shake it. Possibly by being of Slavic stock, one cannot get rid of the inherited ax that sits between one's tonsils and chops the hell out of the words that come through it. Well, tough, because that's the way it is!

The man speaking English to me smiled and extended his hand, not a common gesture in the Soviet Union: "My name is Alexei, I come from Leningrad and I am here on a long vacation." Then switching to Russian he related his background. He was a professor at the university and few months ago, the government decided he should spend some time in Kazakhstan. Where had we heard that story before?

"What made you think I could speak English?" I asked, feeling excited that I was brushing with a little culture. He grinned: "I knew you were exiled out of Poland and guessed you may know either French or English. I felt hungry for a foreign language," and so we weaved a colorful conversation in three languages(my French was better than English), as if we were friends of many years. The conversation became like coaching, as opinions and ideas were expressed very carefully in Russian, but needless to say, we both enjoyed the time spent while waiting in line for a mystery item.

This day particularly was an intellectual gain for me and material as well, for while my mind was being exercised by the language educator, the long waiting turned out to be a bonanza in the shape of "lepioshki," a rare item in a food department. These were the large buns made out of not commonly seen white flour, in the shape of a diamond with ground meat baked inside, surrounded by a crackling crust. (My mind waters at the memory as they were really good.) From the time I was coming closer to the window of the distribution, the aroma drove me crazy and I prayed dearly that the shutters wouldn't come down as sometimes they did, with a nasty word— "out." My fist felt clammy, squeezing tightly the few rubles, hoping I had enough to pay, for we never knew the prices of items being sold, simply because we "shopped" so seldom, living on trades and bartering most of the time. Money was not a subject of great respect in Soviet Russia. One could possibly save a mess of blue printed rubles and of higher value the brightly red "tchervientze," stash them in a box and not miss them at all, being worthless as a piece of *"Izviestia"* newspaper, however they made a colorful souvenir; that is, if you wanted to remember the country and what they represented.

Shortly then I was at the window and the ration of three "lepioshki" was handed to me. With a great spirit and a smile I said, "au revoir" to my new friend and walked away, wondering how to divide the three buns into a bite for everyone! For a brief moment I was tempted to go behind the stalls to hide and to devour the whole thing myself, not a good idea, as one could get sick on such rich food.

It was afternoon and, as I expected, all the boys were gathered in front of the door, playing "pick up stones" with a lot of noise. I caught some words and sentences spoken or yelled in Russian. It seemed the kids were learning to communicate with the rest of the world, getting acquainted with the language, picking up fast the training at the school and to them what mattered most was their half-full stomach and some clothes on their back. Their real homes were far away; the image of the past life was dimming slowly, and to their young minds, the politics didn't make any difference. Today was important because only the present had meaning.

When I walked past them through the door, they didn't even glance my way, being so wrapped up in a game, except one of them, the terrible Stash, who had gotten a whiff of the baked goods. The kid was clairvoyant when it came to locating food and, at times, was a holy terror. Nothing ever escaped his sight or smell and right now, he was jumping like a Ping-Pong ball, yelling loudly, "there is food; I smell food!"

I ran quickly inside and was glad to see Baska. "Help me!" I cried, showing her the "lepioshki." She closed her eyes and inhaled deeply the still clinging aroma, but only for a second, as Stash was yapping at my heels, waving what seemed more than two hands: "let's eat; let's eat!"

We had a difficult time trying to explain to the bunch that there wasn't enough to eat, only to taste, even minimized the craving by fibbing about the quality of meat, saying it came from a camel, but it didn't work, nobody cared, at this point the rarely seen animal flesh was meat and what carcass it came from, was quite immaterial! Each little palm received a shard of a bun and all the young boys, realizing that was it, walked away with disgusted faces except Stash, who didn't give up and tried to move us with his freely flowing tears.

Baska shooed them out and locked the door. I really liked her. She was so open and honest, no nonsense or mincing words, always in control, even when under pressure. If I had a sister, I would have liked her to be like Baska, although in appearance we differed. She was tall, with a lovely figure and beautiful long legs, wavy dark-blond hair and striking green eyes, compensating in a way for rather plain facial features.

We confided in each other, our secrets, our worries, the joys of simple moments not being too frequent, for there didn't seem to be too much leisure time. But we tried to make the best of it. Baska worked wherever she could get the most of the free food for the kids and to stop the continuous whining brought on by hunger of their growing bodies and the age that cried for nourishment. Some weeks she worked long hours at the bakery, the good source of stale bread, quite edible and plentiful, trying to fill those mouths, the biggest of them, being Stash's. Later, for a short period she washed the dishes at the railroad station restaurant, which served to the weary travelers soup mostly, with more sophisticated "lapsha" noodles, meaning there were more of them floating around than in our meals served on the cattle train coming to Russia. She didn't last there long, confessing the trains made her nervous and a few times, she felt like stowing away, riding into the unknown, hoping to be caught or arrested, but only the thought of her sister being left alone with Stash and the rest of the brood, stopped her from taking such desperate steps.

We were learning to avoid feelings associated with despair. Once we gravitated slightly toward it, we felt as if a tangle, an invisible network was pulling and closing, weakening all defenses and zapping our badly needed energy, leaving us helpless and susceptible to depression and detachment from reality.

Time after time, we had to push back the fear in order to maintain the strength to go on. It was immaterial what age was affected, the old as well as young were vulnerable this first year of our exile in Russia—a number of them had their resistance broken down by clinging to the past, living only with memories, without clear thinking or reasoning. The task became even harder if the health was threatened, for there was neither medicine nor advisors to guide you through the illnesses, physical and mental as well. One had only himself to help.

****

So far, in our small group, everybody seemed to be doing quite well. Perhaps the smell of our grandma's "microcid" didn't allow the germs to congregate on our premises and attack in force, at least thus far.

The summer was nearing its full course and the heat was brutal with a glare from the sun hurting eyes, bringing drowsiness in every idle moment. Inside, where I worked at the production of the "valenkys," the sunlight seldom came in, the air was hot and steamy, a sauna at its best, as long as the machines were in motion.

One morning after reporting to work, I was told I could have half a day to myself, while the machines were being repaired, also having been given a hint about a soap distribution. That was the greatest news in weeks! The precious soap was needed so badly, with the horde of kids starting to smell to high heaven, mostly the boys whose common entertainment and delight was stepping into the dung freshly dropped by the camels or donkeys. The water did help in cleaning, but some particles of excrement still clung to the skin, mainly between the toes and those fragrances we had to contend with on hot summer nights.

All the machines were silent already and the place seemed deserted, evidently everybody was heading for the soap line, the rare item in Soviet hygiene, although there was a handout during the span of a year, often enough without a regard to a "piatiletka." Could you imagine the odor around the country if they rigorously followed the mind-boggling innovations of their "red" industries?

I stepped outside and looked at the stalls in the bazaar; sure enough, there was already a long snakelike formation of people, of all ages, shapes and

51

features. I walked fast and stood behind a tall blond woman, searching through the long line for Alexei. I couldn't see him anywhere and felt disappointed, for a long waiting in line would give me a chance for an interesting three-way conversation again. I kept glancing back, wondering why would he pass up a chance for this rare item—the bubbles? Maybe it was the heat, it was August and it was incredibly hot!

The line was getting longer, I kept looking back; suddenly, the tall blonde woman in front of me, swung her elbow and almost knocked me down. I swayed back for a second but was not surprised, as lines usually became a war zone, where feelings and manners evaporated, bodies became like punching bags and hair had a tendency to get detached from the scalps, all of this accompanied by loud screaming, sometimes in several languages. The result was only what mattered and of course the prize to walk away with, at any cost.

I was quite surprised when the blond woman turned to me with a frightful expression, repeating, "excuse me, excuse me; oh, you little soul." (izvienitie dushka). She kept apologizing, very concerned if I had been hurt. I was stunned, and thought, who was she? Certainly not from this area! Her face looked delicate, features thin as if chiseled by Modigliani, not exactly an image of Gzaroon and the steppes. She looked no more than forty and her voice was soft, while she kept repeating "so sorry."

From my accent, she must have guessed I wasn't a native but of foreign origin, and her tone was most pleasant and friendly when she spoke to me. Yet staring straight at the mob ahead of her and behind, she bristled: "Scum!"(A ta svolotch) she spat the words, surprising me when adding some really ugly material, which didn't quite match her external personality. Well, it was a simple case of looks deceiving, or maybe only the angry mouth.

As the long line forewarned of an extended wait, the blond woman opened up with a long story, talking fast, her past life, a very sad unfolding in detail. She was from around Moscow and by profession, danced with a national ballet. (She, being tall, I wondered.) Her husband was a chemist, both were so young and in love when they married, a very happy couple by Soviet standards, until suddenly, without any warning, he was sent to a Siberian "taiga" to a labor camp and she never heard from him again. At the time she was pregnant and soon after, lost her baby, followed by her deportation to Kazakhstan, leaving her grief stricken and so lonely—not quite fit for hard manual labor, but surviving. In as many words as I could find in my clumsy Russian, I extended my sympathy, to which she answered bitterly, "We are all in the same predicament. My whole country is suffering injustices, so many…only God could help us, but I am not sure if He can hear us any more."

Her eyes were getting moist, but she stopped the tears from coming; instead, her mouth became loud and vulgar, swearing at the red government, looking around as if in challenge to see if anyone was willing to listen. But on this hot

August day, the crowds were pushing from side to side, anxious to get ahead. People stood close as if glued to each other, seeing only that brown chunk of soap, which smelled like medicine. In my mind, I visualized already some suds clinging to my flesh and felt a pleasant feeling of going to sleep without having body odor.

The line was now moving fast and without any incidents of bloody clashes and hair flying in the air! Clutching happily my brown-colored trophy, I heard my name. It was Baska standing at the end of the line. "Do I have a chance?" she asked, pointing to the counter. "You do, Basia, there is enough for everyone here and the rest of the town." "That's great, the boys could really use scrubbing; they stink!" I pointed to my large ration, saying, "We will share if you don't get it." After all, we lived together in one house and the smell was everywhere. But she did get one bar and that evening was full of fun for the children. It was a lot of work for us, yet it was worth every moment. General cleaning of the bodies brought a restful night as if with washing away the dirt a part of our anguish flowed away back into the past, where life once was different and easy. But the barriers were so great and time was moving forward, leaving us with moments of synthetic and temporary inner peace, as if life meant it to be that way.

The "bronco" was being harnessed and the wild struggle was subdued to redirect the energy to survival and in helping others do the same. The simplest chores and actions, being one time normal everyday functions, became the markers and sometimes capers, masking the apprehension and anxiety in the face of months ahead and grim thoughts of approaching winter, the unknown and dreaded, Russian winter…

By this time, our hopes for the return to Poland or being rescued in any way, had vanished completely.

******

The world was in turmoil. The nations in western Europe were embattled in their own fight for survival, each sinking under the pressure of the black swastika, bewildered at the immense power and speed it subverted their strategy of defenses and scattered the armies in confusion and flight. Europe was being enfolded in black mourning ribbons and the shock of the conquest and surrender was received in painful silence over the occupied territories in the West. In the East the red hammer and sickle went berserk as the new allies of Hitler undertook the task of dominating and imposing on the iron rule over the freshly seized countries of eastern Europe. The combined forces, triumphant in their zealous expansion, were showing the rest of the world, the supremacy of their ruthless military masterminds.

Most of the information about world affairs would come to us through letters (uncensored) from home with hints and codes (just in case they were censored), without exactly naming the names of persons or country and the political events.

The missing puzzle pieces we tried to find in the news from *"Izviestia"* or *"Pravda"*. Pravda, meaning the truth, sometimes brought a cynical smile even to the Soviet citizens, who knew better what to believe but seldom expressed their opinions outwardly, especially in our presence. The news though, no matter how slanted and distorted at times, was always a source of information and inspired many of us to concentrate, while trying to sift even a fraction of truth from a lot of puffed-up salutes. Most of their boasting and flatteries were directed at the "red paradise" and their leaders, so there would not be much of a mention about the war and the advances of the German army. The radios were no different, blaring propaganda from the loudspeakers, posted high on the telegraph poles in the center of town and at the railway station, creating an ear-piercing noise, with the repetitious routine of praises and wishes of longevity to the great father (batko) of the state, Joseph Stalin. It almost made one ill, but there was no escape from the voices reminding you that the man so constantly revered, was responsible for ours and their countless afflictions and untold crimes to his own people.

We hardly heard any words of criticism, protests or complaints from the native comrades. It felt as if they were surrounded with a false euphoria of gratitude, with their blessing the government for proclaiming everyone equal and given a chance for a new way of living and new era of the 20th century. They were the true "reds," the ignorants who tried to preach to us the misleading doctrines of Marx, Engels and Lenin, and perhaps, themselves not quite understanding but believing, because maybe that's all they could do, believe in it, blindly.

Over the end of a summer, we came to meet with many of our countrymen, who since spring were scattered around the wide range of areas as laborers in "kolchozes" and "sowchozes," some being collective farms with grains and produce, others a mixture of everything that could be raised.

The visitors from those faraway places brought ugly tales of extremely hard work and dreadful living conditions. The acclimatization took a toll on life, brought sickness, hunger and mental depression. The weak and very ill didn't stand a chance to survive the ordeals, although on the other hand, some of them with a poor medical history became stronger, complaining only of not enough food.

Many we thought to be strangers, we found were close friends of our family back in Poland, in close-by towns. Through the learning of the names we became very close in friendship, ready to help as much as we could, knowing we lived under much better conditions than most of them, being estranged from the rest of the world, in the deep steppes. We were lucky, so we thought.

Sometimes we felt very charitable and saved luxury items such as sugar, canned milk and cream of wheat, things hard to get but helping to sustain the health of the young, the babies and small children. I became active in that cause for partly selfish reasons, mainly I was influenced by my personal feelings, as I was very attracted to a young fellow who came almost every week to trade the flour and millet for other foods not seen at all around the area where they lived in a village, twenty-five miles away from us.

I saw him quite often and being of a ripe age, sweet sixteen, I found myself falling head over heels in love with him. He was so polite, so handsome! What was I to do?

On the day of "wychodnaye," I would walk through the bazaar, hoping to see him walking with a whole group of young girls and guys, for their weekly trading and visits from "Novaia Zyzn," the name of the village where they had lived.

All of them would come in the early morning, quite tired from the long march, then sit down at the edge of the market, the bazaar, take off their shoes to massage their sore feet, with their noses turned away! In spite of the fatigue and gobs of blisters, the whole bunch always seemed to be in good spirits, laughing and joking, as if there wasn't a care in the world. Observing from a distance, I envied their untroubled disposition, a sort of camaraderie and bond that extended only in their circle, because of the life they shared and because Mietek, my heart's dream, was a part of it.

Being quite timid at first, I didn't know how to approach them, until I had learned the reason for their frequent trips, almost weekly, to the town of Gzaroon. It wasn't long before I became a welcomed person, simply because I kept bringing food they made the trips in search for. My secret love was very gallant and grateful for the extravagant things I brought, which took time and effort on my part, but for his smile and soft "thank you" tone, I would have starved myself. All those coveted foodstuffs were for his sister's little girl - a consolation in a way, knowing it was a noble cause.

Even over the lengthened number of visits, my idol, Mietek and I didn't get anywhere; except for flirty conversations and mushy-eyed contact, things just didn't develop along the love line. This was just as well, for we were to face problems of a monumental nature, something we always feared—hunger, illness and death.

In the early fall, we had changed living quarters again. All of us, the three families, moved to a huge, one-room house, belonging to a local school, where I was given a job, equivalent to being a janitor. It was labor, Soviet style—very rough, and as much as I can remember today, I still shudder, recalling those days. I had to get up before dawn, still in the dark hours, to fire up the long line of the "pietchkas," each heating a separate classroom. It required continuous cleaning of the grates, hauling ashes out beyond the school area to dump it, time after time…then starting the fires with tumbleweed and small chunks of wood (wood was precious) and running like hell with the buckets to bring the coal to feed the hungry "pietchkas," making sure the fires were burning for the rest of the day.

The stoves were built into the walls of every classroom and in order to maintain a comfortable temperature during a cold spell, I had to hop pretty fast to service all of them properly - feed the coal, shake the grates and carry out the ashes, a perpetual story of a bad-luck Cinderella! Without much chance of a breather, there were also the classroom floors and corridors to scrub, twice a week.

How I detested the cold water and the heavy shreds of the rags seldom protecting the palms of my hands from the splinters, entering freely while dragging them over the old worn-out wooden floor boards, a job so hopeless in its attempts to eliminate the dirt, but instead it seemed as if the mud was being spread in large circles, leaving an appearance of soiled rings, as if all the work done, was useless for its results. Whenever I had a few spare moments, I spent them by the window, trying in a hurry to pick out most of the splinters, before handling the heavy buckets of coals to ease the pain from the pressing weight into the splinter-peppered hands.

At the beginning of a school year, the weather seemed quite fair and my chores at first were light. The word "pryvyknesh" kept its close distance and my ration of dark bread came regularly, every day. I also got paid in rubles, which wasn't a big deal at all. The school itself was through the seven grade with a lot of teachers. Today, I don't remember too many faces, except one woman and a man. The woman teacher was in her twenties at the time and always gave me orders in a sharp and shrill voice, glaring at me with her cold, bulging, fish eyes, as if I was a villain of some sort. I don't recall seeing her ever smiling, although she was attractive. The other teacher was a young man, very blond and handsome, the "Ashley" type from *"Gone With the Wind"*. Soft-spoken and well-versed in literature and the arts, he greeted me politely, sometimes carried on a pleasant conversation, while I listened determined to absorb the words, some of which still sounded so strange to me, but I felt grateful for being treated almost as equal, overjoyed by his openness. Of course it didn't matter that according to their constitution, everyone should be equal and free, easily said, but in truth, their laws and rules were tucked away in books, documents and grandiose speeches. As I look back at their inflated dogmas, I could easily insert a triple capital "B" — "Bolshevik's Bolshoi Bullshit!"

With our status as prisoners or forced exiles, we knew we shouldn't have expected to be treated as citizens of the USSR, feeling still the hostility, not quite being explained to us in so many words.

In the middle of the autumn, the Kazakhstan climate changed abruptly. The cold winds blew through the steppes from the north, strewing sand and debris, breathing a blustery cold and setting off a continuous and sorrowful whining. With that change, the tempo of my work increased greatly. No matter how hard I tried, I could not keep up, fast enough in maintaining the fires in the "pietchkas," for distributing the heat evenly. Most of the time, the coal was wet and the flames barely flickered, being smothered and clogging up the grates, although some burned too fast and had to be relit. Each day I ran from "pietchka" to "pietchka" with a small shovel and tried working miracles. At the top of this frenzy, teachers were harassing me and the school kids - the little bastards! The jeers and dirty words were a common, daily occurrence, sometimes frightening when I found myself knocked down with coal scattering around and chunks of them flying in the air, with me as a target. It was terrifying, and being an outcast anyhow, I could not expect help from anywhere. Being still healthy and strong I fought off the dirty sons of bitches, but I also kept biting my lip so as not to show the tears forcing their way from anger and despair. In Russia, it was a disgrace to cry in public, a sign of weakness, which was hardly tolerated by the Soviet people. In this land, as in ancient Sparta, the aged and disabled didn't fare too well. The government being inclined mostly toward the strong and fit, the fanatical believers in sacrifices, with their strength and health for this detested country and a rotten leadership!

I hung on, not having any other choice, with all of my energy, to earn the bread, to share and fill the gap when others couldn't. In the middle of October, illness broke out in a number of places, attacking first children, then the elders. We faced an epidemic of great proportions involving violent stomach pains, vomiting and diarrhea with a dreadful diagnosis—Typhoid.

Only once during the crisis, we had a visit from a doctor, a Polish woman doctor, one of us, who in plain words, explained to us, there was nothing she could do to help, except to advise us to protect ourselves from the wider spreading of disease. She was quite helpless, without the medicine, as she could only diagnose but neither aid nor cure. Hers was a dilemma, the anguish of a doctor who had to stand by and watch a disease spread and people die.

In our household, we had four children fighting for life, the wild Stash included. They all belonged to Basia's family. The little creatures were so pitiful, lying on the pile of old coats and blankets heaped on the cold floor, with sunken eyes, bluish lips, laying so quietly, sometimes their skinny bodies shaking violently, without the strength to cry.

They all pulled through and survived, thanks to Basia's incredible efforts of caring for them day and night. For hours she sat by them like a watchdog, oblivious to the surroundings, until her older sister relieved her in the evening, after working, in the sewing shop. Then she went to the village, virtually begging for food, anything related to help the little guys to get better.

Each day was a battle in the dark, with death hovering so close by and fear unending with the question, who may be next?

Throughout those difficult days, I went to work as usual, at early dawn, confronting the heavy winds that brought the continuous rains, without stopping until the freezing weather changed it into snow, creating another nightmare of cold days and not having fuel for "pietchkas."

When I walked to work still in the dark, the howling winds came from all directions, penetrating every inch of my body, moving like an invisible force from which there was no escape, in those hours before dawn. The loneliness, the feeling of dejection and lack of any hopes, made our circle of depression a little wider with each day.

The last part of October became a mountain of crises, piling one on top of the other. The typhoid epidemic was raging and had reached a dangerous stage, with deaths being often reported, followed by a slowly creeping hunger. We began to dig deeper into our wicker basket containing our main food supply, realizing suddenly how little there was left from what we had brought with us from Poland, from care packages and trading over the summer. The sight was hopeless, each time we opened the lid with a fearful glimpse of fewer and shrinking sacks of barley, millet and handfuls of kasha (buckwheat).

The outlook was truly grim. The rations of bread we all pooled together and tried divide evenly, eating slowly to make it last, saving a few chunks for drying, to make a soup, a last resort, when everything else would be gone.

The painful anxiety began to gnaw inside, producing a feeling of panic, not known so much up to this time, drying up the saliva in our mouths. In some moments, when the hunger became intense, we imagined chewing on unnamed things, just to muffle the dull throbbing of hunger pangs, coming in waves, nagging until you imagined swallowing something, and it didn't matter anymore what it was, only to suppress the faint nausea and choking feeling at the base of our throats.

HUNGER

The heavy work took up a lot of my energy, but staying after school hours, even when my chores were done, gave me a chance to look for discarded food under the benches and banged up long row of desks. At times I was lucky, finding chunks and hard crusts of bread greasy from melted butter, covered sometimes with floor dirt, and the unlucky days brought only sour tomatoes and empty shells of pumpkin seeds. Whatever the finds happened to be, I ate hastily, without actually inspecting the form; besides, it wouldn't matter anyhow, the demands from the stomach didn't call for aesthetic appeal, but only the filler.

Only one time I got slightly disturbed - perhaps I shouldn't even mention it, but this has been a burden in my memories, a thorn, a sickly barb, whenever it occasionally crosses my mind.

One afternoon, I couldn't find a bloody crumb in any of the classrooms. My stomach was churning, badly. Walking through an empty corridor I spotted a piece of bread lying by the coal bucket, a nice chunk. "God is great!" I said to myself and bent down to pick up the dark lump. My hands eagerly grasped it, but before I lifted it to my mouth, I felt something slimy and moist under my fingers. I didn't want to look at it, guessing what it might be, thus preventing me from swallowing. I closed my eyes, ran the sleeve over the repulsive matter, wiping off as much as I could of the awful nasal discharge, then ate the bread. The nausea never came, I was hungry.

There were more incidents similar or less offensive in that nature, but we never took time to dwell on it; bad and worse, we tried to put all behind us, bracing ourselves for unknown surprises. And there always were plenty of them around the clock.

On one of those days, I worked early at dawn as if in a daze, being awake most of the night by the cries of the two small children, who whimpered continuously, wanting something to eat. They were at that stage of recovery from the typhoid and their little systems were craving decent nourishment. It was so great to see them getting well, yet the hardest part was to stall them with promises that there would be food tomorrow, with us only guessing and hoping. Basia's energy seemed to be endless, spending hours in the village, going from house to house, begging for milk and eggs or a piece of animal fat to concoct a broth for the young children. The results of her efforts were most pleasing, bringing tears to see the weak smiles on the puny, pale faces, slurping happily the soup speckled with the rest of the barley out of the wicker trunk. The last of the grain was disappearing too fast, though we tried to conserve it for the worst of times, not realizing completely that this was the worst and we only hoped what was left would last for a while not so much for all of us, but the little ones and grandma, who lately wasn't in the best of health. She kept repeating how much she missed Poland and felt quite melancholy after all, she was over eighty-six years old. But I thought that whatever bothered her, would pass. It didn't.

That morning, it was already November, I felt completely drained, moving slowly, wondering if the typhoid had bypassed me and I now had second thoughts about being claimed as one more victim. By the time the classes started, some of my "pietchkas" were still stone cold, not lit. Very strong winds kept shutting off the tiny vents and the air wasn't flowing freely. I tried to hurry, but my muscles didn't seem to be in working condition, and frankly I felt so numb, I didn't give a damn!

The classes were already in session, when one of pupils came and yelled that his teacher wanted to see me, right now! I guessed that "fish eyes" must have some problems, the heat, undoubtedly, but braced myself for a lot of barking and reprimands. It wasn't the woman, though, it was my blond friend "Ashley." As soon as I walked into the room, I knew a storm was in the air by the complete silence. It didn't take but a minute for me to find out, the kindly teacher had another side of his personality—a cruel beast, I thought. I couldn't believe it was the same person, looking at the sight of his face, distorted from anger, eyes so cold, enraged: "How dare you leave this classroom without heat? Is the work too hard for your "bourgeois" hands? Are you too delicate, lazy? Better learn to live our way and don't wait for your God to save you, He isn't here anymore, He doesn't exist!" He kept on as if the matter of a heated room was secondary, being only taunted by anger, provoked by his beliefs, exercising his authority in a lecture I couldn't quite catch fully, in a rapid flow of words, in a language I was still struggling to understand. His voice now became louder: "I don't want this ever to happen again or you and your family will be out of here in a minute. Tomorrow I will have heat in this room-I don't care if you have to start at midnight-here are the keys for the school, make sure you are here early!"

With that long and bitter harangue, he threw the heavy ring of keys at me. One of the keys with a sharp edge, caught the top of my ear, tearing the flesh away from the scalp. I winced, then bent down to pick up the bundle of large keys and felt a trickle of blood on the side of my face. My hands were stained with black soot, so I hesitated touching the cut with a dirty finger, but I could feel the slow, steady seepage over my cheek, hoping my ear was still attached. Hastily I grabbed the heavy ring, before he would start preaching again and without a glance or word, left the classroom.

At a fast pace I made a circle of "pietchkas," shook the grates harder, watching the flames flare up, but the fire, although steady, burned very slowly.

The winds blew with whistling sounds, scaling the outside walls, as if looking for an opening to get inside, trying to chill the warm air circulating from the "pietchkas" through the classroom. My efforts seemed hopeless. The temperamental steppes, being merciless in the heat during the summer, were no less cruel in bringing the frigid winter wind from the north.

I had thought about the type of punishment I could be given for failing in my job, the consequences my family and our friends would suffer. Would I be sent to a faraway "sowchoz," alone? There was much harder work there! So many thoughts passed through my mind, I seemed to forget the time and my search for food, I didn't feel hungry anyway, the worry suppressed the aches of the stomach.

I watched the sun descending rapidly over the horizon, leaving the orange glow in a large circle, beneath the graying clouds, illuminating the small glass panes in deeply-set window frames. For a moment, as it grew darker, the shabbiness of the surroundings had disappeared and there was a glimmer of color, the artistic touch of nature, trying to cover up the imperfections of a tattered human existence. There was something soothing in the deep silence and the afterglow of the sunset, but the spell was very brief, the enchantment was broken, only the flicker of the dying flames in the "pietchka" reminded me that I will have to face the same tomorrow.

I managed to shake off the enveloping feeling and having still enough light I turned my attention to the rows of school desks. The raid produced a couple of thin slices of bread with dark orange spread in between them. Carefully I lifted the sandwich close to my nose out of curiosity; well, I would have eaten anyhow, but I sniffed at it, what was it? I tasted it—not too sweet, not sour, but that certain smell. Somewhere in my memory, I knew it—the faint scent of pumpkins. Another item with which to expand our humble menu. I had seen pumpkins at the bazaar, but that would have to wait until summertime.

I bit into someone's half-eaten sandwich (the little bastard wasn't hungry enough to finish it), the flavor bringing back the picture of October sun-splashed fields of potato vines drying up and among them the pumpkins, fat and glistening with colors of green, yellow, orange and striped with white, heavy like the large round bellies of expecting women, lying in waiting.

I remember how heavy some of them felt while carrying them from the field, with bottoms full of dirt making the hands look muddy while we cut and then pulled the mushy contents to separate the slippery seeds to spread to dry on wiry nets, then roasting them in the oven. Oh the smell and the mess from the empty shells and Dorka handing me a broom with a short order: "Sweep it!"

Dear God, would the memories never end? They appeared mostly when I was so hungry! The half-eaten sandwich filled the void in my roiling stomach, with a slight feeling of guilt for not saving it to take home to share, but I thought it may cause more of a disturbance than good.

The waning daylight just barely was showing the path toward our quarters. I approached the house with an apprehensive feeling. The young children were recovering, getting a little unruly and Stash, the sickest of them all, was in an uproar, yelling for food. The ration place was closed already and I had to walk in, empty handed. All the kids were scraping the small lacquer "tcharkas," filled with white looking paste and I could hear the smacking of lips and see eyes darting to the side where Basia stood holding a large wooden spoon, clean of any residue. She turned to me with a guilty look: "Sorry, they just cried and I couldn't take it any more, they got it all!"

I assured her I feasted on "leftovers" from the school and by tomorrow we should have a double ration of bread.

"Did grandmother eat something today?" I asked, looking anxiously in her direction. She didn't look well. The cheerfulness was gone from her normal disposition and a low-key resignation was quite visible in her declining strength to leave the bed. I walked over to her side and sat at the edge of the bed, patting her hand. She smiled sadly, saying, "Don't worry about me, I don't need too much, you young people take care of each other to stay well." Her eyes became cloudy, then she closed them as if going to sleep. I left her to be alone with her memories and dreams, something those of us working long hours could not afford to do anymore.

Each day now was a continuous challenge of grappling with cold, hunger and worry about nearby illnesses cropping up, with anxiety sapping the energy, trying to stay sane. Time didn't stand still, and without counting, only by watching the light and dark, we knew the days were slipping away and without glancing at the hand-scribbled calendar, we knew November came with whistling blizzards and silent, deep-seething despair.

While walking through the blinding snowstorms, I sometimes felt as though my eyes were deceiving me, drawing a milky cloud over them, making me stumble many times, but that feeling went away and I didn't think much about it any more.

The lack of food was a continuous concern among us, the grownups. Going on seventeen, I felt as if I had finally joined the ranks of the ones who held the privilege of being called adults and was now acting as one and sadly regretting the new aspect, wishing again I was a child being cared for, instead. The leap was too sudden, too great from a young fledgling of untroubled years while growing up to the bitter encounter with powerful elements of life, the hunger, sickness and death. The enormity of change was difficult to understand and trying to build stamina at the same time, disciplining myself in behavior of calm influence around me, to carry the brunt, easier.

Children needed an assurance that everything was well and would be alright and in spite of chilling thoughts of the nearest outlook, we tried to joke and laugh, without mentioning the next day. If we could scrape a bit of food and keep the "pietchka" going, it was a battle won, one round for that one time!

Sometimes Baska and I wondered if the time would ever come for a break in this hype of superficial self-control and thinly disguised ease. That came sooner then we anticipated. It was brought on by a tragic event, the death of our grandmother. She died at the end of November. Although we knew she was ailing now for some time, we were not prepared for the end of her life to come so soon.

I was putting on my coat in the early hours of one morning, going to work at school, when to my great surprise, I saw grandmother raise herself on the pillows and motion me to come closer to her bed. She seemed very excited and her eyes were burning feverishly in her yellow, sunken, small face. I heard her voice, strong as in the old days when she spoke to us with a snap and spirit. Now, her sight was focused on the still dark window, as if she tried to penetrate it, saying clearly, "They came, they finally came, they are here, we are going back, thank God, we are going back!"

She must have been dreaming of going back to Poland. After that outburst and the strain of talking, she sank back on the pillows, looking exhausted, and fell asleep. I could hear her breathing normally. In the evening when I came home, she slept, but her cheeks looked pink and her breathing was irregular. I wished mother didn't have to work so late, but the sewing shop was busy making the winter "fufajkas," the gray, quilted jackets in all the sizes, to keep all of Russia warm, but drab and ugly, without a doubt.

The evening dragged on, and we were uneasy, with fear crouching in every corner. Baska was busy, trying to divert the kids' attention from thinking about food, telling stories and evidently being quite successful, for they were listening without interruptions or yelling as usual. I sat at the edge of the bed, occasionally looking at Gran. One time she became restless and I got up to prop up her pillow. When I reached behind her, I felt a lump, and I knew it was a chunk of dried-up bread, probably two days old. My stomach churned and my mouth got moist imagining eating the crumbs. The bread was still in my hand, I couldn't let it go. I started to shake and while looking at my grandma, I scraped my teeth on the dried-up, dark chunk of bread.

My head was devoid of any thoughts, and I trembled while swallowing the crumbs. Nobody saw me and grandmother was oblivious to what was happening.

Later that night I slept at the foot of the bed, restless, feeling remorse and great shame, waiting for dawn to come so I could run to my job, away from here, from my conscience, so full of guilt!

I went to work earlier than usual and came back at noon to meet Basia at the door, who assured me everything was alright. That afternoon, I didn't mind my heavy work, even the pesky splinters and chapped hands from icy water. That day, I planned to search the classrooms more thoroughly, to find bread such as the one I stole from Gran. I did find soft and clean pieces with sweet cream sandwiched in between, Gran surely will like that—I thought happily—and I will go to the village for some milk. I will make up for what I have done!

It was quite late when I left the school. The wind was blowing viciously and I had to walk against the blinding snow, trying to stay on the ground. For a while I thought I had lost my direction, for there was nothing but the whiteness around me. I strained my eyes, looking to my sides, but couldn't see a thing. The school sat at the edge of town and if I stepped the wrong way, I would easily walked out into the wild steppes and a sure death. I stood for a moment shivering, praying. Perhaps if I closed my eyes, my instinct would point me in the right direction. I waited for a while, listening to the moaning wind, but the cold was penetrating my body and I knew I had to keep going. I opened my eyes and through the curtain of snow I thought I saw a faint glimmer of light. I started to walk toward it and with each step, the light grew brighter and more pronounced. I began to walk faster, knowing I was approaching our habitat. As I kept looking at the distant glow, I began to make out the shape of a house and the window where the light was coming from. Now being closer, I distinguished the brightness as a candle burning with a large flame, sitting very close to the window pane. Behind the glow, I thought I saw a figure, standing.

Alicja R. Edwards

CANDLE IN THE WINDOW

It looked like my grandmother. How wonderful! I felt overjoyed inside, and I forgot the freezing cold and the swirling snow. I broke into a run, without stopping until I reached the door.

Strange, when I opened it, the room itself was dark, except for a small lantern burning by the door. Baska came slowly to meet me, wrapped in a blanket, looking at me without saying a word. I forced myself to speak: "What happened? I just saw grandmother in the window with a candle."

I looked toward the window; there was a lighted candle, I was staring at the dark space where I thought I saw a figure, but there was darkness and silence accept for Basia's whisper: "Gran died two hours ago—in her sleep."

My head was spinning, I was back walking in the snow, seeing the candle and Gran behind it, how could it be? She was dead, but I saw her in the window! I felt numb, as if in a trance, hoping it was a nightmare. My eyes were burning and throbbing. I took my coat off, which was laden with thick clinging snow and lay down at the foot of the bed, wishing mother would come soon. While waiting in the darkness, I went to sleep, not allowing myself to think that, at the distance of a touch, our beloved grandmother was lying in peace, her body at rest in the strange land of Kazakhstan, but her soul already back in Poland.

The next morning, a very cold morning to be exact, I couldn't open my eyes...they were shut as if glued with some sticky matter and through a small slit, I could see everything floating in milky color. I could hear distressed voices, I could feel pain and anguish, but it seemed as if it was happening in a different house, not next to me. I missed work that day, but I wasn't aware of my surroundings. I had stepped into a world of oblivion and perhaps it was a blessing for me, for I vaguely remember the days that followed, except a small portion of hours of mourning and sorrow. Mother didn't have time to grieve or cry. To this day, I can only recall a few episodes, as I was feeling as if I was being sedated with a potent drug. Now and then I could hear the voices and discussions with desperate overtones. Mother and Jez tried to find a place to bury Gran with permission from the local authorities, which was no problem as they had pointed out. The steppes were vast and all you had to do is to dig a hole and cover it, without expecting any help or anything else from them. To this day I keep wondering from where in this ordeal came the energy and courage to keep our mother fortified in each hour of the day and night. It seems as if in the most crucial moments of grief, she had acquired an enormous spiritual and physical strength, to carry her through without regard for her own suffering.

Over the three days, mother and Jez would come home with bloody faces and hands from scratches and dog bites, bringing stolen boards, one or two at the time, then later "acquiring" a number of the rusty nails, to assure a safe burial, safe from the steppe animals, and for Gran's body to rest in peace so far away from home.

It was on the last day, I recall, someone telling me to get off the bed. I did so obediently and with my hands feeling around, like a blind person, I found a corner between the bed and the wall and sat there in silence, while my mother and her friends were busy, I was told, sewing a large linen sheet to enfold grandma's body. It was so quiet. Only at times could I detect a short sob, my mother's. The room was so cold and the floor I sat on was like ice. Someone handed me a cup of barley broth and I drank slowly. Everything appeared to be so remote. Hunger, disease, "pietchkas," even this ritual of death failed to bore through the numbness of feelings, detached of any tender emotions, as if the events evolving around me were those in a play or cinema.

I am sure there is a term in medical language for naming such a state of mind, but a diagnosis or antidote wouldn't have helped me. Probably it was the breakdown each of us feared so much, combined with a strange condition of my eyesight—nothing seemed real, and nothing really mattered. For unexplained reasons, I kept going to sleep very often and this time I dozed off again and when I woke up, though my eyes were still closed, I heard hammering outside of the room and the sound of wood being chopped. My body shivering from cold, I visualized myself leaning against the "pietchka," feeling warm again. It was a second of a short living hope, for I realized that the sounds were those of the boards being nailed together—the nightmare had continued.

To this day, I keep living those moments over again, perhaps because I didn't participate in the rites of grieving and saying good-bye to a person I so loved, who was always like a mother to me and my brother. Whatever was happening, I had to imagine the movements by the sound of voices, low and quiet, almost whispers. I never knew the exact time when they took her away; I never saw her face for the last time, that last day…

I only remembered the stolen chunk of dried-up bread and her shadow behind a burning candle.

Drifting in and out of a groggy sleep, I noticed after a long while, it became very quiet—the small noises had ceased and the silence was ringing in my ears like ocean waves. Everyone seemed to be gone, even children's voices and footsteps had disappeared. I got up slowly and walked holding onto the bed, then feeling the covers, I knew the bed was empty. I was completely alone. I felt alone, deserted. This was a time to turn to God, to pray—or cry. I couldn't do either. I felt my religious beliefs had failed me or I failed them. Was God so angry at us? What powers unknown to us above were controlling the events and outcomes? Our future would become the enigma of our fate, helped only by a strong will to exist and survive!

DEATH ON THE STEPPES

Alicja R. Edwards

The weather was extremely cold and I couldn't quite picture if the snow was falling or blowing as usual in every direction. I sensed the terrible struggle my family would have to endure to dig the grave through the frozen earth—the winds, cold, all left up to women and children.

The hours had extended into the late afternoon, when I heard the voices. They all were back and from the other sounds I guessed the "pietchka" was being lit. They must have found something to burn and by the acrid smell, I knew instantly they brought the "kiziak," the highly prized and popular local burning fuel, comprised of animal manure and dry grass or straw, with mud mixed into it to hold together. Dried up and formed into the shapes of large cakes, it provided a good source of heat if you had enough of it to feed the "pietchkas" all through the day. Everyone was frozen, but there were no loud complaints and not a word about the burial itself. Mother came close to me and put her arm around me. "How are your eyes?" she asked. "I didn't forget you being here alone, I just had to take care of "babcia." She hugged me close; something was caught in my throat, yet I couldn't cry.

With mother holding me, I began to feel warm, listening to the crackling of the "kiziak" bursting into flames.

"My eyes don't throb any more, but I still can't see clearly" I told her. "You will, you will, just rest and soon everything will be over, soon, soon," she repeated as if in a trance. Her grip on my arm had lessened and I was drifting again into a deep sleep. I didn't feel hungry or cold any more. This tragic ordeal created an insensitive vacuum around me, a chasm separating me from the rest of the world, the presence of existence. How mercifully my fate arranged to leave me unperturbed and blocked out to the saddest moments, since our arrival in Russia. The death of our grandmother was very painful loss, a grief of great dimensions and feeling as if our world was falling apart.

It was almost a week after the burial, when I could finally open my eyes and see again the surroundings; in as sad a shape as they were before, but I felt lucky being alive and whatever blindness I experienced, now it was gone, leaving me only with the red rims around the eyelids and eyes watering easily from time to time. I coped with it, accepted it but I also lost the job at the school. It really wasn't so much of a loss, but in that package were included bread rations and the shelter, miserable and cold as it was, still we had a roof over our heads.

******

In a weeks time, we gathered our belongings again, the wrinkled clothing, the "pierzynas," a bed and a faithful but empty now wicker basket, and we moved. The hard winter was just beginning, but mother found a place for the entire clan, a part of a dwelling belonging to a Russian family, on the outskirts of the opposite side of Gzaroon. We were to occupy a room divided in two parts, one extremely narrow with a "pietchka," serving as a kitchen and the other part, a larger one, a "parlor," which also meant a sleeping room. Actually to describe it more correctly, it was a space to stand up in, to turn around in or lie down to sleep. At bedtime, when everyone was settled into the chosen area, the overall picture from a bird's-eye view, resembled a can of sardines in a disarrayed pattern. The green bed made a third move with us and by now, was like a member of the family. With grandmother gone, all three of us slept on the bed, being quite lucky in a way, for the clay floor was always damp and full of crawling bugs, some of strange origin.

Our friends had their straw mattresses stuffed with the prickly tumbleweed to add height, away from the dampness, but that kind of fill was rather unkind to one's "tush." Many times through the night, I could hear some coarse words hitting the airways and bugs splattering the walls, being slaughtered in numbers. Some bugs, I suspected, were committing suicide, to escape the torturous hands of the small children who delighted in squashing them slowly, with pleasure and a lot of squealing. We were safe on the high bed, still bright green in color, with wide slats, reminiscent of "mission" oak, but occasionally the bed-bugs would let us report their presence, while hibernating, waiting for the warm weather, to come out in full force.

But as it was, winter just began showing us the many faces of its ferocity with the introduction of "burians," the severe blizzards, blowing the winds in wild circles, to crisp freezing mornings, when the sharp air hurt our throats and lungs, while inhaling too deeply.

Somewhere, amid the tragic events and concerns for life, we had lost track of time, in number of calendar days. Already it was December and it dawned on us, that the great holidays were approaching—Christmas time. Just a thought of it brought out a resentment and bitterness toward the whole world, as if our imprisonment in Russia, was everybody else's fault!

No doubt, we were the victims but so were a few million others, throughout the world, whose destiny was determined by the scratching of a pen from the twisted minds of some world leaders. The only difference was that our pleas and calls for help either were not heard or just plainly ignored. We knew we were on our own, completely alone!

Approaching Christmas, the most joyous of all holidays, we anticipated it with dread. We barely glanced at the scribbled date of the 6th of December, St. Nicholas day. We had tried not to notice the date of the sixth, on the clumsily designed piece of paper, we called a calendar. In spite of the efforts, we knew we couldn't forget the excitement of that day, the anxious heartbeat, awaiting the night, and then the morning, for it was when we found our present under the pillow.

Way back, when we were small children, I recall staying up late those nights, lying in bed so very still, listening for the sounds—maybe the sleigh bells, maybe the quiet footsteps, fighting off the sleep so, for once, to witness the delivery of the gifts. Nothing like that ever happened, though, the only sounds I would hear were those coming from the kitchen, where two grouchy parents sat patiently, sometimes past midnight, waiting for us to fall asleep. One time only, I thought I almost caught a hand under my pillow, thinking it belonged to a gracious old saint, but as it turned out, it was only my kid brother checking the gift site, thinking in fear perhaps he got passed over for being unruly that year. Yet when came the morning, there were shouts of joy upon tearing the soft, brightly colored tissue paper, not paying too much attention to the outside of the present. To me, the appearance of the gift wrap was a reflection of the year passed, an indicator of my behavior. The most common wrap was red or white crepe or tissue paper, tied with a satin ribbon, but the focal point was a small, bunch of twigs gathered into a bouquet, mostly from a birch tree, also tied with a fancy string, which we had called "roozga," and depending on the color it was bearing, it gave us a forewarning, similar to a report card. With "roozga" painted gold, there was no sense of panic; the silver made you stop and think, but the natural color resembling a miniature broom, made the heart race faster, wondering, should you open the gift at all? And, if by chance, there was a stick with the red face of a devil on it, you knew the grade was bad.

I remember one Christmas morning in our parents' bedroom, there was a huge birch broom leaning against father's side of the bed, (in its natural state), with a large empty bottle with a vodka label hanging from the top and a red-velvet figure of a devil, supporting it with a pitch-fork. It was quite a sight! We couldn't have mistaken the message! (I don't think it came from Santa, either.)

Now, it was all behind us, like an incredible fairy tale of joy and happiness, unfolding an awful truth, that nothing ever would be the same again, even if times had changed to normal, the trauma of painful events had done too much damage to erase it from our minds. Our grandmother wasn't with us anymore and hunger and diseases left the stigma of fear for each tomorrow. The future looked rather bleak and although the food situation had improved a bit, with two parcels arriving from Poland at the worst of times, still Christmas wasn't promising any kind of jubilation or even any comparison to the past holiday time. One of the parcels contained "oplatki," a communion type of bread we always broke among ourselves with holiday wishes during the Christmas supper. The sight of them stirred the emotions and brought the tears to our eyes, but the smell of "kielbasa" and a large bundle of "kabanos" changed our depressed attitude, bringing closer to us the brighter world outside. While snipping off the wrapping, it was so hard to control the reactions. Especially with the ugly intestines prodding and forcing us to drool over them, making it hard to behave in a civilized manner, because we all felt like tearing at the package and devouring the food in a barbaric style. Somehow, we swallowed the wild instincts and behaved like silly humans. Mother rationed the sticks of "kabanos" in small portions, damn small to be exact, then we licked our fingers, inhaling deeply the aroma of the pungent garlic, taking tiny bites, smacking our lips with delight, even slighting the heavy Russian bread, our daily filler. Mother was generous and shared some of our delicatessen treats with our live-in friends, who were grateful after the long months of hunger and illnesses that touched all of us in some way.

Our systems were craving nourishment and vitamins unattainable at this time of year, it being winter, we had to do without fresh herbs and vegetables. Occasionally, in moments of urgency, the Kazacks, mother's coworkers who, in time, became good friends, came to our aid with some food, which was greatly appreciated and also put us in line of the holiday tradition of having at least one Russian dish—the borscht. The donation of a bunch of dried-up beets, was rejuvenated in a crock with few simple steps of the old recipe, with a hope that the centipedes would bypass the cloth-covered crock, making the traditional soup more palatable and raising our spirits for a small celebration of forthcoming Christmas.

******

A week before the holiday, the weather became mild enough to bring people to the bazaar in search for something representing the food and we felt quite lucky, for we had found a lightweight sack of dark flour, a couple of wrinkled potatoes, an onion and a "tcharka" of green sour tomatoes. What a fortunate harvest!

A very bright moment of the bazaar errand, was seeing our friends from Novaia Zyzn, although it was a little disappointing to me, not seeing Mietek in the group, but meeting our other fellow countrymen was like a breath of a fresh air thrust into our gloomy and pathetic struggle, which we had learned, wasn't only limited to us. Others went through some very traumatic periods, also, suffering in different ways without a loss of life. However the hunger and cold were enemies we all had shared.

As the unexpectedly mild temperature allowed, we sat in groups on the wooden slats of a sidewalk and swapped tales of the last few months, with many exclamations of disbelief being heard quite often. We were learning that hardships didn't amount only to a lack of soap and sugar—those were only forgotten dreams—a more serious element kept creeping and reappearing persistently. It was the fear, the fear of not having tomorrow, even what we had today.

There was no crying or lamenting during the out pouring of troubles; in fact, into each tale, a lot of humor was injected, to take the rough edges from the frightful accounts of a first winter miles away from here, deep in the steppes.

When all of the stories were finally told and our feet began to pinch from cold air getting through the wads of newspapers in our worn-out "valenkys," reluctantly, we said good byes, hoping sincerely we could see them at Christmas again, joining in singing the carols.

Surprisingly, the time went fast. I stayed home without a job, feeling rather useless and tried to fill the idle hours with painting, the watercolor painting. The approach and finding the materials was an art in itself. I used old scraps of brown wrapping paper from parcels, smoothing and cutting them into square and rectangular pieces, as usable surface material.

Once during the summer, I remember buying on the spur of the moment, a small tray of watercolor paints, without paying too much attention since, but now after rediscovering them, they became my salvation, filling the listless and long winter hours. The quality of the paints wasn't the best, but it would be despicable to complain about it. All that was necessary was some water and inspiration and I managed to find both.

My small paintings became like vignettes depicting scenes of the past summer—the remembered vivid sunsets and camels resting, silhouetted against the blazing sky, - the Kazakh shepherd walking in a cloud of golden dust among the flock of sheep (like the one I saw in the tulip fields). There was a large variety of subjects. I also tried to paint the faces of great character and interesting features. From memory, I sketched an image of Zoia's grandmother, the old Kazakh woman smoking a pipe, bringing the burst of warm colors of the head cover and the matriarchal face with its multitude of wrinkles, the graying hair, falling in long braids over the white tunic.

I really don't know what has happened to my brown paper "masterpieces," but many times now, I have an urge to do them over again, having all the conveniences of pursuing the art, but somehow, the inspiring and harsh atmosphere isn't there to recreate the true picture.

Not counting the depressing surroundings of our living area, I began to enjoy my artistic experiments although the colors sometimes appeared muddy and gloomy, but then my efforts were but the reflection of our present life, which didn't break forth in rosy tones. Once I tried to recreate a mental picture of the area around our home in Poland—the flower garden, the meadow and the blooming orchard in the early spring, but the impressions came out like a bad negative, without vibrancy, rather pallid, looking dull. In my mind, the pictures were there, alive with the brilliant tones and highlights, but there they would have to stay that way, preserved with other fonder memories.

All through the life of my creative moments, even when I tried, I could never do justice to bring a true image of the ones or things I loved the most.

Although Kazakhstan was a land of dust and snow, the features we had become acquainted so well with by now, surprisingly, I found quite a few exciting themes and subjects to fill the small cutout squares of brown paper out of the parcels from Poland.

One image still haunts me to this day, of a young boy with a lame foot, whom I saw often on my way from working in the steppes during the summer. He usually sat in the doorway, playing a concertina, a foot resting awkwardly by the stoop, with blond tousled hair and pale blue eyes, a lonely and sad-looking creature, engrossed in the plaintive melody flowing from the touch of his fingers. In my mind I can see the dark doorway and a small figure of Wasia (his name) dressed in a white "rubashka," a high-collared shirt, buttoned on the side, his back slumped against the weathered wooden planks of a wide door. Later we knew him as a loner and very idealistic communist, a young "comsomol." I have attempted so many times to bring this picture onto a canvas, but each time was disappointed at the results of wrong coloring and composition—the figure seemed rigid, without character, and I couldn't hear the melody out of the concertina.

One day I discovered I was running out of my art supplies, as the brown paper packages from Poland had not been arriving lately. I thought of another source, a store at the bazaar where once I purchased the water paints—there I remember seeing the stacks of black and white prints of Leon Tolstoy in "Jasna Polana." I always admired that print, with the old writer resting his chin on the cane, but now I thought about using the back of a print for my own use, filling it with my painting. Each of the prints cost only a ruble, however, the vendor lady raised her eyebrows when I asked for every one of them sitting on the shelf.

With a sly look, she asked, "why so many of them?" Those people were always so suspicious. "We have some bad-looking bare walls, and I love Tolstoy," I replied, but I knew she didn't believe me, and I couldn't understand why she thought it to be a problem; the prints were for sale, and I needed some art material.

The old, faithful wicker basket gained one more function, serving as a tabletop studio. I tried with a paintbrush to immerse myself by forgetting the idle days without a job, indirectly causing the forever nagging hunger, the cold and the memory of recent months. The colored sketches created an impression of life around us, the painting strokes had long sweeping affects, projecting the moody skies, monotone steppes and endless horizons. At times, it was hard to convey these onto paper something that was so detestable and alien, yet so beautiful in its own way.

For a while, being absorbed in my hobby of art, shut out from the rest of the world, I pushed aside the loathing for the people and their land, including their hateful credos and rules of the system.

Strange, how arts took precedence over political beliefs, minimizing the grudge and malice toward the subjects my mind evolved around, in an unbiased manner while bringing to life its images. My "wicker studio" didn't supply sufficient lighting either. Although the window, being high in the wall, emitted "muted" northern light, favorable with the artists, it was small in dimensions, just

75

barely allowing some brightness to sneak through four tiny glass panes, giving my winter accomplishments a touch of the "old masters" in my favored but depressing dark umbers and siennas.

Sometimes the sunlight would fill one of the four glass window panes, creating an illusion of a brilliant spider network, but the short-lived radiance would fade away, leaving a pale afterglow.

******

Christmas time was but a few days away. One more visit to a bazaar for a lucky strike in search for cheese and kefir, the missing ingredients in completing our holiday feast, assuring us a fraction of the meaning, of true Christmas and wishing others "wesolych swiat" (Merry Christmas) represented by borsht and pierogi.

During this cycle of pre-holidays, we managed to acquire enough of the necessary food and fuel to keep comfortable and even happy through this difficult period of our exile, so far away from Poland.

Christmas Eve was frigid, with dry and snappy cold. The air was clear, the sky illuminated with stars and moon, created an aura of peace and tranquility, while the snow, crushed under our feet, shimmered in the moonlight like a million shattered diamonds.

As I stood with an armful of "kiziak" for the "pietchka," I listened for the sounds, but all was quiet. I remembered, the Russian Christmas, if it were observed, would fall weeks later, but even in this part of the world, to many other citizens, it was a silent night, a holy night. Whatever the regime or rulers forbade you to believe in, the human mind was still free to any thought and sentiment— and this was a joyous holiday to many people.

When I entered our small place, it was already quite warm and the spicy smell of a two-course dinner, borsht and pierogi, kept tickling our nostrils, driving empty stomachs a little wild.

The breaking of a holy bread was very emotional, and the fragile white "oplatki" brought nostalgic memories and tears to many of us, while wishing for each other the dreams to come true, we all knew by heart.

Mother and Irena (her sewing friend) then became busy dispensing borsht, and someone cried, "Stop! We have to make sure we begin the supper with the appearance of the first star in the sky!" That would be according to tradition, but with the now uncommon and delicious aroma in the air, I knew there would be no wasting time on waiting; besides, the already volatile stomach wouldn't give a damn if the star of Bethlehem itself was falling through the chimney! All we knew is we had borsht with sour cream floating on top of crimson beet soup, giving it a royal or rather, being of Russian origin, an imperial touch, with thick slices of bread, a bread with a lighter tint to its texture and surface covered with yellow smudges of pure butter!

It was the true meaning of Christmas for us at that time, not only as a tribute from the religious side, but in human efforts, to rise above the continuos struggle, to bring back some sign of life as we had known before. No matter how poor quality it may be, but nevertheless to halt the slow dying of mind, spirit and hope.

So we celebrated our "vigilia"(Christmas Eve) in a wonderful atmosphere. The satisfaction from taking in the warmth and a great meal, put everyone at ease. Without any embarrassment there were sounds of lip smacking and outcries of contentment, sounds we hadn't heard for a long time. The voices became louder and soon laughter dominated the small area warmed up by steam from cooking and the happy breath of life.

For now, the tragic memories and bitterness had vanished to give us a chance for a sliver of pleasure in togetherness and friendship of people around us. In no time, above the chatter, mother's soprano intoned an old Christmas carol-it was a sheer delight listening to her beautiful voice, then joining her in our spirited "koledas" (the carols).

The strong sound of the voices was soothing in a way, to our much abused souls and for a short time, seemed to erase the concentration of grief and fearful guessing as to our future. When we stopped for a minute to catch our breath, we heard singing, like an echo, but it was outside. We opened the door and came face to face with a group of Russians, apparently standing and listening to our songs, but the sounds were coming from a farther direction. I ran to the other side of the house and to my surprise, I saw a small crowd of our friends from Novaia Zyzn, standing in the cold, singing their hearts out, Mietek was amongst them. The cold took my breath away, but so did the sight of Mietek. I stood as if frozen (I was, too), tense, not moving till my mother poked me in the shoulder. "Invite them in," she said "we have plenty of food for everybody." Then she went inside. The cold was biting but I didn't feel it. Baska must have noticed my confusion, for all she said was, "Aha,"— she guessed my secret and I felt myself blushing in the dark. That evening we would remember for a long time - our friends and we, at ease, sharing the food and the strong Tashkent tea, even some diluted coffee (so bitter), made out of the roasted fresh beans, sent to us from Poland. The marvel of the evening was the leftover food. Normally there wouldn't be a crumb left, now we were looking at the stack of pierogi, some blintzes stuffed with sweet cottage cheese, without feeling those well-known pangs of hunger. What a jubilation!

We sang "koledas" again. The holiday was a good reason to sing, but Poles generally like to sing—happy or sad, they sing. Except, when we're hungry, then there is no singing. But now was an occasion, very joyful to express yourself, for old and young. Toward the later hour, the songs had switched from carols to folk ballads then into the romantic love songs, taking us back to a time before the war.

In the course of the celebration, one of the young fellows pulled out of his shabby coat pocket, a bottle, medium-size, not unfamiliar to me. The label on it showed a picture of a dark bison and the liquid inside was pale yellow, with a straw leaning slightly across. I was fascinated by it but had learned it wasn't an herbal medicine- it was an alcoholic drink called "zhoobrovka," named after the animal of the lost species, although a few of them still roamed our jungle- like forests in Bialoviezha, in northeastern Poland.

The cork was pulled out and someone quickly rinsed the dishes of the borsht. In a second, the yellow vodka started to flow. I was neither prepared nor expected to be given the drink and was really surprised when Mietek's older sister handed me a small "tcharka" with a jolly wink. "Na zdrovie," she said (to your health)— "long live Poland, let the war end soon!"

The toasts of wishful thinking seemed never ending, neither did the slurps of "bottoms up!" I held my "tcharka" with yellow liquid for a while then joined the other toasters with a nonchalant, nonstop drink. In a flash, my body went rigid and my trachea pipes became clogged as if I had swallowed the buffalo from the label of the bottle. Jimminy Cricket! What a powerful drink that was! For a long spell I thought I would never breathe again. My friend Baska, came to my rescue, upon seeing my face turning slightly purple. She shoved a cold pierogi in my mouth, whispering loudly in my ear, "Never take that drink empty handed, always have something ready to chew on."

When I regained my voice, I asked, "So I should carry pierogi with me all the time?" "No dumb girl, just something solid, and sip it slowly, don't gulp it like borsht!" Then she asked, "You have never had a drink before, have you?" I shook my head, still feeling the effect of the drink, burning in my throat like fire.

The air in our small space became very warm and stale, even stifling from the smoke of the strong Russian cigarettes, giving an odor similar to "kiziak" droppings. I kept wondering what, besides tobacco, the guys were rolling in the newspaper. It was an awful odor, but then who gave a damn anyhow? —when you were among so many friends, sharing the moments of fun and cheers and watching the bottle of "zhoobrovka" circulating, with only one thought in mind, live it up tonight and get smashed, which at this time, to me, didn't seem like a hard thing to do. I should remember, just in case, one "tcharka" —no more!

Later, we got extra help from a visitor, a Soviet neighbor, who risked his pride by intruding on our celebration but nevertheless was welcomed quite warmly, not only as a Christmas guest but also a gift bearer of strong vodka. Stolichnaya and Smirnoff would have paled next to that dragon. He also brought a pack of strong Russian cigarettes, which were strong but at least there was an absence of that certain "kiziak" aroma, and a jar of caviar. Now, that would have been much better than cold pierogi after a taste of "zhoobrovka," but I never did like those fishy smelling appetizers and to this day, I can do without them.

This first Christmas in Russia turned out to be quite a holiday! With standing room only, everyone kept hugging each other, wishing for the umpteenth time the same over and over, except as time moved, the words were twisted, with a slur and a lot of giggling.

By now, my throat had regained its normal size, so I thought I could have another try at "zhoobrovka." I kept looking around and finally located it; the bottle with a fierce buffalo, didn't appear so fierce any more, with a thin leaning straw-it was empty!

Having hardly space to move around, I tried to make my way close to Mietek to exchange Christmas wishes, but actually I wanted him to hug me as everyone else was doing-it was a Merry Christmas! I did get more than one, a very tender hug, giving me a great feeling of being safe and content with his arms around me. Until someone passed the Russian bottle of the fiery stuff and with a tiny sip, I did myself in. Things got blurry and all of my troubles floated away!

Next, as I recalled with a twinge, there was a dull throbbing headache in the morning and a very queasy stomach. The visitors were gone, the "pietchka" wasn't lit and the room was stone cold. It was a real letdown from the last evening's enchantment. Yet it wasn't a figment of our imagination, last night was a holiday and we had a wonderful time, although being away from home, country and civilized comforts of living, we had managed to block our distress (with the help of "buffalo"), cheering each other.

****

After the Christmas holidays, we hadn't seen a soul or other countrymen for a long time. The winter placed a hard grip on the land with brutal cold and savage snow storms. During this time we heard many stories about people being lost in the "burians," frozen to death or torn to pieces by the hungry wolves. We listened, terrified, hoping our friends' winter would be safe.

January dragged on, without any specific change in the weather but occasionally, the very strong winds would blast in. Clearing the snow off the steppes, giving my brother and me a chance to go in search of "kiziak," in its natural form of droppings from the camels, sheep, oxen and donkeys, laying all over the steppe area in nice, flat shapes. Today, it seems strange to describe a pile of dung as something nice, but then, as we searched the frozen steppes, the findings in shape and weight were equal in value almost to that of gold. It kept us from freezing and helped put hot food into us and, most of all, it was free! The fuel was very important and unless one was a native and had it stockpiled through the warm seasons by fabricating it with necessary materials, he would have to, like us, face the uncertain and rough winter. Stealing was out of the question, the punishments being too severe and another reason, the borzoi dogs, a Russian wolfhound common for this area, were very vicious.

It was living again from day to day, looking forward to melting snows and first signs of spring, which sometimes appeared earlier than in Poland. But winter held on, bringing storms after storms, in full force!

One morning, as mother and Irena were leaving for work, they opened the door, then stood speechless. The frame of the door held a wall of snow. We all were stunned, feeling as if we were buried alive, but for seconds only, in no time we were at work trying to dig a tunnel leading to the roof. We didn't have any idea how high the snow had piled up. The worst problem seemed to be the disposal of the white menace. With so many hands at work, we finally pushed the cold mess and dug out a path, out of the door, up on a steep angle. Climbing out was difficult, but coming down was a snap. A real fast slide, which delighted the children with the loud shrieks and whoops, but the older folks didn't take it so well, letting everybody know in so many words how they felt. There were some strange expressions, I had never heard before, but I didn't blame them, mother especially who had a medical history of sciatica (Polish "ischias") and was always fearful of the painful attacks coming back during the cold spell.

I watched anxiously her acrobatics of climbing up the steep path to the opening above the door, without any supports from the sides. The first attempt seldom worked out and we had a hard time keeping kids from laughing. Eventually, the one that made it to the top first would help the one huffing and swearing at the bottom of the stoop.

I can still hear my mother's voice, clear as a bell turning to the Holy Spirit for help and then pleading with her "dupa" (butt) for support to "get up there," without injuring her sciatica! Incidentally, her agonizing pain of "ischias" never reappeared, ever.

In the days of siege by the snows, we worked all day digging out, clearing the paths, as did the rest of the village. With the common predicaments and cause, the usual hostile barriers were laid down and the comrades became quite friendly. I recognized the true spirit of communism, that everyone was equal - equal in his own misery!

The bitter cold kept the snow from melting, keeping the hard crust on the surface and the entry to our dwelling without change in its shape, except clearing the area from blocking it, when the fresh snow would fall.

It became a sporting event getting into the house. It took a toll on our threadbare coats, around the seat, which we tried to save by using triple sheets of *Pravda* to slide on. We became quite skillful, then the weather changed, the snows started to melt away and in no time we were faced with a tons of mud.

While the snows were disappearing, the air was still cold and biting, the icy rains brought humidity, keeping us chilled to the bones. The Ides of March ushered in a series of illnesses again, this time as old fashion "grippe" and respiratory infections.

I came down with a nasty fever, which at night turned into delirious nightmares and the symptoms of irregular breathing and glassy eyes, indicating that something was wrong. There was nothing much we could do but wait for an illness to run its course. Mother sat by the bed and watched during long hours for the breaking point and after the dramatic crisis, when my fever finally broke, I was on the way to recovery.

Being young, I regained my strength in no time at all with the help of many cups of barley and beef broth and huge boiled cabbage leaves, boosting the stamina and spirit, not to mention a lot of gas. But that part also came from the others, accounting for a general pollution of air. There were no complaints as long as the air was warm and not contaminated with germs.

******

One day, toward the end of March, we left the door wide open and felt the surge of a balmy breeze. The white patches of snow were completely gone and there were sounds of birds and insects, sending a wake-up call to earth and its inhabitants.

Something inside us was melting with the winter snows and there was a feeling of buoyancy and expectations from the new spring, a feeling of hope and change.

The changes came, but not to our expectations. The daily talk among the village people had a definite fear of a war. We should have paid more attention to the newspaper, *Pravda*, reading it rather than sliding on it, enjoying the fact that for all its printed lies, it deserved to be placed exactly where we had it.

It seemed Germany's fuhrer was changing his sentiments by suddenly breaking the "golden chains" of friendship with the Soviets implemented by Ribbentropp and Molotov. And now, openly his heavy war machinery was ready for a push— "nacht on Osten" (to the East) was his battle cry, to fulfill his dreams of reaching Siberia.

Being so isolated, we could only guess what was happening in the world. Berlin, Warsaw, even Moscow, were a long distance away. We almost forgot the sounds of exploding bombs and the deadly chatter of machine guns. We thought, if war ever came, it would never reach us here in Kazakhstan, believed to be the most remote place on earth. We preferred to ignore the anxious attitude of the Soviet people, their contemplations upon listening to the news throughout the day. We already had our war and being here as a result, we had chosen to overlook the dark clouds, gathering in the west.

We welcomed the spring and tried to forget the hell brought by the winter, in taking long walks out into the steppes, searching for the early sprouting of green onion, garlic and sorrel. Above all, we loved to hunt for the pinkish-white mushrooms growing under the ground, (no relation to truffles). At first it was difficult to find them, but then we learned to follow the Kazakh women, trying to remember the sites they frequented, harvesting baskets full of the great specimens. However, the crafty expeditions were short lived when the women caught on to our shadowing them and from then on, their trail would lead us in circles, to nowhere.

So we learned the hard way, with great results by finally recognizing the signs of cracks on the surface of the slightly bulging soil, resembling a star. When we dug at the center, not very deep, there underneath, sat a family of gorgeous mushrooms—tan, pink and white in color, all giving us a thrill at finding them, mainly because they were a part of our nourishment, loaded with vitamins and so tasty. The hunt itself was a great pleasure, knowing also they were free, not rationed, something we could depend on, at the right season, when everything else would fail.

At this time, there seemed to be a decline in packages coming from Poland. The letters contained distressed messages, as if something was brewing before the storm.

The disposition of the Soviet people around us was changing. We noticed some became friendlier, others carried a load of suspicion and a lot of hostility.

In the collective sewing shop where mother worked, the tempo of labor had increased and the product changed from being civilian apparel to strictly uniformed garb, for all seasons.

The top priority was now the Red Army. Rumors and gossip circled constantly, with only one subject, the fearful war. The atmosphere among the workers remained quite friendly, especially with the Kazakh men, who shared any unusual developments not reported in newspapers or via radios with our Polish workers. Through the day they chattered among themselves in their guttural language, while working speedily at the sewing, without lifting their eyes from the chores.

Easter came with a nostalgic sigh. We stuffed ourselves with hard- boiled eggs, a gift from our friend Lena, drank some "tutti-frutti" tea and later in the afternoon, three of us and our friends, went out into the steppes to enjoy the short lived splendor of blooming tulips. Those were the last days of tranquility before the sounds of turbulence from the west kept growing louder each day and threatening the complacency of ours and other lives around us. The war was imminent. It was only a matter of short months, we thought, allowing enough time for harvest, which was promising to be a typical wartime horn of plenty.

At normal times, before, the beginning of a warm season usually brought the cargo transports from the south of Russia, heavy with fruits and vegetables, during the afternoon hours of four o'clock. Rarely stopping in Gzaroon, but leaving a heavenly scent of ripened giant looking cantaloupes and huge, oblong musk melons, never seen or tasted by us before, which we named the Tashkent pear, namely because the transports came from the capital of Uzbekistan and the taste of the melon reminded us our winter pears.

Up to now, the railroad tracks, which I always looked at with a twinge of longing, was through most of the day, devoid of any movement or sounds. All of a sudden, we had lost the four o'clock whistle of the Tashkent transport; instead there was a constant traffic of boxcars filled with soldiers, cannons, generally the war machinery at its fullest, causing us to remember familiar sights, the last month before the war in Poland.

The signs and sights had intensified in the unbearable heat, too early for late spring. The radios blasted the air with the military marches and patriotic songs; the loud speeches from the leaders and officials, carried the powerful oaths of defending the mother country to the last drop of blood, which later, they did.

We watched the world around us, aroused and feverish, preparing for a war with anxiety, the frenzied expectations and sad, foreboding visions that would tear the families apart.

We had witnessed all those emotions, without compassion. It was their turn to pay for the injustice they had inflicted on us and thousands of innocent people. While their fears had magnified with each coming day, ours had sustained their level on a day-to-day basis, somewhat without emphasis on the hysteria or stress, for our feelings were overstretched, overspent on previous vital concerns of life and death during the passing year. Like impartial spectators, we listened and smirked at times, while trying to control the urge to shout and screech at them: "See how it feels!" forgetting, their fate, may also be our fate.

******

The weekend before the climax and the official declaration of war, the members of the sewing shop were asked to contribute, as a patriotic gesture, a sort of "pro publico bono"—a free wychodnaye day, to spend as a day of labor on the collective hay fields, helping to cut and spread acres of grass to use, undoubtedly, as fodder for animals, most likely horses to be used in numbers at the front.

The work would not be an enforcement of any sort, it was strictly on a voluntary basis, with a promise of plenty of food and drink; the last of which convinced us to participate in this patriotic venture, with my loyalty stretching only as far as my taste buds, with images of a Russian smorgasbord.

It was Sunday and we all gathered at one point by the sewing place. Men and women all decked out in what looked like "Sunday" clothes, which meant there was some color besides gray and brown, and the women's dresses had more of a cut than the back and front, making them look more like women.

The day was magnificent, the sky so blue with color spread evenly as in a child's painting, without an interruption of clouds or softer hues at the horizon. It reminded me of the sky in Poland, in August, just before the first bombs fell.

It seemed one of many attempts by Mother Nature to persuade the miserable humans how this world could be without destruction, the violence and willful extermination of life and beauty around us.

Kazakhstan still seemed a bastion of serenity and undisturbed calm. Today was sunny and bright-the group of women and men of mixed nationalities sat waiting for transportation and chatted amicably as if they were the best of friends. Someone produced a small camera and took a picture, which is still in my possession-very blurry and dark now, but the faces are there, faces of the past, so long ago, but remembered, even now.

My mother's favorite Kazakh co-worker was an ancient-looking gent, the closest vision to a Chinese god of wisdom, with a drooping long moustache, bushy eyebrows and a dazzling beard falling softly in soft silky waves over his chest.

My mother spoke to him: "Thurum-By, how nice you look today, such rich clothing on you—where have you been hiding this?" as she pointed to the flashing embroidery of silver and gold thread, purple and red around the collar and down the front of his shirt-like jacket, the "rubashka." He looked at my mother sideways and pushed a little skull cap with a pointed top, also rich in design, hard over his head: "Once we were rich tribesmen," he said then looked around, shrugged his shoulders and fell silent.

Mother didn't ask any more; perhaps her thoughts journeyed over the same plane, but in a different direction and time.

But for the circumstances, this could have been any company picnic by today's living, accept for the unusual setting, the language and faces—this was the year 1941, Soviet Russia—Kazakhstan.

Someone called my mother's name: "Marushka." It was chubby Xenia stuffing her mouth with "siemioshki" (sunflower seeds), throwing them rapidly into her mouth, then sliding the shells very artfully, like a garland, below the lip, over the fat chin. I was amazed each time I saw them do it, but I couldn't get the hang of it, though I tried-although it seemed so easy!

Xenia was the youngest of the workers in the sewing shop and seemed to have some special sentiment for mother, helping at times with ideas and food. Mother liked her a lot and practiced her Russian in idle chatting, twisting some difficult words in funny ways, making the girl laugh and Xenia being so jolly, she loved mother's learning efforts and giggled constantly.

Now, she was offering the fistful of "siemioshki," putting them into a little tin cup hanging from mother's belt: "Have some, Marushka, it will make you healthy, like me, see?" She flexed her muscular arm proudly; one couldn't help liking her, for she seemed like an overweight Tinker-Bell, hopping everywhere, offering the sunflower seeds to everyone. Mother, like me, also was trying to learn the art of cracking the little devils, but also like me, she was having trouble. "Here," she said "have some, my mouth gets numb and half of a time I don't know if I am spitting the seeds or empty shells." Well, neither did I, but the efforts made the time pass faster.

We traveled in horse carts, sitting on boards laid down between the edges, made like huge ladders, giving a lot of space for the Sunday volunteers. The meal was distributed as promised and for a while everyone was occupied with the morning meal of slices of dark bread, still warm from the baking ovens, a little squishy in texture, but palatable. A small "tcharka" of thin bluish drink, recognized as buttermilk, completed a breakfast Dr. Pritkin would have been proud to recommend. The dark bread contained multi grains, some we could still identify in their whole form, not being ground properly, so we played the guessing game then ate them anyhow. The opaque liquid, dubbed as buttermilk, kept our enzymes in check and although not very rich in taste, it contributed nourishment to the body, as the drink itself lacked chemical preservatives. My, what we didn't know then. While eating anything we could get our hands on, we seldom analyzed what was passing through our gullets.

It took about an hour to reach the hayfields. We crossed areas of drying out brush and small plants already showing rusty scorched tops, forecasting a hot and dry spell ahead. The Asiatic summer came fast and early in this wild country of contrasts and startling geographic features. It always amazed us with the unexpected. This land of sands and barren steppes we were brought to, was also blessed with a large oasis of fertile soil, being cultivated with astounding results. The spotty areas producing the rich crops, became a destination and labor camps for displaced people from various countries occupied by the Soviets in the beginning of autumn 1939. The rich terrain lay open, waiting to be developed and worked on, but without the help and strong hands which the Soviets were short of, most of the land sat idle. Our arrival in Russia changed the picture considerably. With our slave labor, we were to take the place of their outdated machinery and working animals, doing jobs requiring serious attention. Up to this time, the field work was a distant worry for our family while living in Gzaroon, but today we would have a taste of what would become our days and nights, only a month away.

The fields we were taken to were like a transformation into the summers of Poland: the hazy heat filled with the smell of wild flowers; the buzz of insects almost brought the memories of vacation days spent on our aunt's acres of wheat fields near Rohatyn. I thought of the war threatening again the places and families we had left behind.

We couldn't even dream any more. The fantasizing had to be shelved for a while, given to a cycle that, somehow in our hearts we knew, would never repeat itself again.

Upon our arrival at the hay acres, we were given rakes and pitch- forks and shown the areas where the tall grass was cut already and had to be gathered into heaps.

In a second, Xenia was staring at me: "Where is your head cover?" I shrugged my shoulders indicating I didn't have any. She then thrust at me a very colorful scarf, with long fringes and bright pink roses, the material itself being heavy, almost like wool, but I tied it in the Russian style, low over my forehead, thinking back to where we worked at the "air-field" and Liska putting her flimsy underwear on her head, to shade it from the sun. I wondered where she was now. This being one year later, my underpants certainly wouldn't deflect the sun. The fast wearing out texture, I saved for "wychodneye," using for every day the new line of Russian "dainties" made out of linen, once being a wrapper on parcels shipped from Poland. I didn't mind them being of tough material, a little coarse on the skin, but the format they were cut into was simplified and literally gave one a pain in the crotch. Linen, though, seemed to be in vogue this summer, proof of the continuing affection and caring from family and friends back home, shown in the number of care packages being sent through the months of winter and spring.

The heavy material they were covered with, eventually was converted into unique apparel, simple, rather novel, being sewn from the large square linen patches of blank and printed addresses in red or black ink. Mother, with her creative mind and never-ending ingenuity, would inject a little humor into her pattern of sewing, by craftily placing the large letters of destination— C.C.C.P.(USSR), at the back part of a dress or skirt, exactly across the rump area, so when I bent down, the letters would stretch, giving a view of my sentiments exactly...

As I looked around me, raking the hay, I knew the call of the mother country was answered diligently by her citizens; everyone was hard at work, even my mother, I noticed, was putting her energy over and above her duty. What gives? I asked myself, was she in the race for the "Stachanovka" medal? She looked so involved, yet quite content! In spite of the heat and sun blazing, I worked like the rest of the crowd, counting the hours before the noon break.

The meal we were served was as they promised, plentiful and good! Here we were introduced to a strange drink, a delightful tasting liquid, a thirst quencher, called "kvas"- it was nonalcoholic, having bread for a base and some other ingredients I wasn't quite familiar with, but at the peak of a hot and sweaty day, it was superb!

Years later, we tried to reproduce the "kvas," but it never tasted the same, maybe the formula was too simple or the bread had to be Russian, but it was an unsuccessful try.

This all-labor "wychodneye" was like a picnic, communist style, a little different, but still very generous in food, something we hadn't seen since our arrival in Russia. The group of mixed nationalities took time out from pitchforks, resting in the shade of haystacks, content and feeling drowsy from drifting scents of freshly cut grass. It was quiet, some only engaging in small talk, about the weather, the small gardens by the river, family gossip, but not a word about the war.

If you could draw a blank on the past two years, you could almost wish these few precious moments of today, so different from the wintertime, would continue for a while—even with a faint knowledge, stirring in the back of our minds, that, at this time, there was the beginning of a dreadful turbulence taking place in the land so close to our hearts. But Poland was miles away-it seemed as far as any other planet.

Even with the overheated air and stillness around, the approaching evening was balmy and peaceful. Most of the people meandered about, hesitating to begin the long journey home. As if we were camping on a strange island, cut off from the world and its complexities. Riding back, I watched the sun sinking slowly, leaving the afterglow over the horizon and feeling some joy and gladness, knowing that everything good and bad, must always come to its end.

The word "pryvyknesh" came fluttering close again, disturbing the harmony. Would this word of defeat or solace, change our lives into this meaningless form, without hope, bringing only a temporary contentment, such as today's—What if...

But then we knew the war was coming and we had to live only one day at a time.

******

Oppressive summer heat brought discomfort and tension waiting for the news to break now, any day, any time.

Actually the announcement came quietly over the radio, on June 22, stating calmly: The German forces attacked the Soviet Union. History had turned another chapter, with pages soon to be filled with violence and death—and the foreboding historical facts, the destruction of conquered territories, savage killing in eliminating enemies. Somewhere in that course of action, we were thrown into this boiling pot, wondering who was the enemy and who the friend. Although we were at a great distance from the front lines, we felt that there was danger lurking everywhere. Our status was uncertain; were we still considered captives, prisoners or allies?

We listened to the blaring radios and read the newspapers describing the victories of the "Red Army." The shouting cries of "We will win, we will win!" (Pobiedim, pobiedim) were heard loud enough, but carried a hollow tone with an echo of uncertainty, which made us believe things were not going smoothly for the Russian side.

Now and then the truth would trickle down from the people arriving in transports as we did a year ago, from Poland, Lithuania and other Eastern European countries, who were caught at the outbreak, while being transported, with some casualties.

We listened to them in silent dread, realizing that if there was any chance for our return to Poland, now the hope was completely gone. We all shared, from now on, the fate of the Soviet people. And the Soviet nation fought gallantly, displaying incredible courage, defending its land and cities, but the Germans kept on, overtaking the large territories, moving deeply into mighty Russia, implementing the wrong tactics and cruel treatment to captured people, leaving fear and hate behind them.

The ones who escaped the territory occupied by the Germans, brought tales of disbelief and horror.

However, in Kazakhstan there was no panic, yet. Life went on as before, except for those families whose male members were inducted into the Red Army, to defend the motherland.

Perhaps the war came at the wrong time to this poor country, still bewildered from the echoes of the revolution and at the crossroads of its ideals and beliefs that were supposed to provide its people with a better life. Now it was too late, not ever having a taste of it, not knowing the ordinary comforts of living, their chances were lost now. To survive, to live through it, was all that mattered. The war, the tug between two powers and the innocent people caught in the middle, for us, began a year ago and now it was the turn of the Soviet society.

We thought, perhaps with the sword hanging over their head, the conduct toward us would soften a bit, changing the abusive attitude. We wished, we hoped, but as the tempo of hostilities increased, so did their suspicion and harsh judgment.

The few families living in Gzaroon felt, at times, as if being under surveillance and the truth was, we were.

One morning, mother, while walking to work, realized she had acquired a shadow, following her all the way to the door of the sewing shop. The shadow turned out to be a member of the NKVD, who politely told her to come with him to the local militia station.

My brother and I didn't suspect where she was and that she was being questioned, until I went to visit her at noon, in the place where she worked. It seemed so strange, that everyone was so very busy, without lifting a head in greeting. Mother wasn't in and I sensed, with gripping fear, something had happened, or something was wrong.

"Where is mother?" I asked her friend Irena. She didn't even glance at me, but her knitted eyebrows and solemn look on her face said enough, then finally she looked up: "Your mother is being questioned by police, go home, stay with your brother, I am sure they wont keep her long."

I went home, wondering why it was only her taken to the station. My imagination went round and round, expanding into awful thoughts and guesses—will she come back?

Another hour of waiting seemed like forever but then, mother walked in, and without a word, at that second I knew everything was all right. The unexpected crisis had passed and the routine was back, except mother didn't go back to the shop; instead, she brought out some tasty-looking cheese and a still warm hunk of dark bread. We had a feast as if after a funeral, except the supposed dead was still alive! Somehow the feeling of hunger would never leave us; no matter how great the worry and anxiety, we always wanted to eat.

What now? I didn't ask, for I knew mother for sure was going to share with us her visit with the police, being just too glad she was back with us. For now, she was very calm, rather pensive, as if resigned to some secret burden she carried inside, since she walked into the house. Time stood still. "Something is wrong," Jez said. Mother took a deep breath: "We will be going away, soon—I don't know where, yet."

I felt a chill! "Sowchoz," miles away, desert and sun! I sensed from the time she was being questioned, we could be facing some kind of a change and not a pleasant change, for at this point, any change would not have been for the better.

Mother wrapped the leftover cheese in a piece of material and put the bread in a small linen sack. Irena's children were playing outside while we sat waiting for mother's story.

"It's no lie, how scared I was," she began, "I knew not to expect anything good from them, but I couldn't believe the stupid questioning. The officer sitting behind the desk looked like a Christmas tree, all lit up with military decorations. In front of him lay a revolver and he told me to sit down. "Sadish," he said and when I did, he started to play with the gun, sliding his hand over it, dropping it on the desk and all I could think of, was the two of you and what may happen, in case." In a flash I remembered the cries and whimpers of the two little girls left alone in the transport, while mother kept talking: "I don't think I'll ever forget that bastard! Then, all of sudden, he got up and angrily started to shout, 'Who is Franco? What do you know about Franco?' I was so surprised, I couldn't answer. Again and again he repeated the question and all I could say was, 'I don't know Franco.' It never occurred to me, perhaps he meant General Franco of Spain, but then I didn't know him either and besides, what the hell would he have to do with us? God knows!

"For a long time he just kept throwing those questions, staring at me, so cold and all I kept repeating was 'I didn't know Franco.'

"After moments of those theatrics, I knew he wasn't going to shoot me, so I quieted down, except my stomach didn't."

She looked around: "We will be leaving Gzaroon. The war is coming this way, and you see, they consider us the enemy."

We sat listening, trying to grasp the idea of a change coming to our life again—it had only been a year since we had left Poland, what will be our next destination? Mother had that faraway look, but she seemed very calm: "The war is catching up with us again, we'll have to look at it this way, there won't be a normal life for us, for a long time."

******

We knew what she meant, but the next few days still would remain a puzzle. Our friends also were uncertain as to their future, even though the authorities didn't question them they still remained frightened and uneasy each day.

Mother went back to work, but not for long. She was called again to militia headquarters, questioned again by the same officer, but acted quite dignified after noticing the revolver was gone from the top of the desk. The visit was very short and she was told in few words to pack and get out of Gzaroon, without making it clear how. "Where?" "Just get out!" Get out, get lost, who cared! The steppes were long and wide, and we didn't have a choice!

Mother didn't panic. We surveyed our possessions, which amounted to very little—the bundles, the stately wicker basket and a green bed. It was a short list but one consolation, we would be traveling light. Mother seemed unruffled, even relaxed: "Get everything together," she said, "nothing loose," then she went to see our friend Lena. Baska came from work earlier then usual, very worried about her sister and the family. "Which way will you be heading?" she asked. "Novaia Zyzn," I said, hoping it would be so.

"I can't think of anything being closer—unless they decide to take us to their own choice area." I hated to say aloud the name "sowchoz," I knew it would give me a chill.

"Baska, I hope you will be spared this ordeal." I sincerely wished it would hold true, as it would be so hard for them with small children. She hugged me for a long time. During this past year we had become such close friends, sharing the pains and heartaches and also some of the happiness. There were few tears and although we knew there would be a distance between us in miles, somehow we sensed we would see each other, again.

Mother came back but not alone, she brought with her transportation, a large wagon. Sitting at the head of the cart was our friend Lena's youngest son, Tola, swirling and cracking the whip at the two oxen, which were standing quietly and patiently taking the abuse, but glaring in an unfriendly way from time to time.

For a reason we had suspected, mother tried to hasten us, with nervous jitters. Could it be she was frightened of the NKVD possibly deciding to ship us off to a place of their own choice?

Living in Russia, we had become infected with their own diseases of mistrust and suspicion. Now she feared that the authorities may change the orders and select for us a destination of their own choosing.

Finally, the sad moment came to say good-bye. We carried out our shrinking assets, which by now we could easily fit inside the wicker trunk, and the green bed, now disassembled into a few pieces, taking up most of the space in the wagon. But we felt wealthy, having a piece of furniture to our name.

A few last hugs and we were off into the hot steppes, the journey's end, unknown…

We had traveled north, across the railroad tracks, past the tall grain elevators, on the dirt road leading to Novaia Zyzn. The day was lovely, but hot and sticky. The small cart squeaked and the oxen walked slowly, very slowly.

Throughout most of the trip, none of us talked at all, each of us being engrossed in private thoughts, perhaps of the same nature with many anxious questions, all understandable in the face of an uncertain future. Time had passed, the sun changing its position in the sky, when ahead of us in the distance, I saw the clear horizon, broken by the tall, jagged shapes of the stately poplar trees. As we drew closer to this sight uncommon to us, we noticed some more greenery around. A paradise, I thought! Gzaroon was all sand and a few bushes misnamed as trees. I got excited! "It's Novaia Zyzn!" I exclaimed.

"I am sure it is," mother said, "the first village on the road, as they said, it has to be!"

The road we had traveled on was leading straight as if we were going over a plateau now slanting down, revealing the village nested below in the valley, snug as a bug. It looked enchanting and for a moment I forgot we were in Russia—now completely homeless.

Would our fate be lenient for a change and let us stay here, in this place so vivid and fresh with many tones of green, a soothing picture to our eyes after being accustomed to dirt and sand. Besides, Mietek lived here and a thought of him, raised my spirits with a bit of hope that this could be the end of our travels. The recent events had spiraled down our status to the bottom of the pit, enlarging our frustration, but we still didn't give in to dark resignation, although it seemed the world was crumbling from sudden crisis.

In a while, we could see the people moving around—there was life here in this village, also! We turned from the main road into another one leading toward the dwellings sitting in short rows, some just scattered in disorder. We came close now, entering the very edge of the village and were treated to a full view of the entire area. Suddenly, there was a parting among the trees and my heart skipped a beat. In the distance, the hill, like a green mound, was rising, quite naked but for three towering wooden crosses jutting into the clear blue skies, like ancient obelisks of a bygone and forgotten faith.

Was it an omen or a paradox? For a moment I couldn't catch my breath, but the phantom, the real vision, was there, a part of the landscape looming above the village as a monument of Novaia Zyzn.

The impression was brief yet deep, giving way to the anxiety of a question, "Will they let us stay?" We were wandering into a world of accidental rules, counting on good luck and hope!

Seeing a woman outside one of dwellings, mother asked politely where certain Polish families lived. "Oh, so many of them!" she replied in Russian and pointed to the other end of the village. Mother thanked her and followed her directions, taking us to an L- shaped, squat building, quite large in size. Our cart came slowly to a halt, close to a dark opening with a heavy door slightly ajar. Nobody came out, it was so quiet. We looked at each other, somewhat disappointed. Mother, however, as usual, didn't wait for things to happen-in one jump she was off the cart and disappearing through the dark opening of a door. It seemed hours before she came out with a broad grin on her face: "We're staying here, in this house!" she shouted, "Thank God and bless the lady, I didn't even ask her name!" She kept repeating about our good luck, her eyes sparkling with excitement, her mood spilling over on us, with a feeling of gladness that our search for a shelter had ended and for now, we were spared more traipsing about the hot steppes.

Inside, mother said, there was a corner, a fraction of a space by the wall and floor, we would call our "home" for a while. Silently, I acknowledged, there was a God.

We unloaded our possessions from the cart in a flash, Tola helping with the familiar green bed, setting it inside for us, then gave a snappy salute, getting ready to depart for Gzaroon. Mother, still bubbling with gratitude, hugged him more then once and shoved some "tchervientze" in his pocket, saying he deserved it. Tola grinned and took the money, for I am sure mother was generous; besides, here in a "kolchoz," money wouldn't mean a thing to us.

Inside, my eyes had to adjust to the dim light from only two small windows set on the side of the long building. The room was spacious, a new luxury for body movements. We were to occupy a part in the middle of the dwelling with an unusual feature, a space built into the wall, a sort of a niche behind a "pietchka," which during the cold spell, must have been heavenly, containing most of the warmth from the burning stove. But this was summer and as of now it felt cool and pleasant in this large room. We were impatient to unpack, but mother told us to wait, we had plenty of time-first we should meet and thank the gracious lady for allowing us a place to settle in, perhaps changing the course of our life.

We met her in a short while, as she walked toward us or rather waddled, limping slightly with a smile. She was small and very frail looking, her eyes enormous in a triangular, delicate face. I tried to match the resemblance to someone I had seen before, but then mother was introducing us to her, promising we would be a help and not a burden. She spoke in a soft voice: "This house is full of young people, feel welcomed, you're among friends. My name is Gorecka and my large family lives here, though now during the summer, most of them are out working in the fields." All of sudden I realized the resemblance—we were in Mietek's house. What a twist of fate! Was Dame Fortune smiling on us, mostly me? I didn't burst with jolly shouts, knowing mother wouldn't exactly share my excitement, but then she wasn't seventeen and full of imagination and silly dreams!

Lady Gorecka was our savior and at the moment, was giving us all the information about "country living," which included very hard work in the fields mostly, nothing I couldn't cope with, I thought, until I learned later, but that is a different story.

Our first move, she said, would have to be a visit with a local official, authorizing us to stay in the village, without much difficulty, having a place to live already. For the village, we would be a gain in hands for labor. She assured us there was nothing to worry about; besides, her daughter Zosia had a talent for helping people when the authorities were involved, always with good results. We learned later she had a foul mouth and never feared anybody.

It was cool and pleasant inside this darkened adobe; slowly, we unpacked our bedding and some clothing, then to my great surprise, I was given a space of my own, a private cubbyhole, behind the "pietchka." What a joy! I wanted to chirp like a cricket with praises for Novaia Zyzn and the frail little lady who welcomed us in a most kindly way.

The green bed was put snugly by the wall, the wicker, my ex-sleeper, stood next to it and "voila!" we became instant tenants, with a roof over our heads, turning the busy hours since we left Gzaroon, into a personal triumph of the whole anxiety-filled, long day.

We sat relaxed, mother chatting with the "lady of the house," our new friend, whose family, as we learned, came from a town in Poland, close to ours. The entire clan, having a military background, was arrested, most of them now in prisons or lagra camps, the younger and the very old members brought here to Kazakhstan.

Her husband, being very ill, died in a prison, her daughters' spouses were sent somewhere in Siberia, without any word or sign from them since, a story comparable to thousands of others.

The conversation brought tears and painful recollections with a question forever repeating itself, "Will those times ever come back? In time to live them over again?" The persistent riddle could not be answered, we knew that much, not to predict a week ahead or even tomorrow.

Lady Gorecka got up slowly and limped around the "pietchka," looking into a blackened, large iron pot: "Would you like something to drink?" she asked, "I don't have much to offer, but I could treat you to a good tea, a genuine Tadrzyk "tchai." My dear daughter traded my hand-made pillow covers for a small sack, so now each time I take a sip, I see my long hours of embroidering, going down the drain, but then what is a pillow case worth? What's life worth, here in Russia?"

For now, it seemed as if we had entered a new phase of life in Russia. That first evening in Novaia Zyzn, we felt at peace and minimally safe. The war didn't matter, our thoughts were mostly occupied with speculations of what kind of work would be given to us.

Late in the evening, we went outside and sat on the door stoop, enjoying the air still warm from an overheated summer's day. The sky was inky dark but sparkling with a myriad of stars. Somewhere, a donkey brayed, then the dogs answered with a barking duet, blending the sounds into a cheery serenade. For a long while, we allowed ourselves this visual and audio contentment, leaving the sense of concern for tomorrow, on the side. The eventful day had finally ended but, in spite of its charm and tranquil atmosphere, it was time to get a well-deserved rest.

It was at dawn, when I woke up the next morning to the noise of the country and the pungent smell of a burning "kiziak." Lady Gorecka was an early riser and a busy little person. There was hot water gurgling in a heavy iron pot and a small stack of what we would call lukewarm "hot" cakes, made out of rough grain flour and water, then baked on top of a "pietchka." A great combination if you needed your teeth loosened up…however, I don't recall even that kind of food being wasted, especially in the morning, when our stomachs felt empty more than usual. I dug out from the bundles a fruity brick tea and poured the hot water over it in a tin cup, then picked one of the heavy morsels offered by the lady, encouraging me with a friendly nod of her head. There was no thrill to this early exercise of the mouth and teeth, but it sure was filling. In a while, mother was up, then my brother's blond head with sleepy eyes, completed the group, ready to explore the new system of work, the labor in the "kolchoz."

A huge barn, a "center office," sat on the other side of the village, being also a distributing place for the rationing of bread, grain or any other alms earned through the hours of work.

The official we faced was an older bearded individual, who looked us over and without a long deliberation, gave us the assignment. We waved to each other for good luck, knowing it would be late in the day before we met again to pick up our ration. My guide was a woman of questionable age, thirty to fifty, it was hard to tell from the early wrinkles and the missing teeth. She was quite pleasant in trying to explain to me the work. "I am taking you to an experimental station, where you will be clearing the weeds blocking the growth of oats, planted for research." It sounded boring, but after an hour with sun burning in the sky, it turned into a lot of sweat and a sore back.

I was shown a dimension of my quota for a day, it amounted to a number of hectares in field measurements, which to me at that time, looked as if the land assigned to me, was reaching the horizon, stretching all the way to China. When I stood up and looked ahead, I thought: "Shit! I will never finish it today; I'll go to bed hungry." But soon I learned never to look at the far distance, but work systematically around me, moving step by step, clearing the area—blister by blister, occasionally stretching my sore back.

I was the only one in the field. At least it was peaceful, the only sounds came from the buzzing insects and sometimes the cries of the birds, invisible, high in the hot skies. I worked diligently, thinking about the bread at the end of the day and the fact that it's all I could do or wind up doing something worse. Clearing the weeds was constant movement, a pain in the ass, nothing too strenuous, - still at the end of the day, I felt like a heap of aching muscles and bones. Without a clock, I could only guess the hour by the position of the sun, which sometimes seemed as if imbedded in the sky, without moving an inch. Yet, I found myself racing with time toward the late afternoon and kept pulling the wild morning glories and scrawny daisies with unrestrained frenzy, in order to finish the allotted area. The noise from the stomach helped also in a way and finally an appearance of a horse rider, a "watch dog" inspector, cinched the eagerness in completing my task. I couldn't believe my eyes when I looked over the vast field I had worked on. I earned my grits, or whatever else I was eligible for in the line of food.

Walking through the area, toward the village, I knew, in spite of my puffed-up blisters, I'd eat again, for a few days.

Mother greeted me at the ration barn, dangling in front of my eyes a modest sack of potatoes and the daily bread. The country life was promising us a better diet. On the way home, we shared the thrilling hours of our first efforts and chores on this first day in a "kolchoz" of Novaia Zyzn. Mother was awarded a spot by the huge pile of potatoes, picking the rotten ones out of the existing batch of last year's good crop, not a very exciting job, but it brought home the "bacon," not literally, but the bread and the spuds were almost as good.

My brother Jez got himself a real job; he became a shepherd with a large flock of sheep. The little boy was rapidly growing up, his character developing with his new responsibilities.

The L-shaped dwelling was a welcome sight after the work, a final escape from the still scorching sun, into the coolness of a dirt floor and a few slaps of cold water, over the sticky and rank smelling flesh.

Somehow, we felt, as the year departed us, like a snake shedding its skin, useless and not deserving to dwell upon, except for the still remaining pain of losing our "babcia."

But for that cycle in our journal, we had closed the pages, erasing it in order to gain a new fortitude to go on ahead. Perhaps we faced now the beginning of a harder life, but not so harsh and uncertain as it appeared last year in Gzaroon.

Around our new habitat, we helped with small chores, stacking the "kiziak" and filling the pots with water. Getting the water out of the well became almost recreation for me, walking with the galvanized buckets where it sat in a poplar grove at sundown, when the air became cooler and clear, bringing in the scents of drying hay in the near by fields. I tried not to hurry, enjoying a few moments of my own.

I remember, at art exhibits, seeing paintings of similar settings as the one present, come alive with subject and background. One glance at my sweat-soaked garments told me I wouldn't quite qualify as a model for Wierusz Kowalski, although the hill with three crosses would have created a very dramatic background. I didn't look to that side, though, it scared me even on a bright, sunny day but with evening approaching, I looked to the road leading to the faraway fields where most of the young people worked through the last couple of weeks. Mietek's mother said they were due back, any time now. Time went slowly, the days reflecting each other in a monotony of the productive hours. Then, one Friday afternoon changed the life style of a quiet life in Novaia Zyzn. Finally they came back!

We were waiting in the barn at the end of our working day, while the rationed slices of bread were being weighed according to the hours we had spent on the job, when we heard the noise of loud and jolly yelling... The Soviet official looked out of the door and spat with gusto. That was another art the Russians had mastered, shooting the saliva through their teeth, especially if in anger, at an unbelievable distance.

He squinted his eyes, listening: "The mob is back!" he said, then went back to weighing the rationed bread. I grabbed my portion and ran out to the road leading out of the village where the intensity of sounds was coming from. The wagons with long ladder sides, were rolling in with dust clouds trailing behind them. I never realized there were so many young Polish souls living here in the steppes. I felt excited with a prospect of joining their group, eager for new ventures, new life! After all, that's what the name of Novaia Zyzn meant: "new life!"

The returning laborers were already at the door, dropping their bundles of dirty clothing at the back of a dwelling. It was a normal activity as I have learned, before entering the quarters and for the simple reason not to contaminate the entire household with common parasites, clinging for life to the filthy and sweaty flesh. The fast outside shower with a minimum of soap, comparable to "smigus-smigus, dyngus-dyngus," did help with some sanitary measures, but didn't quite eliminate the itching and the awareness that the nasty vermin were still around, bugging everyone to no end of embarrassment. But after a year or so, this seemed to be a minor problem to the younger set, one they could live with, even turning it into a fun guessing game: "Is it a blonde or brunette?" and as there were lice, there was also a will to exist and scratch...

The Gorecki's household was full of shouting and signs of gladness, at being back in the village-all five of them—the four women and Mietek, all burned from the sun, complaining of fatigue, but healthy and energetic looking.

We stood on the side, watching the family reunion, while their mother tried to explain our presence, cautioning it was her wish that we stay with them. For a few moments we felt uneasy, but quite unnecessarily, for we were greeted warmly and were welcomed. Into the late night, we sat listening to their lengthy tales of living and working in the heat-drenched fields during the past few weeks. All of them looked great, tanned and full of pep and gestures describing the involvement with (dangerously sounding to me) scythes, sickles and pitchforks, which would soon become my Waterloo, many times over.

I couldn't sleep that night, with the visions of hot fields drifting through the dark room, plus I was listening to the healthy snoring and thought Mietek was so close—

The awakening feelings of affection or would-be first love, came naturally with age, with the same rapid heartbeat and longings, the same desires as would be everywhere, except for the props... no silver sandals, no bouquets of flowers, nor waltz or promenades..." The imagination had suppressed the reality with a wide-awake dreaming, till eventually sleep ended it all.

I was at my job earlier than usual, as working seemed easier in the cool of the morning. I had doubled my energy, tearing at the weeds on the experimental hectares of oats, with last night's stories still floating in my head. Being young, I only sifted the excitement of novel change, even a thought of a romance, from what lay beneath a hard labor in weeks of long ordeals. If only I knew what was waiting for me in the next few days, I would have lingered at the weeding of daisies and morning glories, much, much longer.

For now, all able and working hands were staying in the village, where the chores were waiting in different areas. Also being eligible for a change, away from the weeds, surprised, I found myself in a large group of women; among them were, Zosia and Irma, Mietek's two older sisters. I recognized Zosia's voice immediately after the overseer announced the location of the next work, out of the village. I listened to some snippy phrases and foul words I hadn't heard for a while. I didn't realize one could talk back to these country overseers, but my hearing was good, and Zosia was loud, yelling, "What kind of shit is this after working out in the fields? I sweated my ass off day and night, now we have more of the same?" the overseer heard her, though: "Your ass is your problem, woman and you may be eating shit if you don't stop complaining, the grain isn't ripe yet and the stalls are empty! Watch your mouth, it's wartime!" Knowing Zosia never dodged a hard day's work, I became frightened, wondering what "this" meant, something that upset her for she kept mumbling, "Eat shit, work with shit, that's the story of my life in this damn country!" I asked quietly: "Zosia, why are you so upset?" "Upset?" she whined— "No, I am not upset, just mad enough to spit!" She made a face and spat, Russian style, hence I moved slightly to the side, for her aim was quite good.

The large group of workers, women mostly, had to walk a short distance to the edge of the village, where sat a huge sheep barn. My instincts and smell forewarned me, Zosia was right by repeating the word describing the stench—the shit. It hit us as soon as we walked into the barn. The numerous buckets scattered around needed to be filled with water from the outside cisterns. At first, I didn't catch the concept of this project, but slowly the inkling was setting into my head, we were to scrub the surface of the floor, which was covered with layers and layers of accumulated sheep crap.

I stood with my mouth hanging open and my stomach climbing fast toward my throat, while someone handed me a wooden tool, a spatula—it was Zosia. "Get going, they're watching us," she said. In a flash I went down on my knees as did the other workers, then for a moment I hesitated and clutched my middle, good God! it seemed a physical impossibility to avoid the sickening feeling of nausea, and I threw up. My friend splashed some water on my face and scolded me quietly: "That was stupid, now you will have a double mess to clean up! Try to tighten your stomach muscles, it will help. I couldn't tolerate it at first either, but it will pass, believe me, it will pass." She lied. I threw up again! In desperation, I spilled a whole bucket of water, flooding the area of my vomit and also softening the caked layers of the sheep feces. I began to work at my revolting job. Most of the women around me were Polish workers who evidently were familiar with this type of a "clean up," for occasionally I heard the laughter and humorous swearing. I could have sworn also, but being so glad my stomach felt normal again, I kept my mouth closed tight and tried to avoid deep breathing; working my arm fiercely in a circle, smoothing out with water the rough surface, trying to forget that the matter I was working with, was a stench reeking dung. How low can you sink? I thought we had hit bottom but even there we had become immune to the smell and touch, except on rare occasions, when discovering with a shock, that among the sheep droppings, there were also human feces, and by that time we were numbed, accustomed to it, in a way... "Pryvyknesh" leapt out from hiding, challenging my weakened frame of mind, —would Freud argue the point if he was here? But old Sigmund was dead and I was alive, solid,—surrounded by shit!

It took about two weeks to complete this repulsive task, by whose end we had even learned to joke about it. On our last day, I still remember so clearly, while waiting to receive our rations, we heard singing outside. A group of young guys had decided to serenade us with a pre-war song: "Tonight I kiss your hand, Madame," a cute reference to our smelly pads, as if we needed a reminder. Zosia wasn't amused. "You young bastards!" she muttered, but the truth was, that kissing ladies hands, one of the habits of the continental culture, was still popular, although a slowly dying custom here in Russia, under the circumstances and for reasons as solid as the recent operation of "sheep-shit" scrubbing. Keeping up with a tradition was one thing, but to be subjected to a wild guessing of the hands' involvement in these irregular and harsh times, was a cause for casting aside temporarily, this traditional male gesture of respect and admiration, for women.

Today at the ration barn, we were treated to an extra portion of grain, that being oats, something I have always associated with horses, but here it was accepted by the workers with a lukewarm enthusiasm. I couldn't quite envision what we could do with this grain, still with husks on and long sharp needle-like spears at the ends of it. I was puzzled, examining my portion, quite a heavy sack, so I asked: "What happens to it now?" Zosia didn't seem suprised: "Well, see what we'll be doing in the next hour, so let's hurry up before others get there." I was still looking at my sack, asking "Is it for us?" My new friend Marynia was grinning: "That's to help with a change in your diet, a little variation for your guts, fill 'em then blow 'em out with a noise!" she laughed. I looked at Zosia thinking they were pulling my leg, but she smiled. "Don't worry, I'll teach you how to convert this heap into food, you are going to learn things you have never dreamed of, little one!"

She wasn't much bigger than I, but she had a tremendous strength of body and spirit. Considering our status as captives or prisoners or whatever else we were, she often displayed an incredible courage; fighting for her and others' rights, knowing quite well each time she opened her mouth, she endangered the welfare of the family. Standing up in defense and hammering at the wrong deeds and sometimes the cruel behavior of the overseers and guards. Women young and old looked up to her and welcomed the help which she never declined, but offered readily, although her mouth, once starting to rattle, kept spewing words, not exactly ladylike, to make your ears wilt. The rough swearing didn't seem as shocking anymore, we all were gradually shedding the polished facades of civilized upbringing.

Continental "Bon-Ton," a counterpart of American Emily Post, once a model for a standard of behavior, was becoming a shadow and an echo that belonged to a different era and time, lost to unforeseen events and circumstances, the ties that didn't fit or apply anymore. The ugly swear words spoken now habitually and so freely, may have not changed the quality of life, but somehow fortified the insecure frame of mind, changing slightly the personalities by putting rough edges to withstand the upheavals and the repercussions of the new and survival lifestyle.

Since leaving Poland, over this span of time, the tolerance grew among the groups of young and old, with necessity blindfolding the previous indoctrination of morality and rights of innocence, leaving the blemishes on the individual reputation, without too much fanfare.

Now, with our rations in hand, I wondered what kind of a miracle would transform this hairy grain into edible nourishment? Actually, the marvel of the grain would lie, as I later found out in exactly that, passing it out! But as of now, even after a tiring day, Zosia hurried me: "Get moving, you will have the first lesson in how to grind flour."

We didn't walk too far. "Here we are," Zosia said as we entered a large one-room place, very empty, except for two heavy stands, topped by two gigantic round stones, connected in the middle with an iron handle. This was a flourmill. The contraption sitting at the center of the dirt floor was of a very primitive character, used by the villagers from many years back and now Zosia giving me a lecture on how to operate this simple archaic device. I lifted the wooden handle attached to the large round slab of gray stone and turned, till there was a space between the bottom part, free enough to throw the hairy oats. Then I lowered the top slab, making it tight and started to turn and lo and behold, my hairy grain was changing into a true flour! My arms grew sore, but my sack was filling fast, except among the fine meal, there was an abundance of sharp whiskers and husks that didn't get ground. I asked Zosia if it mattered, but she suggested I could spend hours being "picky," otherwise, just forget it. So I did, until the next morning.

At the moment, I was so proud of myself, knowing what was involved in the production of these precious few pounds of an oat flour. With a loving touch, I tied my small sack and sat by the wall, squatting Kazakh style and waited for my friend to get through. Finally we walked away, tired but for me, feeling triumphant in the accomplishment of this simple task.

At the age of seventeen, I marveled with irony, what a path to success, with a career—a sheep-shit scrubber and a newly acquired skill, that of a grain miller. It seemed a farce of any parents' dream, with aspirations for a future, however the choice of the present pursuit, was neither theirs nor mine...

At home, nonchalantly I slung off my shoulders the heavy sack with the precious contents, grinning and imitating the horse laughter. Mother looked at me strangely and with a worried sigh, asked: "What's in there?" she pointed to the sack. I answered with another hee-haw, at which time Mietek stuck in his face with a chuckle: "I see health food, today we dine—tomorrow we whine!" Then, there was no rhyme to it and the reason was unclear, but something about these oats kept bothering me, however I dismissed it as unimportant for I had volunteered my hard-earned rations and services for the evening meal. What a mistake!

I should have crawled behind my "pietchka" and died for the night from fatigue. Instead, I went through creating the oat "delicacy." There was nothing to it, ingredients and timing being so simple. But it was summer, hot, sweaty and "kiziak" didn't want to catch the fire, so I kept feeding the "pietchka" while shaping the dough out of my priceless flour. Occasionally glancing at my dirty hands, although it didn't matter any more what went down the food pipes, it seemed that our brains, senses and stomachs, struck up a pact of tolerance and accepted anything in order to stay well and alive. The small oat cakes, hard as a rock, baked themselves on the hot blackened grill and when they were done or burned, it didn't diminish their taste, for the taste wasn't there in the first place. Yet somehow, before the evening was over, the oat "monsters" were gone, disappearing in a flash, without compliments or thanks to the chef.

As evening approached, the young people gathered outdoors at the far side of our dwelling, where an old tree trunk lay across a grassy knoll, a welcome sight after a hot day, to chat and gossip and talk of the day's events, the feelings and concerns for days ahead. When the small talk had ceased, someone would start a song and that was always a signal to fill the rest of the evening with singing. Into the late hours, the melodies would float through the warm summer's air, with tempos changing from the lively mazurkas to vigorous military lyrics and then to the sleepy ballads of the time past. Each of us, absorbed in singing, was lost in his or her own personal longings and hopes.

The song was a magnet, drawing us together and perhaps for few moments, lessening the weight of everyday ordeals, even imagining a different tomorrow.

And tomorrow came for me, early next morning, but it started awfully, with solving finally, the riddle of the horsey oats. A nudge from Mother Nature made me get up early and it was then I discovered the menace of the prickly husks and sharp needles I had left in the ground flour. There is no way to describe how prickly they were, unless you yourself were pricked by them. So this was what all the chuckling was about, the jokes and painful smiles. Well, this was no joke to me!

It was a small case of agony, as much as I can recall. The sad thought splashed through my mind then, there was still a sack full to be dealt with. Eating wasn't a problem, but disposal of it was.

These were not especially glorious moments to remember and dwell on, but they were a part of our life; the insignificant and laughable events, today standing out as much as the tragic ones. For like a long and continuos chain, they made up our existence of tough and seemingly endless three years in Soviet Russia.

****

July came with a hot breath of summer. We lived in a strange world, ostracized from the rest of the universe. The news of the raging war west of us, where the German troops were advancing steadily, exactly where, it was hard for us to pinpoint. We hardly had any chance to read newspapers and the Soviets didn't readily volunteer to share with us the progress on the war front, which also heightened the credence of how grave the situation was.

With a heavy workload and barely meeting our daily needs, we didn't quite care who would be our next prosecutor. Now and then, the rumors began circulating about the release of the prisoners, bringing them out of "lagras," out of the coal mines and far distances of north and far eastern Russia, even creating the volunteers army to aid in the war's efforts, fighting the Nazi's alongside the Soviets.

Those being only rumors, they incited, perhaps falsely at times, our feelings of self-discipline, which set in to adjust to the kind of living we had faced from day to day. It disturbed us, but at the same time injected a wedge of hope, a hope for change we were once dreaming of. Nevertheless, we were alerted to every whisper and piece of gossip concerning us and other members of the families, imprisoned far away, our fate and future. Some feared that this fantasizing might become a habit, knowing in the past how many illusions had turned into great disappointments.

All the expectations and secret star gazing didn't deter or interfere in our dawn-to-dusk hours of hard work. When reporting each morning, we were always amazed and startled at the variety of chores awaiting us, foretelling a lot of gymnastics and sweating.

The grain in the field was ripening, but the harvest was still weeks away. Around the area of the village, there lay fields cultivated for experimental purposes only, such as the hectares of oats I hade worked on before. The early sown millet was ready to be cut and that's where our next assignment was. As horses and strong, able hands were at the war's front, we were the substitutes and replacements to carry out the job.

Men and women of able age were given the implements, outdated but available in large numbers, the sickles and scythes, half of them rusty, some sharper than a devil. My sickle was fine, but I had to grip the handle tight, for my hands were small and fingers short. Our overseer, for a change, was a jolly fellow, with a grizzly beard and a pleasant disposition. The work was not easy, with the sun beating down and the insects pestering and biting us! Considering my stature, I was doing surprisingly well in our assigned area. The grain laden stalks lay in neat rows, while I attacked them with a fury, earning my bread, until a small slip of a sharp blade and off went my left pointing finger. Well, not quite off, it was hanging by the skin... stretched as if elastic and dangling—a gruesome sight, even at a quick glance. Things became fuzzy at that time and all I remember was so much blood, someone cursing and pouring a clear, stinging liquid over my finger, then I must have passed out. When I came to, my finger was swathed in a bloody cloth and faces were around me peering, anxiously asking "How are you feeling?" I felt alive, a little woozy, but alert enough to hear a loud tirade coming from the jolly overseer who, at the moment, did not sound so jolly. He was fuming and ranting at the top of his voice: "Clumsy girl! Where were your eyes and fingers, stuck behind you? (a curse) I had to loose a whole ration of vodka on your stupid finger! A one whole month (another curse) down the drain!"

He went on blowing his stack for a while, then spat noisily! In spite of the heavy cursing and blaming me for a lot more than I deserved, I was touched by his Samaritan sacrifice of the precious booze. Knowing it was rationed, but being of good character, he perhaps saved my life by pouring the high-proof alcohol on the ugly cut, thus preventing an infection and its consequences.

For the life of me, I still can't understand how I did not suffer any ill effects from this unfortunate accident. Mother was worried, naturally, but nothing else could be done to help. By the next day I was back at my workstation, cutting away the stalks of millet, although without my previous speed and energy, having the finger covered with a thick roll of bandage from a torn pillowcase. There was a throbbing in the injured area, but that was to be expected. Most of my worry was to keep the flesh together, to grow and heal faster so as not to interfere in a major operation coming soon, a planned raid on the watermelon fields. During the entire week now, the area was scouted, without any concern for the weather, as it hardly ever rained in summer, but we were not quite sure if the melons were ripe yet. Truly I was hoping they were not, so as to give my finger more time to reattach itself and grow stronger for that important event. Today, an assault on the watermelon fields seems so adventurous, a stunt or young persons' prank. But at that time and place it helped as seasonal nutrition, aiding our systems during the fluctuations and changes in our bodies from the lack of normally ingested vitamins and generally something we used to recall fondly as food.

My slashed finger, became a mystery, a wound hidden under the soiled and dried-up bloody cloth. It was on its own, I hoped healing itself and growing together. I restrained myself from peeking inside of the dirty bandage, praying there was no permanent damage. Friends and older people brought a lot sympathetic advice and home remedies some of which I tried and hoped for the best.

Among my younger peers, I had gotten amazing treatment while at work with everybody pitching in, donating labor with a kind-hearted understanding and help, easing the anxiety of my burden, in unexpected incidents. Whatever happened, we knew we didn't stand alone, sharing the joys and pain, except in personal emotions of the heart. There, we had to work out the problems on our own. I, myself, was a good example.

Being infatuated with Mietek now for over a year, I discovered, with dismay, there were other young girls vying for his attention. From my close observations, I singled out one rival, a tall and rather plain but sexy-looking girl by the name of Miroslava. Mira, for short, was soft-spoken, very athletic in appearance, with a deep tanned face displaying forever a pleasant smile, which I learned to detest whenever I saw her with Mietek. Although she called me affectionately a "doll," I just sizzled inside. Doll, my foot! I wasn't stuffed with wood chips!

I was seriously thinking of transferring my affections somewhere else, but it seemed the availability of young guys in Novaia Zyzn amounted to a few that were not romantically involved or not unappealing. Well, there was one, a great-looking individual, an aspiring lawyer, who was possessively guarded by his lady-friend, whose husband was known to be alive and heard from, but unfortunately he was still imprisoned in north-eastern Russia.

Amorous awareness was not a priority in our present life, it came secondary after breathing and eating. The first two, were a must, but love? It could come and go. We mourned and moped for a while, then forgot about it. The circumstances made it easy, for hard work kept us occupied and we learned with time, control and restraint in romantic and the emotional encounters.

The approaching Sunday, was to be our watermelon jaunt. We felt excited, conveniently overlooking the fact that this adventurous hike, was nothing less than stealing!

The Ten Commandments and other moral reminders got swept aside, not being in harmony with our plans. Perhaps the conscience was still alive, but in silence, hiding somewhere and there was no time to feel guilty.

When the time came, we gathered all available sacks and heavy spreads to hold the weight of the bulky watermelons. My finger, happily didn't throb anymore and everything was progressing smoothly.

The night turned out to give us a great cover of haze with the moon hiding behind the thick clouds. We all met at one point then scattered upon reaching the field, stretching for acres, wide and long. The idea was not to go deep into the "forbidden" territory in case of being caught, but spread out widely for a quick departure. After a while, caution was thrown to the wind as we crossed the fields and became selective in picking out the bulky melons, busting them open to see how ripe they were, generally disregarding the need for alertness and for a change, having fun with an enjoyment of stealing!

With the first step, for a mere second, I thought the sky would open up, exploding with lightening and thunder of supernatural ire...

But the night was warm, rather humid, with a veil of mist hanging about, creating this whole daring episode as wild, madcap fun. From time to time, we called to each other, checking upon their safety while sinking our teeth and mouth, up to the bridge of the nose, into the red and juicy flesh of delightfully tasting, cool, watermelons. Finally, with reluctance, we passed the word around, like an echo, that it was time to go back, to gather up the loot and get back to the village.

Now it took a little longer, and we walked slower, being full of liquid and Mother Nature required of us a few stops in order to get rid of it.

The disappearing clouds gave way to a dark but clear-looking sky which the bright moon moved slowly across, touching softly the fields with its brilliant light, illuminating the area and occasionally catching the dark silhouettes of figures, as in the game of musical chairs, squatting down and going up, without a sound.

We were on our way out, almost leaving the field, when someone from the back yelled, "The guard! The guard! Run! Run!"

Nobody looked around or questioned the warning. We all broke into fast strides, a difficult attempt with the bulky weight on our backs. I had slung my load over my shoulders and held on tightly, not paying any attention to my knuckles clutching the folds of heavy sack, until someone passed me running faster and yelling, "You're losing your finger—do something!"

I looked down and in horror I noticed my severed knuckle was opened and bleeding profusely where it once was healing so nicely. My bandage of dirty cloth had become unraveled and was swinging in front of me, while I tried to avoid tripping on the damn thing! I wasn't quite sure if I should let go of my cargo or push the bloody finger to hold it in its place. I kept running though, with the heavy load, keeping an eye on my flipping finger and holding on to the sack with the watermelons—hoping for the best! We all made it safely to the village without being caught, my tormented finger included. (It's still attached to the rest of me, showing only a faint scar, proof of my toughness or good luck.) We were lucky that night, escaping the punishment and for many days to come, enjoying the contraband fruits, even contemplating jokingly, a watermelon festival!

Soon, the memory of it was gone and the entire community was besieged with hard labor. There was talk of getting ready to go again deep into the steppes for harvesting the ripening wheat and millet, which also meant bivouacking close to Mother Nature, under the hot skies with only haystacks for protection from the scorching sun. For me, it would be a new experience in the field work, for others, a second summer was an old story. I felt excited, a little anxious and somewhat frightened at the prospect of being alone, so far away—living outdoors. In spite of being healthy and quite strong, my limited height was in a way a handicap, but even so I was ordered to join the assigned group and get ready to leave on short notice to an area a few hours away from our village.

Mother was watching me, throwing extra clothing into a sack, some feeding utensils, (hoping there would be a use for them), otherwise, we traveled light. It was another stepping stone in my advancing years toward maturity or just simply one of the many sides of growing up fast. A rude awakening that soon I would reach the age of seventeen and perhaps, by then, would master some more of the crafts, without any specific profession, skills I had never dreamed of acquiring, and in a normal life, would have never thought of.

The working group had gathered at dawn on the outskirts of the village where long carts awaited and without wasting any minutes we were on our way to the fields only known to us by the numbers of the hectares they covered. The larger the stretch, the longer the stay, and harder the work. The early morning hours didn't encourage anyone to talk, this being still a sleepy time, our heads with eyes half closed, were bobbing from side to side, as the carts were creeping over the rough terrain.

The sun was at its full force by the time we arrived at our assigned work area. The first object I noticed immediately, was strange looking equipment or call it a contraption with a pair of oxen reined to it. There were two tractor seats, one directly behind the animals and one next to an octagon-shaped, fan-like cage, made out of the wooden slats that turned, as everything went into motion.

In no time I had learned that I would be the one to generate the motion. Thus, I became the "wabohreika" and the oxen driver. I was told to get on the iron seat and was given a whip with double leather strands, a form of persuasion, for the animals to get in motion. I wasn't alone though, I had a partner who occupied a second seat and really did the greater share of the hard work, pushing with a pitch fork, the cut stalks of millet, through the turning wooden blades. The good results of this chore would depend on the harmony of the two workers. From the very beginning, I felt sorry for my partner, for I was green and quite clumsy, while learning the rudiments of the simple field labor. Back in Poland, my partner's family was once rich farmers, working the land for generations and passed it on as an inheritance with great love and honor. Now, everything was gone, his family dispossessed of everything they ever earned and owned, leaving them with heartbreak. Here in the steppes, the fieldwork was not strange to him. He was very patient in explaining to me the handling of this new implement and the hostile-looking animals, the oxen. I tried to absorb everything, for it seemed like a snap to follow his advice in cracking the whip to the left or to the right, while yelling loudly at the top of the voice, "sop" for the turn to the right and "sobea" for the left. The correct command would cut a precise path through the rows of ripened stalks by the contraption I was to guide, the one called "wabohreika."

Controlling the oxen was surely an art and struggle leading them in the right direction, so as not to miss and wander in streaks all over the field. I am sure there were times when my partner would have liked to strangle me, for at the very beginning, my confusing commands, did just that, confuse me and the oxen, make them meander without any discipline and uniformity. From a bird's eye view, my part of the field must have looked like a pattern of granny's "crazy" quilt... I felt such a failure, my throat was dry from the yelling and parched from heat. The water was rationed and besides, there would be no interruptions once I placed my butt on the iron seat.

Under the blue dome of a sky, the work was in progress, the harvesting of millet had begun. The low and high-pitched voices were heard in unison and at intervals with accompanying wooden rattles of "wabohreikas," raising wispy puffs of dust, hanging lazily above the ground, engulfing everything around and choking it from dryness. Except for the work, everything seemed as paralyzed by the oppressive air and heat from the blazing sun. This was Kazakhstan as I saw it for the first time… in its scorn and agony!

My time was absorbed in concentration on my performance of the newly acquired profession. I couldn't quite achieve the balance between the right words of a command, whipping the shit out of the oxen, straining the muscles to hold on to the reins and at the sharp turns, trying to keep my ass from sliding from the sweat-drenched iron seat. The hours stretched into infinity, and I swore the noon break would never come. I surely thought I was going to die from exhaustion. But I didn't. I went on yelling, whipping, cursing and as the hours slipped past, so did my anxiety and fear of what, to me at the beginning, seemed a superhuman undertaking.

The simplicity of the Soviet common sense came back to me again and for a brief moment, I understood the word I hated with a passion. The sound of giving in, actually was help in disguise to survive during the worst of times.

I managed to get through the first line of crisis and all of sudden I realized, the activity in the field had stopped and relief had come with a break for a drink and, I hoped, some food, which I knew I had earned. I got off the "wabohreika" and walked stiffly, feeling my muscles tight from the tension and physical strain. I glanced at the others and although their faces looked fatigued, I heard laughter in a line being formed around the stall where the meal was being "served." It was nothing exceptional, the same or maybe thicker slices of a dark bread and chunks of goat cheese, salty enough to strip the lining from a mouth cavity but relief from the burning with unlimited "kvas," if the time allowed. The cool liquid was stored in an enormous wooden barrel that sat alone in a small cart pulled by a mule all the way from Novaia Zyzn the day before our arrival, amazingly keeping the liquid deliciously cool.

The mule was now champing peacefully on the green brush, growing in the ditch, loaded with unfamiliar berries, almost as large as blueberries, of the same color, but quite different in taste. At the moment I cannot recall their name, but the berries became our frequent desert and source of recreation. In the brief, idle moments, sometimes stretching over time limits, when a young couple would cross into the world of caprice, an interlude from the intense and hard work, off into the heat-induced tender touch and flurry of kisses, a sweet diversion and a morale boost to carry on through the rest of the day. The blue-stained backs of linen dresses, provided evidence that the short while wasn't so idle, at all. The smudge from dark juicy berries became a hallmark and the cause of raised eyebrows and blushing on the girl's part.

The hour of noon rest passed quickly and while the muscles relaxed, the hay made us feel drowsy in the shade of a huge stack. In no time, there would be a call... "Davai, podnimaish, rabotai..." (Come on, get up, work), the words, like a drill we had become so familiar with, kept rattling off repeatedly, making us jump automatically in haste.

On the way back to my "wabohreika" and my oxen, Zosia walked with me. "How are you doing, little one?" she asked. "I am trying as best I can," I smiled back, praying my "best" would improve sufficiently for my sake, my partner's and Mother Russia.

The afternoon session, except for the breaks for quenching the thirst and other natural reliefs, lasted way into the flaming red sunsets, with just enough time to find, while still in daylight, a small area to fill with freshly cut hay, cover with the extra garments, then pitch my aching body down for a well-deserved rest and sleep...

Being my first night in the fields, I learned that even simple tasks such as getting ready for "bed," produced some unexpected frustrations. With the sun setting fast, I hardly noticed what others were occupied with, feeling good for having Zosia as a sleeping neighbor, assuming that women had a separate area for the night hours, separate from the men, that is. Well that assumption slipped fast away, as I watched a huge figure of a guy throw his bundle on the other side of my roost. Zosia noticed an alarmed look on my face, and without a word, she shook her head as a gesture to assure me it was okay. Right!

To find yourself at the age of seventeen sleeping next to a healthy young male, whose name I didn't even know, was normal? The upright teachings from the past, were doing high summersaults in a moral sense, smashing the barriers erected by social ethics, in normal living. But this was far from normal, in every step we took, the enormity of changes in our lives was hard to grasp, to submit to, every turn a challenge and a denial of everything we were raised in and accustomed to, way back, though it seemed like centuries ago.

I glanced around and my panic had subsided slightly, while Zosia tried to quell my fears. "Don't get excited, we have rules—nobody here gets bothered; no matter how "bothered" they get-our guys still remember to be gentlemen, it's only if you happen to stray on your own, that's your problem-and trouble; otherwise, sleep well, we'll be up at the crack of dawn."

The dawn came, too fast. It seemed that only an hour ago I was talking to Zosia and now I watched the horizon light up with a pastel tinge of yellow, listening to the braying donkeys and the clatter of rusty machines, getting ready for a morning's work.

I wasn't quite ready, but the overseers were. I stared at them kicking the bare feet of those who were still lying down and in order to escape having mutilated toes, I got up fast and tied my worn-out canvas shoes with a string, hoping the rubber soles would last till the end of the outdoor work. I felt sweat already trickling upon my scalp and neck, being irritated by the noxious loud encores of "davai!"

*****

Day after day passed and though the hours seemed extremely long at times, the time itself didn't stand still, but was filled with continuos hard work. We had learned to cope with unexpected difficulties, accepting this cycle as everyday existence or call it a living. I began to discover amazingly fast how to discipline certain parts of my body, beginning with bare feet when walking on the field of cut wheat or millet. It was a very painful experience at first, leaving the tender soles bleeding from opened cracks of sores filling with dirt and drying blood. With the help of gnashing teeth, minimizing the stings till a thick layer of skin formed, tough as leather, giving blessed protection and indifference to the sharp spikes, covering the surface we had continuously walked on.

Of course there was a slight problem, similar to what Cinderella's stepsister had faced, trying to jam the shoe on the larger foot, which we solved without any pain. We simply shaved off the excess rough flesh, in order to make a true fit, something the wicked stepsister didn't think about, but it left us with just a little tenderness and without great discomfort.

Some dilemmas could be resolved with patience and time, some only helped slightly as it was with a menacing head and body lice. Those we tried our best to eliminate with hopeless efforts, facing constant sweat and dirt, without having water to wash with.

Each day, toward evening, when there was still daylight, we sat in circles like a pack of monkeys, mashing between our fingernails the nasty creatures infesting our heads and torsos. It would sometimes give us a "hair raising" appearance, not precisely in its meaning, as no cause for alarm, only trying simply to show us their presence, in large numbers. The itch and scratch became a normal occurrence, as there was no immediate remedy for that predicament.

The field labor grew harder as time passed, but with that came a passive feeling of acceptance. Sometimes there was a breakdown, mostly for the young women, a fear which materialized monthly, bringing distress and a rather shameful feeling for not being able to hide it completely from those around us. Our companions tactfully tried to divert their eyes at such times, pretending not to notice the dried-up residues of blood streaks, sometimes leaving traces all the way down to the ankles. Most of the young women and girls tried to ignore it, as if the pain and the sight didn't matter that much, but it did. Everything mattered, yet we had to keep our sanity on an even level, so as not to give into the wild mood swings, which at times, seemed to have the tendency to keep us off the balance.

Alicja R. Edwards

On many evenings, when our bodies were not completely exhausted and our minds were still alert, we made bonfires and enjoyed sitting around into the late hours of the night, singing our hearts away. One of our friends had an old battered guitar and with an accompaniment of strumming in background, the melodies would follow one after another. In the darkness of the heat-absorbing steppes, the songs of strong and many beautiful voices floated in harmony, bringing a therapeutic touch, like a balmy compress over our fatigued flesh and souls.

The labor of harvesting the grain lasted over the summer, with long periods out in the fields, a few days at "home" for a change of, literally speaking, truly loused-up clothing and a deep scrubbing of accumulated dirt, something not easily done, having a limited amount of soap.

I remember during one of those "homecomings," my mother standing by a wooden tub, trying to separate oily suet from the twisted, bloody intestines of some animal, possibly a horse, who knows what it was? We didn't bother with an autopsy, but the stench from it, was unbearable!

Now and then, mother's stomach kept quivering with the strong urge to puke her own guts out, but she kept working, till all of the blubber was cleared away. Later she added some lye to the slimy fixings and through this simple chemical process, we became the proud owners of soap. Not exactly the "Schiht" brand with a jumping deer, but omitting the smell, it was a cleansing type, something that mattered most to us. Just the idea of decimating the pesky varmints, the lice, made us tolerate the odor and the memory of its origin. At times with my eyes closed, I tried to imagine it being of a pastel color and a scent of lily of the valley, at least to dull the senses, while getting clean. The primitive soap helped our hygiene to some extent, eliminating the itch and whiffs of raunchy sweat, acting as an antiseptic in the areas threatened with infections.

Boils sometimes sprung up in clusters, taking time to fester, before maturing in accumulated pustules that would burst open at the worst time. It usually happened during the field work, when the abscess seated under the armpits, all you could do was furiously flap our arms like a chicken to help it split open and let the yellow fluid seep down the side of the body, while holding your breath.

I seemed to be blessed with a fertile zone for those painful boils and mother kept laughing, pointing with a warped notion about all the evil leaving my diminutive person. The ugly pustules were sheer torture but, as with everything else, they passed with the season, without appearing again.

*****

The war seemed so far away, as the rumble of bombs and fear of bloodshed hadn't reached us yet in this corner of the country.

110

In late summer, the trio of our family went in different directions and to various types of labor. Mother did a variety of jobs right in the village, while Jez was a full-fledged shepherd, guarding a huge flock of sheep. Although being so young, at the age of thirteen, the long and lonely hours in the isolated fields gave him a chance for meditating and may have instilled in him a foundation for self-control and logic, which became his primary guides during his later life.

Through the hot days of summer, I went periodically to the fieldwork, altering in stages, as the gathering of grain had rushed ahead. Depending on which grain was ripening the fastest, it was cut without delay and stacked up in large heaps. Our workforce was moved swiftly from hectares to hectares, without regard for time or physical condition of the people. I had a trying time attempting to handle the pitchforks, the size of them alone, making me shudder. One given to me stood higher than my short figure and its weight kept throwing me off balance, but after some deep breathing and a few snorting maneuvers, I learned to manage the devil, although it slowed down my work. I faced the lonely hectares again and the norm of daily ordeals which I would begin with plenty of confidence, till the pressure of the pitchfork put a few cramps in my forearms, halting my efforts for a while and watching my companions disappear out of sight, ahead of me. My spirits would fizzle out, but there was hardly time for crying or pity, the ration still would be the same.

Over the summer, the labor had intensified. We found ourselves working nights also, with small intervals of rest in between, bringing loads of gathered oats, wheat and millet into the area where huge thrashing machines sat waiting like hungry monsters, surrounded by clouds of dust during their activity.

I recall, one night, it being my turn to receive the grain stalks from the wagons carrying the loads gathered in the fields, to distribute them alongside the thrashers, to create a long and tall mound, easy to slide into the wide openings of the noisy ogres.

The night was unusually warm and humid; the moon, normally bright, was hidden behind wispy, vapor-like clouds. I was tired, dead tired as everyone was, working in the last few weeks from the early dawn, and all through the night. Lord, I was tired! I felt beat, numb, muscles drained of any energy, it was as if being out of body...being buried somewhere with stalks thrown on the pile, except my brain was floating around somewhere.

While waiting for the rest of the loads to show up, I must have dozed off, right on the top of a mountain of millet. When my friends came back, they thought I was taking a break, not being able to answer their calls. In my deep snooze, I didn't feel the weight of layers and layers of heavy stalks being slung on top of me. I was being buried alive! It could have been serious, if not for someone's lucky maneuver with a pitchfork, that accidentally found my rear and jabbed me hard enough to snap back to a reality of what was taking place. I thrashed for a few seconds through the heavy greenery, gasping for breath, then jumped as if shot out of a cannon with millet leaves sticking from my hair like a grotesque halo, looking like a mad Circe. Someone pulled me down and shook me, slapping my face, a little too hard I thought, but finally bringing me out of the "zombie" stage to the point where I began to feel the sting of the pitchfork. I knew then I was wide awake!

For the rest of the night I contented myself with my favorite pastime, whipping the hell out of the oxen.

Toward the end of summer, we had gotten a new wave of overseers. One of them was a vicious-looking, a curly-headed Tzigan(Gypsy), from Bessarabia. Everybody feared him, women the most. His presence was always known by the sound of a cracking whip made out of braided black and white hide, resembling a snake. Its long leather straps many times came close to our heads and legs, keeping us watchful to duck in time, escaping the whistling of the wildly spinning, sharp tips.

With instinct and being continuously alert, we had learned to escape his never-ending fury. One day, my luck didn't hold. We were at the wheat fields, heaping the golden, rich grain into the wagons, while the curly-headed bastard was dashing madly on his horse from place to place. His face expressed uncontrollable rage, his mouth spewed obscenities at us, complaining there was too much wheat left in the field, that we were good-for-nothing and lazy "bourgeois."

He caught me standing with my pitchfork idle by my side, while I was wiping the trickling sweat over my eyes, which was blurring my vision. I was unaware of his movement. He was fast. Without any question or warning, he raised his whip and, like lightening, cracked it across the right side of my face. The sudden pain was a shock; it stung, and it burned. I touched my cheek with a finger and saw a few small red drops, where the leather cut through the skin. I stood petrified—and everybody around, for a second, watched in silence. Then, out of nowhere, Zosia came running and with a rapid movement, shoved a pitchfork at his black leather boot, when he was still in a half-standing position over the horse, with a whip ready for another strike!

I realized at once, he was going to whip her, but Zosia's mouth opened up like a sewer, yelling and cursing at him at the top of her voice: "You dirty son of the bitch! You curly-headed fucking bastard, you pick on defenseless people, enough of it! You will get yours one morning with a dozen pitchforks stuck in you chest! Watch yourself!" Then she pressed the tines harder into his boot. He glared, taking into account all the hostile looks on the faces of the laborers, then spat at Zosia, leering viciously: "Yop tvoiu mat!" (fuck your mother), he screamed at her and turned his horse around, riding fast away.

Zosia threw the pitchfork after him, yelling loudly: "Yop tvoiu torze" (fuck yours, too). Still fuming, she turned to look at my cut, which wasn't very deep, but it left a scar for a long time, a reminder of the barbaric rules and times. Today, there is hardly the trace of a mark, but the memory, even now, is vivid and throbbing, sometimes as if it happened only yesterday. The images of boundless wheat fields, a deep blue sky and a black-leather clad Bessarabian overseer, are still imbedded in my mind like color slides, mute but intense.

THE WHIPPING

The fear in us must be the sculptor carving the intaglios of events that cannot be easily erased from our memory, bringing them back in a flash at will, with dismay and awe, but not hurting anymore.

The fearful Tzigan wasn't with us for long after that; they said he was called into the army, making everyone breathe easier in the grain fields.

But the pattern of work remained the same, hard and long with days advancing into the new season, as the summer was coming to an end. The monotony of labor was changing into the new phase of harvesting, with an emphasis placed on the precious grain. The hectares of the far-stretching fields, lay lonely in the hot sun, silent and naked, but for the dried-up, cut stalks, and squawking dark birds, gleaning the dusty rows.

The thrashers and scattered mountains of yellow glistening grain, became the center of activity. Carts boxed in with long and wide planks as containers, were brought in and for us or, rather me, the novice, a new experience had begun. I remember using to the utmost every muscle in my body, while handling the shovel, filling the cart with grain to a heaping mound. When the grain was loaded, we formed a caravan with our carts and while coaxing the lazy and stubborn oxen to get a move on, slowly we departed for our destination, the elevators in the town of Gzaroon.

It was a long journey across the forlorn and wild land, covered with clusters of rough, sharp-edged grass and overgrown tumbleweed. The mixture in the soil was that of sand, reddish-looking earth and various sizes of pebbles. The barren panorama didn't have much to offer our eyes. Now and then, there was an echo of a cracking whip and an angry command "yaow."

The heat was still intense, although the whining wind thrashing around the tall weeds was taking on the pitch of a dreaded November "burian." Each cart had only one driver sitting in front on a flat board and another to rest our feet, with reins attached to the wooden yokes, leveled at our elbows. The trip, although monotonous, was a great relief for the aching muscles from hours and hours of working at the field chores.

For a while, the mind and body relaxed, stripped of all troublesome thoughts and aches, letting our vision roam over the endless horizon, without focus. Mindless and passive, with only a heartbeat signifying our living presence, the time moved slowly, without revealing the hour of day. In a strange way, it was peaceful in this desolate wilderness through which we had passed when exiled from Gzaroon.

From time to time I could hear a sharp cry of a bird, invisible it seemed, till I learned to spot him by a tawny coat and white glistening chest feathers, resembling a large hawk. It could have been a distant cousin of the species I recalled seeing in Poland during hiking excursions. In fact, we had one of them at home, stuffed, with the wings widely spread, sitting on a mossy branch which hung in a corner of the living room, keeping company with a white speckled owl, placed on top of a tall oak wardrobe. I have always felt, as both of them were staring at me with their artificial beady eyes, it was gruesome and disrespectful to have dead creatures on such display, like a silent zoo.

The bird flew in wide circles under the brilliant blue skies and when it came down suddenly to claim his prey, I shuddered, frightened by his size, as he was huge. The span of his wings, would easily cover the length of a wagon. I blessed myself quickly, out of habit, and thanked God it was only a runty "suslik" (a prairie dog) carried away in his claws, and not I.

During the slow-moving caravan of grain carts I observed life on the steppes, its creatures and plants, trying to fill the slowly creeping hours with some interest, over the long stretching miles, while it seemed as if time stood still. One thing I learned on this first run, was never to fall asleep at the "reins," especially if we were the last ones in the train.

I discovered the hard way, when I found myself waking from a nap, which I took without being aware I was sleepy, and finding my two beasts lazily munching on a bountiful growing plant, the very bitter wormwood. While they were enjoying their lunch, I began to panic, realizing all of a sudden, I was completely alone. The lazy bastards, the oxen, must have halted their march quite a while ago, when I first slept. Looking over the horizon, ahead on the trail, there wasn't a trace or a shadow of a single wagon I was following behind. The heavy imprints of the cart tracks were in front of me and all I had to do was follow them, quite simple. Not quite! The beasts decided to stay put. The whip and my dried-up lungs didn't do a thing. The two sons of bitches were casually champing away, without heeding my threats, not even turning their heads at the whip slashing their hides. I got off the cart, looking around and to the skies; I don't know what I was expecting to find, but I noticed the bird above me...circling. I shivered. Was I going to be his prey? "Matko Boska!" I prayed aloud. I checked the wooden yokes, and discovered one of the straps was loose. I tied it with a rope, hoping something would get me going, for I didn't contemplate spending the night alone in the steppes.

Holy Moses! It dawned on me, that could be a strong possibility! The coyotes, the prairie wolves and other wild creatures I hadn't met yet, the thought terrified me.

It seemed so unreal, like a dream, no, a nightmare! I looked up to the skies, and the bird was gone; well, the hell with him! There was one less danger to deliberate about, and the oxen? Damn them! I could have killed them, but that wouldn't have solved the problem, either. I was at their mercy. Once they picked up a step, but it was only in search of fresh wormwood. Perhaps if their bellies got full, I could coax them to move on, so patiently I waited, only to witness the spectacle of shit gushing out of both of them, with some of the spray reaching my face. I swore quietly and wiped the smelly mess. Again, the oxen

116

moved a couple of feet and my hopes soared, thinking we were on our way, but that was another of their hoaxes. The feeding went on.

Dear God! Was I really going to spend a night here? There was a hiss to my side. I turned my head, thinking I heard a rattler. I climbed back on the wagon and sat, resigned…hoping some miracle could change this situation or the dumb oxen would decide to plod again.

In my disgust and heavy brooding, I didn't notice a figure appearing ahead of me, on the horizon, until I saw a definite movement of someone walking on the trail. Something else to worry about? No letting up on my misery!

I strained my eyes and almost started to yodel from joy! It was Tomek, our young friend, whose cart I was following in this, my first caravan. When he got closer, his face showed concern: "Are you all right?" he asked. I nodded my head, still choked up from the thrill of getting rescued. "What got into you? I turned around when we were crossing the ridge and you weren't behind, what's the trouble?"

I hated to tell the truth, but with embarrassment I confessed my stupidity: "I went to sleep during the ride and when I woke up, I couldn't control the dumb oxen and make them move."

Tomek looked irritated: "Your cart's the last one in line, and you decide to take a nap? The heat must have gotten to you! Move over, we have to catch up with the rest of them!"

Feeling very humble, I moved. He took the reins and the whip, cursing and yelling like a maniac. It took more then "sob" and "sobea," before the stubborn animals decided to budge. In a short time we were over the ridge, approaching Tomek's cart and in the distance we saw the rest of the caravan. This time, Tomek let me ride ahead of him, for safety I guess, his wagon now becoming the end of the train. I kept my eyes on the road, wide open, all the way to the Gzaroon elevators.

It had been a few months since we were banished from the town, but it was exciting to see it again. After unloading the grain, we wandered into the familiar bazaar where, a year ago, I had watched this same group sitting down on the wooden sidewalk, rubbing their tired feet as I was doing now, except mine were only sweaty from being shook up from the scary ride through the prairies.

The town hadn't changed. I wondered where Baska was—hoping for the sight of her, but not making any effort to find her, feeling exhausted. I sat and watched the familiar surroundings with myriad memories rushing in. It being late in the afternoon, the bazaar was almost deserted, except for few vendors, lounging around the large, dark barrels of pickled tomatoes. I had an urge to walk across the empty square to the sewing place where mother had worked before, wondering if her friends were still there. I watched the place, trying to recognize people going in and out, thinking, should I go in to visit? Then I decided against it. Next time, I thought.

Without any feeling of remorse, I walked back to the elevators to join the rest of the group, getting ready to go back to Novaia Zyzn. Again, while crossing the railroad tracks, there was that slight pang of yearning, to follow them far south or east, somewhere to a distant land, where life would be free and people, different. But it was only a brief moment, an encounter of ideas and dreams, I had learned to keep to myself.

The trip back was a snap, although nightfall was descending when we reached the village. The indigo firmament held a profusion of glittering stars, hanging so low, I almost wanted to reach and pull them down. The beauty of the evening dispersed the recollection of strenuous past hours of a trip to Gzaroon, lifting the spirits, in a way being glad of coming "home."

******

The end of summer and beginning of the fall season triggered preparations for a long and bitter winter. There was a certain similarity with drawn-out months of harsh existence we had known a year before in Gzaroon. In contrast with past problems, the food wasn't so much of a worry, the clothing was. The outerwear we came into Russia with was getting pretty shabby and thin. Everything needed extensive repair. With time, the patches grew larger and became of exotic quality, being fashioned out of the bed covers, tapestries, drapes or colorful and sometimes heavily embroidered doilies or tablecloths. I remember one morning, one of the young guys coming in with an excited look on his face, repeating, "Spring is here, spring is here." We thought he was going "buggy" (no surprise in that, it was a common occurrence), but suddenly he turned around, as if he was going to moon us. Lo and behold, his butt was covered with gorgeous embroidered red tulips, which once perhaps served as a table cover now condemned to keep someone's ass warm, with a hope that it would survive a Russian winter. However, the weather was still balmy and work in a great variety awaited us each day.

As I recall, at that time, my brother, the shepherd, became sick and asked our mama to substitute for him, at least for one day. Mother was enthusiastic and cheerfully claimed it would be a welcome change for her, being alone with nature (she loved the outdoors), feeling the ruffles of the steppe winds, blowing away her troubled thoughts, maybe even dashing a few letters to our friends in Poland (she forgot it was wartime).

MY BROTHER, THE SHEPARD

My brother, however, was a bit apprehensive and worried, cautioning her to be careful, giving special instructions how to handle some problem sheep, especially the male ram, who always acted as a leader and was quite a nuisance, sometimes even uncontrollable. Mother listened politely and didn't seem very concerned with all of the advice given to her (which was a mistake), and waving nonchalantly a long willow "shilale," she made her exit with a smile: "I'll manage" and she was on her way. Until late that afternoon, this particular day was uneventful. For a change we had an easy job of husking the huge heads of sunflowers outside the long sheds, right in the village. The work itself was boring, without any muscle strain, making the time drag very slowly. I still hadn't mastered the art of shelling them, as a snack, in the native style. Even today, it remains a mystery to me how those seeds were cracked and the empty shells slid alongside the bottom lip, like a garland. As many times as I watched, observing them closely, trying to imitate them, even in my best efforts, the empty shells somehow always wound up on the ground, by my feet.

After a while I gave up, knowing it wasn't a life-threatening exhibition anyhow, then just enjoyed chewing on the fat white seed, which helped to eliminate the hunger pangs and contributed a significant amount of badly needed vitamins.

So this was a carefree day, the weather so pleasant, no reason for sweating or scratching, with a mind completely blank, feeling great for being alive and well, and looking ahead to a peaceful evening and a good night's sleep. At the dwelling, I was glad to find my brother's condition much improved.

The tranquility of the late afternoon hours, however, was shattered, when suddenly, mother appeared at the door. Her dress was festooned with a tattered hem, she limped, moving slowly and her face was stained with tears. She was almost sobbing. My brother, the conscientious worker that he was, looked at her a little shocked, but with great concern, he asked, "Mama, did you bring the sheep in?" Mother somehow managed to shout through the tears and anger, "Like hell I did! They brought me in," and she sobbed again. Jez nodded his head, peering at mother with sympathy: "He booted you all the way home, didn't he?" I knew Jez meant the old ram, who as Jez told us in a lot of stories before, considered himself to be a leader of the flock and hardly ever tolerated any supervision from strangers, including from our mother, the intruder.

Mama was still simmering: "Cholera nie baran!" (He is not a ram, a plaque!), she cursed, her teeth chattering. I helped her while she hobbled, hissing like a snake. I pointed to a small wooden bench for her to sit down on, but she gave me a nasty look: "As if I could? Suki syn (son of the bitch!), "his horns were at my rear all of the way home!"

We had to suppress our laughter, it was funny, though mother didn't think so, for a long time. Later, when reminiscing, she could joke about it but shied away from the areas where the sheep were grazing and swore off the products that smelled or had anything to do with lanolin.

Although the weather was still very mild, the days were growing shorter, compelling us to spend more time inside of the murky dwelling, lit only with candles and lanterns, which in spite of their numbers, didn't give out sufficient light. Living as guests of the Gorecki clan, we became like a part of the family, contributing and sharing our work and rations we kept earning daily.

Each of us had a favorable interest in passing the time during the long Kazakhstan evenings and nights. Telling stories was the most common diversion among the grownups. It was the easiest of entertainments, requiring only a big mouth with narrative talent and there was an abundance of it, with the older folks. They had so much to recall from the past and a long life, except for a slight void in the war stories, as those were still too fresh in everyone's minds, for a need to dwell on, having enough anguish in present living.

We all enjoyed the "bedtime" stories, listening quietly, but now and then I got distracted, watching Irma, Mietek's sister, being deeply involved in reading fortunes from the old playing cards. Her mouth was constantly moving, as she shuffled and spread them out in four rows, engrossed in a study of the symbols in telling her own fortune! At times, her eyes would open wide, with a smile she would slap the table loudly, delighted evidently with an outcome of the position of the greasy cards.

Predictions of the unknown had always fascinated me. Even as far back as I can remember, when being a "little" girl, I would get so excited when the Gypsy caravan came to our home town in Poland. My very close friend and I used to empty our banks, to the last grosh, to spend on the fortune telling. I remember my silvery metal bank, made in the shape of an old tree trunk and a hare sitting by it, as if guarding the treasure, which I had always had a hard time to keep inside. With a key in grandma's pocket and a hare as a guardian, I still managed to shake the coins out through the slit bottom, so we could sneak out of the house and run to the edge of town, where the Gypsies camped. What a thrill it was! We had to get the old cigar and pipe smoking woman Gypsies' attention, showing our palms and rattling the groshes; otherwise, there was no fortune reading. My heart used to beat fast upon listening to the predictions of a great future, great loves and riches, voyages and prominence, fame. What fantasy! Yet, it was exciting! The hard-earned groshes were gone, but there were times filled with dreams and great expectations, until the war came, with an unforetold journey to Russia and all the misery accompanying it...

Irma was not a Gypsy, but she might have been one. Clever and cunning, always with an answer to every question, right or wrong. She was a "know-it-all" wizard, an adviser, surprisingly quite respected among our own people and the Soviet villagers as well. At places where she worked, the Russian women begged her secretly many times to visit their homes and tell their fortunes, with a

121

promised reward. Occasionally, Irma had mentioned and now was evaluating all the offers, but not exactly committing herself in the open. Superstitious acts such as fortune telling were not quite legal and not very beneficial to the soul in the eyes of the red government. On one of the evenings, half listening to the tales, I sat, hoping to get sleepy, as I watched Irma shuffling the greasy cards, just shuffling, without putting them on the table, as it seemed her mind was working overtime. Suddenly she pounded her fist on the table top: "We have got to get some more lighting for this winter, we can't go on like this for another year!" Her concern was genuine, but the idea itself seemed like nonsense when we realized there was no chance of walking to the nearest store and buying anything of this kind. We sat, not saying a word-she could have been hallucinating, but Irma was serious: "We shall have the light this winter, maybe evens sooner, don't doubt me!" Her voice took on a superior tone, then she laid out her plan, very simple, but it scared the daylights out of me for it involved Zosia and also, me.

Irma was going to tell a fortune to a Russian woman who was very anxious to learn the fate of her husband, a Red Army officer from whom she hadn't heard for a long time. While she, Irma, would keep her occupied with card reading, we would be busy—stealing.

The day came, we left dressed in oversized clothes, easy to hide the stash or whatever we were after. I was scared but went along with the plan, knowing that if caught at it, we all could get our asses kicked out of the village to a faraway "sowchoz," where, as the expression went, even the devil kept saying "Good-night!"

There was a chill in the air, an indicator that even the warm October was slowly succumbing to the oncoming cycle of prolonged darkness, a dreaded wind and the cold Asiatic winter.

The thought itself made us more determined to carry out this shameful act. Irma, the leader, wasn't jittery at all. Her composure seemed to have a calming affect on us and we trusted her shrewd schemes.

The Russian woman's house was on the other side of the village, among a grove of tall poplar trees. She greeted Irma warmly and once again, I felt ashamed for such deceit and what we were about to do, then the images of long, dark evenings appeared briefly, and I brushed off quickly, as we walked into the house. It was a warm place, clean and cozy, the wooden dishes decorating the walls, linen-covered table and heavy iron pots gurgling on the "pietchka," emitting an incredible smell of vegetables, even a trace of meat. At this point I would have trouble recognizing a savor of this kind, but it wasn't important. I watched Irma concentrating with an artistic flair, laying out the greasy cards, holding the woman's attention, while raising her eyebrows constantly, the lips moving without a sound and her victim, the anxious woman, standing stiffly, holding her breath, eyes questioning, awaiting a word of doom or encouragement.

The brassy-looking lamp sat by the door stoop, next to it a tin can with an awful but marvelous smell of kerosene—we hit the jackpot! Just in time, for Irma was putting the cards away and the woman customer, smiling happily, was handing her a packet wrapped in a newspaper. I knew our errand was a success. Zosia was already out of the door, walking fast, not even waiting for us and I had to be careful with the smelly liquid swishing under my oversized coat...

My hand holding the can was burning, not from the fluid but the act itself of stealing! I had an urge to turn around, fearing the woman may be running after us, but the feeling of self-preservation overpowered the guilt, the trampled touch of decency. If later there were any echoes of remorse, they sank, without a plea.

The three of us walked in silence, Irma tried to cheer us up; "Don't look so gloomy, we didn't ask for the kind of life they forced on us; they preach equality, think as we're trying to live by their rules." Maybe Irma was right, the Russian woman had more oil lamps then she needed and we had none. I don't know if that had something to do with equality, but that evening we sat around till late, messing up the dirt floor with sunflower seeds and chatting with friends whose curiosity must have been enhanced by a brighter light coming out of a window. Their visit was a welcome sight, for each of them contributed some advice or other wild ideas to help us get through the trials and tribulations to ease the way of living in this so-called "Red paradise."

Over the last weeks in October, everybody, including all of the Soviet comrades, the villagers, was ordered to work in the potato fields. We had a friendly group, a mixture of exiled nationalities and the native Russians. Each of us worked equally, from morning to sundown. First we had a short stint revolving around the vegetables from collective plots. The specimens we were harvesting were of an amazing size and taste, so rich and flavorful. The earlier tomatoes we never tired of eating whenever we could and later the carrots and turnips were used as the meals for the day, though raw and covered with soil, they filled the stomach, bringing all of the nutritional benefits. The fields were not very large and took but few days to bring the stock into the sheds for storage over the winter. Some of the rejects we were allowed to keep and those made very tasty soups, while the rest of it we kept in a dugout, to last longer, through part of a winter.

And now, it was potato time. Each morning, we checked at the entry of the field to pick up our working tools, the spades, forks and baskets, then we would take a long walk across the wide and long area, the size of it, telling us how many days we should be digging and picking.

So far, the weather was cooperating to everyone's relief, lucky for us, for it would have been an awful mess and muscular strain if the rains interfered and turned the rich black earth into heavy mud. I felt sorry for my mother, seeing her bending down continuously, digging deep to bring the potatoes to the surface, her gray hair falling in wisps over her forehead from under the sweaty scarf wrapped tightly around her head. I noticed, though, she didn't seem to mind the work or the effort. Sometimes, to this day, I keep wondering where all of her strength came from, remembering our life in Poland was a relatively easy life.

It was as if the energy was flowing to her constantly from unlimited sources. Once in a while I even heard the humming of a tune. During the noon break she would get into the heavy debates with our overseer, a man of middle age, who spoke the Polish language quite well, being himself of Polish descent. I can't count how many times she had tangled with him in the heated arguments, making my blood run cold; for he was a dedicated communist, a loyal patriot and mother was walking a tightrope, trying to prove to him the points that could have pointed us out of Novaia Zyzn, to God only knows where! Yet, there didn't seem to be any animosity and at the end of each day, there always was a chunk of a dark bread handed with a friendly "do svidania."

On early mornings, we anxiously looked out of the doors and sighed gladly, noticing the clear skies and sun coming up, still sending forth, its warm rays. We had but a few days left to finally complete the potato project and this morning I observed our mother pulling a heavy string through the hem of her crushed velvet jacket with a silvery fur collar. The once-elegant garment, now worn out and shabby, could hardly be recognized as a fashionable article once designed in Vienna, where it came from, a few years ago. I watched mother fumble, hissing impatiently, till finally she managed to tie the bottom of her jacket, just below her hips. I stared and wondered aloud: "It isn't that cold yet," I said to her, but she mumbled something about a plan, her mind was spinning, but she didn't explain what it was! The day started as any working day, but somehow, I still remember it so well. The sun kept going in behind the clouds, the air was balmy, but in spite of that, mother was wearing her velvet jacket with the silvery fur collar.

At noontime, we were allowed to build a bonfire and roast the flat and great-looking potatoes, almost like our Idaho's. Everyone helped to gather the dried-up vines lying all over the field and those produced a terrific fire, burning fast and hot! I sat gazing at the dancing flames, sputtering and crackling and for a while, my mind went back to Poland again. Back to our clearing beyond the orchard and a group of our school friends gathered by the fire like this one, all of us waiting impatiently, poking at the roasting potatoes to test the tenderness, sometimes not lingering long enough to wait for them to be done, blowing off the hot ashes and sinking the teeth in and burning the lips and tongue on the hot mush. The best of the gourmet dishes could never compare to this simple and primitive delight of greasy fingers from the runny butter, melting along with dirty ashes, smudging our mouths to look like clowns, but always with an expression of carefree happiness. Only then, we didn't realize, how precious those moments were, taking for granted the peace and harmony of our own surroundings, not ever dreaming that it could be taken away from us. Not then, but now I could see the pastel pink sky before the sunset, the tall thistles growing along the weathered fence and a frail gossamer blowing gently in the wind.

Damn the memories! —And bless them in some way, to bring a joy and torment. You can't bury them. If only you could keep the images at a safe distance, dimmed enough not to hurt so much—yet to remember whom you were and who you are. As the saying goes, you can't go home again, but through the mirrored reflections of the years past, you could view them in a light, that you would wish to remember.

Listening to the soft crackling of the fire, we ate the crispy skin and soft potato flesh, though without runny butter or other additives, they made a great meal, and we did enjoy those simple moments, while there was a chance, as soon the changes would come again, some expected, some unknown, so we tried to think and live one day at a time.

It was a very pleasant day, at the beginning, scary at the end. We were ready to leave the field, gathering our work implements, when mother waved me to go on, saying she would catch up with us, and eventually she did, but I noticed her jacket was buttoned up, the string tied at the hips, dangling as she walked. She looked sort of chubby. Before the war, she was a trifle overweight and to my recollection, kept always complaining, being quite concerned about it, going through torturous and breathtaking wrestling with girdles on many occasions. Her downfall was the continuos baking, which never ceased, contributing to her weight gain and our great pleasure of eating. Baking sweets was like religion with her, occupying time and concentration on creating desserts of her own ideas. She loved it and so did we. The vision of the sweets had slid in front of my eyes, the big stack of "pontchkis," full of rose petal and cherry jams, the mouth-watering "chrusty" before Lent and the aromatic mocha filling in the layered walnut and almond cakes. Ah, I am forgetting the best of them all, the richest of them all, the creamy Napoleons, which she baked only on certain occasions. She passed up the "Josephines," claiming they were too sweet, (as if the others were not).

Since our arrival in Russia, mother's weight went down considerably, with her admitting it was the only plus in our present existence, so when I saw her walking off the field displaying a pre-war figure, I was puzzled for a moment, but shrugged it off, enjoying the warm breeze and the smell of the burnt potato vines in the dying fires. I followed the line forming at the exit to receive the daily ration and to my great surprise, found a fat slice of farmer's cheese beside the usual dark bread-a gratifying ending to a hard working day, at least it would have been.

While waiting on the side for mother to come through, I witnessed a scene, giving me a shiver at that time. While mother was putting her portions away, our "tovarish," the Polish overseer, took a swing at mother's shapely rear, yelling good naturely: "Marushka, you're getting to look more like a ballerina every

125

day!" He didn't quite finish, for the string holding mother's jacket, broke and a flurry of large, flat potatoes, fell to the ground. I froze. So did our companions, all of us watching in panic, with visions of "pierzynas" getting packed for a long trip, deep into the steppes, a punishment for stealing!

But it took mother only seconds to recoil and spring back(she was good at that). Turning around, she started to yell at the standing and slightly baffled, overseer: "Look what you have done! I work my butt off for you and your state, breaking my back. Now help me with those damn potatoes, that's the least you can do!" Then she took off her jacket, laid it down and started to throw the tubers into it. Good God, we couldn't believe our eyes, the overseer was down on his hands and knees, saying, "Nitchevo…nitchevo…" while helping her with the rest of the potatoes. I was holding my breath—here was an open act of stealing, a crime according to a Soviet constitution and mother was getting away with it! Something was amiss. The Red world was turning upside down or the war on the front was going very badly! Mother's face was flushed, possibly from a hidden fear and anxiety, but she held on tightly to her velvet jacket, folded like a sack, full of illegal produce. We walked away, heading for the village, at a faster pace than usual and all the while I kept sneaking glances, to see if we were being followed. There was no one in pursuit. Mother had gambled again and came out a winner.

The last warm October days were abruptly driven away by November, bringing rains and the penetrating winds. The sun stayed hidden behind the thick blankets of dark clouds and the earth beneath our feet felt like mush, giving us a feeling of a physical sinking, when walking. In this deep and muddy mess, the "valenkys" didn't stand a chance and with a diminishing quality of our footwear, we were hoping for an early snow, which would have been one of the lesser evils. But the rains came, day after day! On the outskirts of the village, the three crosses at the top of the mound, towering over the countryside, swayed in the strong wind from side to side, as if some irreversible power tried to harm whatever stood in its path.

The sounds of those whistling winds still ring in my ears on dark November nights-whining, sobbing and threatening as they did in Novaia Zyzn, filling the small valley with dreadful sounds, till the wind rolled out through the fields, toward the steppes and somewhere, got lost in a total freedom.

The shorter days became the idle days, restless for us, being accustomed to grueling hours of daily work. Occasionally we were called for some easy chores such as cleaning vegetables or grinding corn and other grains, nothing to sweat about, but it also meant less of rationed bread which even in grams was missed. We had to fend on our own and create meals out of produce we were gathering and storing for that reason.

The life in Novaia Zyzn made us feel more secure in that aspect of survival. The families shared and helped each other in need when it arose, being our own doctors and nurses, trying to substitute herbs and other weeds, even leeches for pills and drugs unavailable since the war.

During long evenings in November, young people would convene at homes having the most space for self-entertainment and what we would call enjoyment. Forgetting the war and the surroundings, momentarily creating hopes and dreams and banishing thoughts that this may be the dead end of our life's journey.

Even being so isolated, we also knew the world was in a great turmoil, with the latest events and the major developments of war being filtered to us only through gossip and occasional glances at the *Izviestia* or *Pravda*. Nonetheless, our morale was hovering on decent levels, with hopeful wishing for that opportune ending that may come some day. One day, we felt it would come perhaps soon. This awareness kept appearing and seemed to be supported by an eerie feeling, like the whispers from a mysterious extra sense. At times, I thought I was going off the beaten path in my mind, but never mentioned it, for it appeared as coincidental when I was near some disaster, though I could sense it before it happened. For a while I thought I was becoming clairvoyant (What a triumph it would have been over Irma's greasy cards), but it wasn't so. I didn't take the time to analyze this phenomenon, I only knew that I was directed to get out of danger's path, on many occasions.

It was as if I acquired an invisible antenna, keeping me alert and wary for unexplained reasons. I had never confided in anyone about it, assuming I would get strange looks, as if I was off balance. That itself wasn't anything unusual, either, under the circumstances it was tolerated and understood, but even under tremendous pressure, we tried to keep up the pretense and act as normally as possible.

To this day, I get this erratic feeling at certain times, at certain occasions or meeting certain people, then I tend to listen to the remote whispers against the normal judgement, leaving me with contradictions between the inner feelings of the heart and cool calculation of the mind. If only I would have shared my new findings with my friends, I would have been relieved to find a lot of company in similar encounters.

It must have been the continuos living on edge, the uncertainty of our duration, elevating our psychic anxiety to the point of guessing the handouts by Lady Fortune ahead of time. Strangely enough, it helped with day-to-day living.

The rainy season kept us inside and the only bright moments highlighting this term, were the evenings when the young people met at dwellings, for fun and games, many of them of folklore nature. Our lives in Poland and now in Russia, still were greatly influenced by myths and spirited customs, based on traditional and old country legends. Our calendars were filled with days intended to honor the memory of various saints and those we celebrated with religious rites and sometimes carried to colorful pageantry, observed by a whole nation.

Each of the name days signified events or markers of a change in seasons and giving helpful hints to various occupations. With gloomy and idle November days, we awaited snow eagerly as we did in Poland, being tired of mud and drenching rains.

The eleventh of November was a seasonal marker honored as St. Martin's Day, whose legendary appearance on a white horse, signified the beginning of winter in Poland, when at the same time in England, he represented a late summer, a counterpart to American Indian summer. (I imagine St. Martin was a double agent.)

We looked forward with excitement to the first falling snowflakes, on this saint's day. The very first snow back home, also brought an early ritual, which we didn't quite cherish as children. Our grandmother, a self-proclaimed health enthusiast, insisted that we fight fire with fire, but in this case, a cold snow, with cold feet—our feet. On the first snowfall, she would drag us out of the warm beds, at early dawn, make us dress, except for the bare feet and out of the door she led us into the wet and cold snow-covered back yard. I remember standing on the stoop of the door, my mind and mouth rebelling silently against this entire ordeal, but obediently making the first step, then breaking into a steady trot, following my brother, about ten times around the yard.

Our yard wasn't very small, either. In the middle of it, sat an ancient linden tree, beautifully shaped, like an umbrella, a delight in summer months when we sought protection from the season's heat. I can still smell the aroma of the tiny fuzzy flowers covering the surface of the tree, drawing to it the hordes of bees and wasps, filling the air with loud buzzing sounds, all day long. Those were such warm and sweet days of summer, with a lot of activity around the old linden tree. When the period of blooming had ended, Gran would gather the blossoms into a large sheet and leave them to dry for later use as a tea or some other obscure herbal medicine.

On this snowy week of November, though, while we shivered and counted the rounds during our health race, the majestic linden tree stood unmoved, stretching the dark and bare branches in its lethargic state of winter hibernation. I remember, by the fifth circle around the yard, I was ready to give up and cry out: "Please, no more!" but grandma stood by the door, with her arms folded over her flat chest, glaring like a proud little Napoleon-unimpressed. With the last round, my feet were so numb from the cold, I couldn't even argue that such stupid gymnastics may cause us to get sick, but it never happened and I didn't dare to tease her with: "I told you so."

And as the legendary rider traveled through the land, blessing the winter's cover, two of us kids, on our own trampled freezing flakes, then would run for the door and a warm kitchen where hot cocoa was waiting. I remember reaching for the handle of a dainty filigree holder, containing the tall glass filled with warm liquid and a fluffy cloud of a sweet meringue floating on top of it. My cold hands relished the warmth exuding from the glass and, sip after sip, bringing back a state of a well being.

Now, with grandmother gone and days not identified on the calendar, the first snow trampling was only a memory, perhaps remembered briefly when the worn-out "valenky" or the soleless rubber boots came in close contact with the icy snow.

However, by the end of November, an evening of St. Andrew would be well remembered here in Novaia Zyzn, by a young crowd and most likely, by me. In Poland, St. Andrew's evening was always celebrated with great parties, dancing and entertainment. As children, we were excluded from the adult social gatherings, but we observed the tradition in a different way. We had a rather simple but enjoyable chore, with grandma supervising again. In the orchard, we would break off a long sprig from a cherry tree, each to our own liking. At home we would put them in a tall glass jar, placing it on the ledge above the brick oven and there, among the colorful tins filled with exotic teas and spices, it sat in the warmth, spreading its spindly branches, with us inspecting it each morning, looking for a sign of greenery to appear before the sweet smelling blossoms. We knew it would be in full bloom by Christmas Day.

Here in Russia, those were but sweet memories, lovely and simple to which I silently said goodbye, sensing they would never come back again.

When told we were to celebrate St. Andrew's Eve at Gorecki's place, we all felt excited, as if our life was being steered onto a different course, a cheery one—for change.

Friends dropped in by early morning, bringing delicacies such as chunks of pumpkins, wheat flour in a lighter shade, millet whole and crushed—we were already loaded with potatoes, thanks to our mama—and a lot of cheese and kefir (yogurt). No sight of a caviar—damn. Preparations took on a feverish speed.

We made dozens of "pierogi" out of "well" ground flour, small cakes made out of millet, resembling "kolache" stuffed with pumpkin filling, a true feast, comparable to a banquet. What an excitement it brought to our dismal style of living. It was pulling us all out of apathy, out of hopeless and dull existence, elevating us into a level of temporary ease, and putting a spark of vitality into everyone, for this evening.

The dwelling was swept clean, and by sundown, the lamp (our booty, not so proudly claimed before, but with time the guilt vanished, and it was proudly displayed) was lit and among the smells and warm steam of food being prepared, we all waited for a crowd to step in.

When shadows had disappeared and the gray of the evening turned darker, the door almost stayed opened, till the last old and young joined the "party."

129

The inside was like a beehive. The laughter from the jokes bounced from wall to wall and the exchanging of gossip-type news, starting with... "We heard that..." would bring on an instant silence and attention from everyone.

The strongest of the rumors, repeating itself perpetually, was the release of the Polish prisoners—the men. There were a lot of hopeful sighs from the young women and old, dreaming of the freedom for their husbands, sons, brothers...

We couldn't entertain that, once being informed that our father was gone, but we were glad for the others. The joyful news, or if just rumors, was a part of the inspiration for this gathering tonight. No matter what development was taking place in the grim front, we felt as if slowly we were being rehabilitated and without being told to our face, we sensed our status also was changing—a grade up from the present.

With loud shouts and greetings, there didn't seem to be any boundaries between the young and old. Each person, overlooking his age, appeared to have an understanding of the needs and problems created by our welfare conditions, blending the feelings of mutual compassion and congeniality.

In a true spirit of St. Andrew's Eve, we began with the strange tales, a warm-up to games of a traditional folklore touch. I remember, sitting as if petrified, listening to the ghost stories with a genuine fear, but at the same time, they fascinated me as much as the Gypsy fortune telling.

At our home in Poland, it was a favored pastime for our maid, Dorka, to fill our heads with the spookiest and goriest stories before bedtime, sometimes herself believing they happened and at the same time, enjoying the fright reflecting on our faces, while she went on and on, weaving her village ghost fables.

Dorka was like a friend to our family, normally a very good-natured lady, but at times she would change her kind and stable disposition, playing tricks on us, causing a little chaos. For example, one time, on April Fool's Day, she prepared our school lunch, putting into our ham sandwiches thinly sliced chunks of creamy soap, cutting in the holes to resemble Swiss cheese, so we really had a reason to foam at the mouth! Her ghoulish tales, told in a half-Polish, half-Ukrainian dialect, always left us limp and sweaty with unwelcome side effects. I slept night after night with a light on and a cover over my head and even during the day I would not dare to climb the stairs to my favorite hideout, the attic, or walk through the orchard path, after dusk.

This evening though, in Novaia Zyzn, we sat listening with excitement, knowing the spinning tales were but the products of an over active imagination, flavored by history and legends handed down from the generations. It was great fun, at that time...

Absorbed in the pleasure of the evening, I heard my name being called: "It's your turn today, get those water buckets filled!"

Wow! I never tried to avoid my duty, but venturing out into the darkness, walking to the well with all the ghosts and demons fresh in my mind, wasn't exactly what I cherished at the moment. However, to show myself as chicken-hearted, would have been an embarrassment with jokes without end. So I grabbed the buckets and before I reached the door, someone yelled, "Watch your step, so something doesn't pull you down into the well!"

What a grand send-off! I shivered from cold and more from the fear, looking to both of my sides, as I walked. Outside it was pitch dark and the tall poplar trees were visibly swaying in the wind. The well wasn't too far but, at this minute, the distance to it seemed miles away. I hung the bucket on the hook attached to a chain, then began to lower it, turning the handle of a wheel. All of a sudden, there was a sharp cry piercing the silent darkness—a coyote, no doubt, or maybe early wolf—at this point I didn't bother to explore the cause. I left the handle spinning fast on its own, the bucket riding down on the unraveling chain, hitting finally the water level, a sound which I didn't even hear, for I ran without knowing there was ground under my feet. The fear almost lifted me in the air, until someone grabbed me. I screamed!

"Hey, it's only me—Mietek!"

I was so out of breath, my vocal cords were clamped shut. I couldn't utter a word. Mietek was holding on to my arm: "I thought, tonight wasn't a pleasant night to make a trip to the well alone," he said, then looked at my empty hands—"Let's get that water."

I was still shivering, but followed him, waiting while he brought the bucket up, then left it on the ledge of the well. "Drink some," he said, "you seem to be all shaken up."

And why shouldn't I be? The dark night, the animal cries, the wind and wild ghost stories, and now, Mietek so close to me...St. Andrew! Is that what you had in mind?

But St. Andrew was not here. It was Mietek pulling me closer to him. My heart beat so fast, it thumped so fiercely and loudly...all of my blood left the upper section of my body and had settled in my feet, like a ton of lead. Something was happening, in a biological sense that I wasn't aware of before. I recalled reading about these phenomena of love and passion in novels, had seen them in sizzling movies (ones we were not allowed to view, but did anyhow). Yet it was happening to me, every touch and move a surprise...the strange sensation I had never felt before. True, being of the ripe age of seventeen, so far I hadn't been kissed and never had I realized, that all this biological turmoil, preceded the contact of two lips!

But when it happened, it was so sweet, such a new and tingling feeling...once, then twice—then more and more. And with more kisses, it became sweeter. What a shake up it caused in my entire body!

I wasn't quite prepared for the reaction, being uninformed in that area of growing up, having my mind occupied with books mostly and attending an all-girls school, kept a distance from the young men, with merely an imagination of innocent romances.

The pounding of my blood, must have affected my memory also, for I completely forgot the surroundings and the windy night until Mietek abruptly let me go, saying, "We have to get back, they are waiting for us…"

For a chilly second I was startled at his rudeness, but sometime later in my life, I realized he was being a gentleman, even more so, in not using that cold bucket of water…

Was it a first love, attraction, a passing fancy, or just a simple case of a first kiss? Who knows!

Yet when walking back to our dwelling, I felt like a hawk, soaring, detached and a little disoriented. I thought my whole life had turned around, but for a short spell until we entered the warm and noisy place where the games were in progress. They were throwing the melted wax on the cold water, a ritual for predicting the future, a form of fortune telling from reading the shapes and the contours of silhouettes reflecting on the wall away from the light. Each of us, while maneuvering the hardened piece of wax to interpret the shadow, had tried to stretch the imagination to bold and hopeful guesses, showing more favorable signs in predicting the future, for we all were curious and concerned of what a third year in Russia may bring to us. A melted candle would emerge as a symbol, perhaps of a voyage out of Russia), flowers in a wedding bouquet, or maybe the most everyone hungered to see, was a silhouette of a man, an omen of freedom, out of prisons.

The excitement of the traditional amusement held wishful thinking and rising hopes that the imaginative games would follow through in the predictions. When I finally had my turn, I was astonished at the stubborn appearance of a dark silhouette of a ship, a very accurate foretelling of my much, much later life, because when roaming the world as a U.S. Army wife, I spent quite a few days crossing the seas. As the fun of this game had worn out, we played a shoe contest, involving only the young and unattached by placing the smelly dilapidated footwear in a line-up from the end of the wall, facing the door. With a first shoe over the threshold, the owner was pronounced "lucky," however, in Russia, it didn't quite hold true—the wedding bells, if any at all, seldom rang for the young couples, knowing there hardly could be any ambition in planning a future here.

Tonight, no one had a serious thought, tonight the "Andrzeiki," as we called St. Andrew's Eve was to celebrate with fun and enjoyment, forgetting the heartaches and hardships—and I am sure that everybody did, into the late night hours.

Finally, when the bash was over and everyone had left, I watched Mira linger outside of the house, apparently waiting for Mietek, but then I saw her walk away—alone.

Yes! Tonight I had claimed my prize, tonight I grew up a little! There was no stopping or bending the will of time against the normal changes of needs inside of you, to burst and thrive without explanation and follow the feelings of the moment. Tomorrow was still to come, with only a few hours before dawn. Mietek was with me, we sat together, whispering only sweet, meaningless words of tender nonsense, letting the mood change into unspoken words, and a quiet pleasure derived from the warm and long-lasting kisses.

Youth has no limits in place or time, no preconditions to impulses or consequences, it is simply to live for a moment and cherish it! But then those were the most unusual circumstances and one always gave a heed to warnings so as not to cross into a danger zone.

When later in years we all had parted and went our separate ways, perhaps we all forgot the tender moments, diminished with passing time, but today, I remember, sadly, because youth is gone, but happily the memories still linger on, as sweet as the kisses of the seventeen-year old, in a tight embrace, behind the "pietchka," on St. Andrew's Eve, in the village of Novaia Zyzn.

*****

Christmas came, uneventful, though we tried to make it more festive than any other day, but the extreme cold kept everyone inside. The fear of war was coming closer, becoming such a grim reality that we might feel it as far as here, in distant Kazakhstan.

The frightful thought of bombs and faded sounds of explosions kept a steady pace with our nagging anxiety. Again the memory came back, of dread and nightmares of running.

Suspended time had hung in the air, although we knew that the fate of us Poles as Russians would be predetermined if the Germans defeated the Red Army and would advance deeper into Soviet Central Asia. Even if the war action looked distressing on the European eastern front, there was still hope, and we prayed that in other places in the world, the situation might change in time, to halt the Nazi expansion.

For us at least, there seemed to be a current of a different air in subtly expanding freedom, our freedom in vocal expressions, in communicating with the Soviet people. Our status as that of a laborer and a prisoner, was changing and slightly improving in their treatment, sometimes making us feel almost equal, which of course didn't alter the fact that we were stuck here in this godforsaken desert, by their own damn doing.

But the visible omens were there, like wild spring flowers, still hidden under the cover of the last autumn leaves, sending a scent, without showing the color. A faint twist, not a complete turnabout, but getting us onto a road of belief that nothing was lost and much yet to gain.

There were rumors of a formation of a new Polish army, through the voluntary enlistment of our prisoners being let out of the "lagras"-to create needed help for the crumbling defense line in Russia's western front. The Soviet people tried desperately to stop the steadily moving German army from overtaking the vast territory of Russian land and cities. It seemed logical to recruit the people whose country was also under the Nazi siege, whose interests of regaining its property was as great as the Soviets defending their own.

The first harbingers of the liberation came from far away, north of Siberia, Kamchatka, at the tip of Sachalin. By Christmas, we saw the first members of the "lagra" communities. Slowly, more and more prisoners were let out. Bewildered men were going from place to place, searching for families and access to a new purpose of life and a reason to go on living in this strange and hostile land.

Those we saw were young, old and middle age, with sunken faces, eyes still clouded with the pain of cruel treatment and longing for lost families or grieving their unknown fate. Some of them came to Novaia Zyzn. They brought with them horror stories of survival, incredible tales of ill treatment, diseases and death taking a toll on many of their comrades. We all listened with shock, not wanting to believe, with a dreadful feeling of wondering how our father would have suffered if he were condemned to that kind of life.

Each of the ex-prisoners was treated royally while staying in the village, each of them determined with hope and a belief, that there would be a way out of Russia, not an easy one, but there was a chance to see the civilized world again.

Their presence, like a magnet, drew everyone into the small dwellings to listen to the stories, arguments and the political discussions, their guesses and deliberations about the future and fate of all Polish people scattered throughout the Soviet Union. The "lagra" visitors' stay was usually short, a few days, getting well fed with deserved rest but impatient to be off, to continue a long journey, taking them to a terminal goal, somewhere in the very distant east and south of Russia, a centralized arena for a newly forming Polish army. At this time we weren't exactly sure of the region or its' name.

The Nazi threat was as great as ever, but for us as a part of a nation, we had felt uplifted spiritually and although we were wronged without a cause, we were proud that our number counted in this chaotic world of politics.

We stood as survivors, with patience and endurance, waiting for the right time, reinforcing the fact put into the words of our national anthem: "Poland is not lost, as long as Poles are alive!" (Jeszcze Polska nie zginela, puki my zyjemy.)

The winter days seemed to rush by, keeping us tense and aware through continuously changing hearsay of slowly developing critical decisions concerning our people in the Soviet Union.

When the January snows came, the communication with the outer world ceased for a while. Being cut off suddenly from desired news and watching the victuals diminishing from our pantries, we decided it was time to venture out, to seek the world reports and whatever food we could find and trade.

Gzaroon would be our place to visit. The old bazaar was active through the seasons and there we were hoping to do some trading with our accumulated grain, that we had earned through the sweaty summers.

A group of us started out on a nice winter day. The pleasant road we have traveled on during the summer was now covered with a heavy snow and visible tracks where large sleds went through. We followed the trail but still our feet sank in the white powdery fluff, slowing down our walking. The sun came out and shone, creating a sparkling field of a million diamonds. We had to rest at times, giving arms a break from aching muscles from the weight of grain sacks. The most important were our feet, being wrapped in newspapers inside the heavy "valenkys'" felts.

We made it safely to Gzaroon, did some good trading at the bazaar, then headed back to the snowy trail with a feeling of buoyancy, knowing the heavy sacks of grain were replaced by golden chunks of butter, cheese and even some hunks of beef. Our imagination already was steering and tickling the taste buds and palate. Obtaining the luxurious foods spun the vision of forgotten menus, which, in a normal life, were nothing but simple, yet here in Russia was a delicacy.

Halfway through, on the way back, we lost the company of the sun. The gray skies now blended with the snow-covered fields. After a few kilometers, we felt flakes brushing our cheeks, and soon we were walking in a blizzard. We came face to face with a true winter storm, a dreaded "burian." It was so quiet a white, pristine calmness all around us. So beautiful in its whiteness but scary. Somewhere, close to the village, we noticed through the curtain of swirling snow, the shadow-like shapes following us at a certain distance. Our group moved closer together, as we knew the shadows were the steppe wolves, looking for prey.

We walked faster; I broke out in a sweat. The village was close, yet this last kilometer seemed an eternity. Once, the wolves came close enough for us to see their features, but then with a blur of snow, they disappeared, till we spotted them again, behind us. There they stayed until the first dwelling appeared on the horizon, then we felt safe again. We were lucky this time, as there were many incidents, where only bodily remains were found after the spring thaw. The village looked so good, even the stacks of "kiziak" piled in front of a barn with accumulated sheep crap again, I greeted with a warm feeling. All the familiar sights were welcomed—after the wolves and the snow.

*****

WOLVES

Spring came again to Novaia Zyzn. We didn't take time to walk into the fields of colorful blooming tulips. The good earth was awakening with an urge of bearing, producing and giving a general call for work around the clock—and for us to answer, anywhere, anytime.

The grinding circle had begun and life went on as before with small interruptions of news from the front, waiting for travelers from the north to visit briefly, just long enough to share fresh information and strengthen the hope that changes might be coming our way.

There were so many unanswered questions. Right now, we were but guessing the odds, basing them on political events and the progress of war. It was impatience and speculation creating the unrest and wonder: Will the true help ever come? We began to hear repeatedly the names—Churchill...Roosevelt, others in the military—Sikorski, Anders, Montgomery? (Who the hell was Montgomery?).

There were connections we tried to make, but even our wild imagination could not place us at the right guess.

Unknown to us, there were secret agreements made by powerful leaders, transactions and bartering behind our backs, hush-hush pacts, a selling out of a soul to the devil! Except it was part of our country! Already we had paid such a high price, with blood, hunger and diseases, yet it wasn't enough!

The tragedy of war demanded sacrifices in unlimited amounts piling up in heaps, as on an ancient pagan pyre, but the future would reveal it was a betrayal! In haste, without compromises, the great blunders were committed, in a blind disregard to consequences for the Polish people...

The hectares of idle fields lay waiting for seed to be planted. A hundred other chores cried out for steady and strong hands to start the wheels of never-ending hours of hard labor. We fitted into every slot and sometimes more than one. Working in night-day cycles, kept us still alert for the news, making the work easier, for the occasional visit from the travelling ex-prisoners, would bring cheer and a small envy, knowing they were making their way south, leaving behind a touch of yearning from us, to follow them all the way to the Russian borders where freedom could be waiting, across the Caspian sea.

Time had dragged on. The variety of work was far from being monotonous or easy, intensifying in speed and long hours, putting pressure for an output of grinding the stored grain and other supplies of food in any form, to feed the fighting men at the front.

We did our best, simply because we ourselves had to eat. The efforts had been doubled knowing the Soviet "bread basket," the state of Ukraine, was already overrun by the advancing German Army.

The early spring was a time to scrounge and utilize the "horn of not so plenty" or equal to it, leftovers from the past year. There were still "prickly" oats and mushrooms to dig out, some sprouting greens in the steppes. I remember the crumbly kernels of millet, which became our main staple almost every day, in various consistency and taste—thin soup, thick soup, boiled into a sticky mush, flavored sometimes with a few spoons of elusive milk or burned onion. Other times, it was sweetened with crushed pumpkin or, on rare occasions, sprinkled with saccharine we kept for "rainy" days from the first year when the care packages were still coming regularly, before the war, in June. Whatever we consumed in any combination and taste, it was welcomed, without any complaints.

In the middle of May, the long hours had everyone exhausted. One of those sunny and warm days, I was on my way back from the outlying fields (weeding the morning glories again,) when at the edge of the village, I met my brother, alone. His protégés, the sheep and the fierce ram, were already safely locked in the barn. We walked slowly, talking now and then. When we approached our dwelling, we noticed some or our older friends standing outside, engaged in a loud discussion and upon seeing us, stopped the chatting. A strange feeling came over me—had something happened to our mother? I looked at Jez, then we both ran past the group, all of them looking at us, without saying a word.

The door was wide open. Inside, we noticed the figure of a strange man, sitting on a large sack of millet. Although the weather was balmy, he had on a heavy black sheepskin coat. For a second, the sight stabbed painfully at my memory. His back was turned to us and we couldn't see his face, but on the other side of the darkened room mother was standing, crying quietly.

We stood on the stoop of the door, sensing a silent, unexplained aftermath in the tense, charged air. In another moment, the man turned around, his face now in full view. It was familiar! Good God! It was our father! Underneath the sallow skin, the bones were protruding, the eyes looked sunken, full of pain but with a sparkle upon seeing us, then breaking into a grin, showing only a few teeth left in his distorted mouth.

It wasn't the same person we saw last, in October 1939. He didn't get up right away. We approached him slowly; it seemed my breathing had stopped and a fist-size ball was obstructing my throat and wouldn't go up or down.

Then, all of a sudden, there was free air, bursting with emotion. Jez and I both began to hug him with the overjoyed cries: "Tatush, tatush"—we carried on, sobbing through the tears, then laughing, shouting broken words without correlation or order, till the frenzy had eased. Father's choked-up voice soon became steady, yet somewhat hesitant, trying to explain the last two years of hell and degradation, of his life in a "lagra," the death camps and torture for political convicts and the innocent as well. Father lived through this nightmare and survived with a slim hope that he might see us all, one day again.

Each of us perhaps, unknowingly, possesses the strength, when faced with paramount agony and suffering, somewhere, deep within us lies a hidden will and force befitting Hercules in order to fight our own demons and failures. It may be that concealed grit was the guide and encouragement for our father's tough determination and survival. Whenever, throughout our life in Russia, the blackest of an hour emerged and the anguish raged to no end, at the final turn, we held on to that thin thread of hope, with a will to live and get through it, no matter what the odds were.

The weakness of submission didn't have a place in the time of waiting for changes. Father's goal, once set in his mind, was a guide, that brought him back to us. Granted, we all have lived through some parts of private hell, yet we could not compare them to his ordeals as he tried to recall his days and months of labor in the coal mines in the Ural Mountains, around the Svedrvolsk area.

However, while relating stories from both sides, his and ours, father respectfully conceded to mother's courageous spirit, claiming the burden of the responsibility for taking care of us and our grandmother, outweighed the horrors of the time he spent in the "lagra" camp. His life was a torment, but as he maintained—he was alone.

Now, the family, except for our "babusia," was together again; we stayed with Gorecki family, but not for long. Father decided to strike out on his own and headed for the great city of Gzaroon. After a brief rest and recuperation, he thought he might get a job more suitable to his skills, working with the machinery.

His hunch paid off; he found work at the grain mill, as a machinist. We had stayed behind, sweating for hours again on the hot fields, earning bread, grain and other life-supporting fares, among them the crumbly and indispensable, millet.

Labor, without a change in its character, became a bit lighter, with the knowledge that this was not an end of the world, after all. Somewhere, there will be a way out of this dilemma and the tide of events will have to improve now that we had a father figure in charge of the family!

The Soviets were releasing the pressure on our people and the relationships. The stigma that adhered to us in the previous years had diminished since the beginning of the war. We were looked upon as civilized individuals and began to be treated as such; according to their thinking, giving us a chance to blend into their Soviet workforce and culture; bringing us very close to the level of their lifestyle, without an attempt at converting us into bloody-red communists. Knowing damn well, there was no earthly enticement that would propel us to embrace their ideology—having lived with it, so closely in the last two years.

Slowly, the anger and disciplinary threats were being eliminated, leaving only the habitual cursing! (Lord, how they could swear!) We were so accustomed to it, which was a way of life in Russia and sort of a prop to a daily existence, depending on in what tone of voice they emerged. It was a minor offense, we didn't mind being cursed at and most of the time, we swore back.

I loved their lengthy airing into the ancestral past, bringing out the threatening curses all the way from great-great grandfathers and uncles, each quarreling party trying to outswear the other with superlatives of ill wishing. Sometimes you could stand for hours, listening to menacing but flowery saber-rattlings, seldom ending in violence, depending on who got tired first.

With days rapidly passing by, we began paying attention to the news of the Far East, the war with Japan. That part of the globe was nearly a blackout to us from the very beginning. We knew, vaguely, there was an attack on the U.S. at Pearl Harbor on December 7, 1941. Then, from time to time, we saw only brief articles, mentioning the various battles on the Pacific Islands and the seas. Frankly, we were too preoccupied with our own lives and predicaments to pay close attention to the conflict so far away from us.

Our father's return was a great uplift and a step up to a more hopeful future, improving our frame of mind, reminding us of the constant changes, making us almost believe in miracles. We took long trips to visit him in Gzaroon, mostly shuffling back and forth on foot, other times riding in donkey carts, with me avoiding the oxen like a plague.

During one of the hottest months in the summer, father paid us a visit, arriving in our old friend, Lena's hired wagon, drawn by the same pair of obnoxious oxen we have traveled with, the first time to Novaia Zyzn, a year ago. Father stepped off the wagon, himself looking more like a "bourgeois" squire than a plebian gristmill machinist does. He sure had done well on his own! His teeth were still missing, but his face looked so much fuller, and he was all smiles as he came to us with a tempting offer to move us to Gzaroon, as soon as possible to a huge place, owned by the mill, with fuel provided for all seasons ("kiziak," no less) and maybe occasional ration of soap and sugar, even a liter of vodka, purchased under the counter. A true promise of an easier life, nothing like the past two years. Father didn't have to beg us; we would have been ready at the moment's notice! But we knew there could be some difficulty from the village in releasing us from work at the peak of the summer, with the harvest just around the corner. It seemed quite improbable, considering it was wartime and each pair of hands was vital in working the precious grain, a food supply for the fighting men.

So we were greatly surprised when told we could leave Novaia Zyzn in the last month of summer, making everything quite easy in planning. We said good-bye to the Gorecki clan, extending our warmest thanks for their hospitality and as for me, I even faced Mietek with a friendly handshake, wondering how fast my great love had evaporated, probably vanishing with the sweat on the hot steppes. Then we didn't waste any time asking questions, hastily we gathered our hard-earned grain, the faithful green bed, a couple of heavy "pierzynas" with lumped-up feathers clinging to one side, the bundles of threadbare clothing, all our wealth and possessions-the symbols of crude, material poverty, but ourselves rich in spirit, earnest, prepared again for the change, we hoped, for the better.

Life back again in Gzaroon would become a leisure time for me, at least. On the day we moved, my old friend Baska appeared as if out of nowhere, with a happy grin, hugging everybody more than once, while helping with the unloading of our belongings, this taking but a few minutes. Her eyes were misty and being quiet by nature, she surprised us by nonstop chatter of the stories from the past year, asking questions in between without waiting for the answers. I was amazed at her changed personality, but it was so wonderful to see her again and to be back in Gzaroon, at least for the present time.

The day, being unusual for us in settling in to a new place, was a beginning of a new phase, an important event, having the hard work on the steppes behind us, feeling somehow comfortable and safe.

Baska and I didn't wait, we left the small chores to cope with to the rest of the family. We called ourselves family so proudly now, having our father back, as a protector and a bread winner, making me at the same time feel rather carefree and unconcerned about tomorrow or the next day.

The heavy block of responsibility was slipping down, away from my conscience, leaving me being aware of only myself, aware of my age and my needs, bringing on the very selfish traits, creating a sort of a rebellious stand-off to the elements of time and place.

So when Baska said, "Let's go somewhere!" I didn't ask where. We just closed the door, slamming it noisily, then headed for the only exciting place, the popular and old bazaar. The town hadn't changed in its appearance—it was the same quiet place we had left a year ago. Sprawled over the sand, barred to the east on one side by a slight rising hill, which later was discovered as a source of copper.

Walking through the bazaar, I noticed a lot of people, unusual for this late time of day, almost comprising crowds. Strangely enough, many of the faces belonged to youngish men, who, by rights, should have been in uniform and on the front.

Being away from the town for a while, I thought of the many things that must have had occurred, but I was curious: "Baska, who are all those people?" I asked. She smiled then explained. These new faces, which we would see often now, were displaced Soviet citizens of German descent, now being deported in large numbers from the Ukraine and other regions of Russia. Evidently the Red Government didn't trust their own people near the front or in the army, mainly because it was their misfortune to be of German ancestry at the wrong time, it being a war with the Nazis. Their fate being similar to ours invoked a touch of sympathy; otherwise, we didn't get too concerned about them, it was wartime anyhow and everybody seemed to suffer some repercussions.

We strolled among the crowds, but I noticed Basia looking around anxiously, almost if she was expecting someone. And she was.

From a short distance, two men walked slowly toward where we stood, and she ran eagerly to meet them. To one of them she held out both hands: "Wie geht's, Alex?"—she greeted him in German. Standing aside, I watched with slight amusement her delight in seeing this person she called Alex. No wonder! He was a looker, a typical heartthrob and from the expressions of my friend, I gathered Baska was in love. Times had changed and while I drove the oxen and worked the fields, Baska was upgrading her social life, even dating.

I guess, each added year brought in many of us new discoveries in feelings, an awareness of growing up. As I looked at them, I also noticed Alex's companion, standing to the side, looking at me. I got flustered. Since my first emotional kiss and smooching with Mietek on St. Andrew's Eve, I would feel quite uneasy whenever a man stared or even glanced at me. Sometimes it gave me that funny and queasy sensation in the form of premature hot flashes and shortness of breath, harmless though it seemed. I suspected that, in this abnormal mode of living, there must have been a subtle transition of leaving early adolescence into the still uncertain area of young adulthood.

In Poland, I would have been in my last year of Lyceum, deciding for my future studies and the final direction in a choice of professions, and at the same time enjoying the loveliest cycle in life, going to dances…dating. I brushed off the spider webs of what could have been. When I looked up, Basia was introducing her company. Alexei's friend was German also; his name was Peter or Pietia, as he was called.

I thought him to be about twenty-six or -eight years old, of medium height and of slight build. At just a glance, I decided I liked him. He mentioned he was married; his wife had stayed behind in the area where they lived before he was deported. I liked the honesty and the straight talk, no secrets or presumptions. His main interest was music; he was a pianist and now a teacher.

Our conversation was light and pleasant, as I managed well now the Russian language, except his eyes never left my face, making me feel rather uncomfortable. I can still clearly remember his deep-set gray-green eyes and a shock of the wavy hair falling in a light clump over his forehead. He spoke softly, with a slight hesitation and a most charming smile. I was completely disarmed by his look and personality, and it took great pains on my part to conceal it, for in the back of my mind the warnings were flashing, allied with mother's stern advice and threats of emotional involvement and its consequences, while still being in Russia.

Having both parents now hammering at me the meaning of the virtues, I had felt a continuos stress laced with hints for a clean behavior, mainly now that there was hope for leaving the USSR and a chance of finding a new life beyond the

Russian borders. A very sober idea, a valid guide in attaining this long-awaited goal, easy with patience and determination.

Yet, in between, there were the blind spots, sometimes blocking the way. It was my age, being eighteen. The most beautiful years of my life were drifting away, slipping rapidly, taking with them the gossamer thread of unfulfilled hopes and dreams—and time, like a guard and enemy, would not stand still to give us a chance to extend the year of being eighteen, at the right place!

But time moved on and since the war nothing seemed to be right, nothing appeared to matter except survival and a hope for change. To me though, time and things mattered; I was young, I was healthy. Nature, being quite oblivious to the world's upheavals, didn't bother to suppress a development of senses or the body's physique, keeping the pulses pounding strong and vibrating life with energy and spirit, enough to let the whole universe know, we were alive!

Very much alive! But at this time, our whole world, seemed to be quite limited, whereas in those small contours of existence, the rigid mind had maintained its annoying rule to intervene in physical craving, with stupid notions to wait, to postpone, while your entire being was aching with longing for a tender touch and affection.

In that frame of mind, I met this person-the pianist, Pietia. What a change from the yells of "sob" and "sobea" and the rattles of the "wabohreika" to an unexpected evening of soft-spoken words and sentimental moments. I spent a delightful end of a day in his charming company and most of all, quickly forgot the hot fields and buckets of sweat, the countless hours and ballooning blisters. I wondered how long our good luck would hold.

Perhaps the tide was changing, for the better. We stayed in Gzaroon. Father's job was surely a blessing, supplying the money and food, and plenty of it. For the first time since our arrival in Russia, the earned rubles and "tchrvientze" gained a slight prestige and respect, for in the course of time, they would buy us the tickets for the intended, long journey into the deep south of the USSR.

Our visions of the change were still a little hazy, but slowly we had begun to discuss the eventuality and the first steps in planning to reach the region bordering the Soviet Union and the old Persia (or the new name of Iran). The new and strange names of those faraway places and the steady progress of the growing new Polish army, became constant subjects of discussion and heated debates.

Should one jeopardize a firm roof over the head and sure slices of bread in exchange for the unknown number of days, bivouacking under the burning skies of Uzbekistan, picking cotton in fields, existing on fruits and raw vegetables only, contracting malaria, bloody dysentery or other tropical diseases, possibly risking life, as many already had done?

But here, our freedom was at stake—and the price was high! Our people were distraught, confused, on the crossroads of decisions and judgment to be made by each individual alone…whether to cross that Rubicon.

For us, the time hadn't come yet. We still had to review our next steps and plan carefully, while enjoying the present living, which according to the Soviet standards, was a good life.

Mother was in seventh heaven, having the abundance of flour through father's work and my brother's crafty trips to the mill with large containers packed with noon meals(mostly large vessels filled with water), and coming back with all shades and brands of flour, giving mother a joy in concocting some strange dishes, each of them passed off on us as a surprise, which many of them really were, considering the Soviet stores, with mostly bare shelves, could hardly offer any necessary ingredients for cooking, not to mention baking.

Yet some of her efforts turned out to be quite tasty and were put away swiftly, sometimes even with compliments. Pierogi stuffed with mashed potatoes and cheese, a one-time delicacy, now became as common as the thin millet soup, once keeping us alive in Novaia Zyzn.

She made a great variety of fillings, playing games with us, making us guess what was inside…sometimes we hesitated, wondering, but no matter what she came up with, we were always stuffed to the gills, without waiting for holidays. Rubles bought eggs, cheese and other luxury items, making us feel like gourmets, dining every day and as long as we had pierogi generously doused with butter, what else could we want?

There even surfaced a question of a weight watching, something unheard of among our people here in Russia, but it just proved the point how life can change so drastically even under seemingly hopeless conditions.

All through the passing days, we felt our life as being on amends, not normal by any means, but happier, so much happier. The little town of Gzaroon became more active than usual, being connected with the rest of the world by railway. The usually quiet, small Victorian yellow station, was now surrounded by crowds, civilian and military.

I remember the cool October evenings, the four of us taking walks toward the station, Basia, Alex, Pietia and I, with arms linked together sometimes without talking at all, simply enjoying a silent contentment of being alive and young. In those pleasant moments I discovered and have learned about the Russian spirit, their heart and soul we once thought were never there. When we came close and reached beyond the protective shell of their psyche, we detected a different personality, somehow quite open, flamboyant and very honest.

One of those quiet evenings, Basia and I sat on an old bench beyond the station, reminiscing about the past two years—the anguish, hopelessness and despair during the hunger days and typhoid epidemic, the fear of waking up each morning, not knowing what evening would bring and grandma's death. The war, at present, sad to say, made it possible for us to temporarily look on the brighter side. We were not mistreated anymore and so far, not touched by the violent fighting. Miles away, to the west of us, in Russia and in the greater part of Europe, thousands were dying of war-related destruction and holocaust. We being so isolated, felt compassion and concern, but were living through a hell of our own, so our feelings were spent and drained of pity or extra sympathy for others who were caught in this horrid global conflict.

But as in the more civilized part of Europe, so here in the Asiatic steppes the time went on, filled with an anxiety and hope for some supernatural miracles to intervene and change its course. But the miracles didn't happen. The serenity of the beautiful evening put a stop to our bitter recollections, it seemed so futile to drag out the past, but in a way it left us frightened, wondering if menacing events could repeat themselves again.

I saw someone's hands covering Basia's eyes, and without turning around, I knew we had company. Basia was ecstatic I am sure and my heart skipped a few beats, hearing Pietia's voice. (Bad sign, I told myself.) The end of the day was tapering off to a perfect evening. While miles away, the war went on, its hateful sounds now deadened by the great distance and echoes that couldn't interfere with peaceful sundown or hush out the soft chords of the balalaika, coming from the other end of the village.

My favorite pianist was quiet. The wistful melody of the balalaika filled the void of unspoken words, a moment of solitude and silent bond. We sat close together, watching the warm October sun sinking slowly beyond the steppe lines, each of us engrossed in our own thoughts. The sun was setting fast and I couldn't hear the balalaika sound anymore, but from nearby speakers attached to the telephone poles, the music started to blare, sending a medley of military marches. The sentimental spell was broken, the loud volume suddenly broke off and a soft woman's voice began to croon a song about "a demure blue scarf," the melody haunting me to this day, in trying to remember the missing words in Russian of love and longing, bringing back with amazement a recognition of feelings, I never thought, at the time, were there.

When the song had ended, it was still very quiet. Without saying anything, Basia patted my hand and walked away with Alex. The horizon to the west glowed with a vermilion streak, like a bloody twisted ribbon, a reminder of the time and fading shadows. The golden sky became dark. I turned to Pietia and in that moment, was startled by the look in his eyes, holding an unspoken emotion of tenderness and sadness. I felt his arm gently drawing me close to him...I stiffened for a second, my expectations soaring, only to feel his lips, brushing my cheeks lightly. We sat in silence for a long time, his arm holding me tight. We never kissed then, nor did we later. I could have loved him, perhaps I did. But then, I didn't know it. After that evening, I didn't see him, until spring.

*****

With cold days crowding long November, we became involved in welcoming the volunteers heading south to join our own Polish army. Our humble but large place became a stopover for anyone who needed food and bed, a few encouraging words for good luck and a promise, "We'll see you soon, in Uzbekistan!" Groups of our young people spent free time in a building donated by the local officials (we had come a long way), as a sort of meeting and information center. This was our first public place for gatherings and sharing the latest news through word of mouth and radios. The room itself was spacious, lacking furniture at first, then later acquiring some rickety chairs and a large table. On the spur of the moment, one could even do a wild polka, but dancing was out of the question, still being too daring.

We spent many hours meeting with strangers, both young and old, who came from the faraway north, in cold Siberia, bringing stories of their own woes and accounts of living in a "Taiga" belt.

In one of the newcomers we had found a cousin, whose husband was a forest ranger in Bialovierza and whose short life ended in the Katyn Forest. As a professional nurse, she knew her destination already, spending a few nostalgic days with us, then headed south to join the army.

Others came from the far limits of our area, "kolchozes" deep into the steppes and farther yet, from the "sowchozes." People walked long miles for days, lured by the spirit of freedom, hoping to find a pulse on life, a purpose and motivation to go on to determine their unknown future. For the three years wasted in forced labor and oppression, this became a year of steady search and rebirth of the identities for our young and old, even those who stopped believing and completely lost confidence and faith in God and themselves. All of us, rebounding to a freer life, shared the mutual vision of the primary dream—to get out of the Soviet Union.

Our usually outdated information was relayed by word of mouth or mail, which was slow. We were thriving mostly on more believable news brought by recruiters, coming back from the south to encourage the young and old to journey where the action was intensifying, a preparation for a great exodus of the newly formed Polish army toward the Caspian sea and, from there, across to Iran.

In this stretch of time, each day was a diversion from the other, for we lived in a feverish state of anticipation, knowing there were plans and a quest already put into motion, to help our people. We had to keep contact and be constantly alert for any special news or even gossip and rumors, while our meeting room became a beehive of activities.

In a matter of weeks, we had an unexpected excitement. A priest wandered in, pausing in our small town for couple of days, on his way south. The news traveled fast! A representative of God we hadn't seen for almost three years. His arrival brought a strange mixture of feelings, that of gladness and common respect but less of the idolizing fear and homage we were taught to maintain for the clergy as children in school. Now, a revered man whom we always saw in a black habit and high collar became more human in dress, in sharing the pain and misery of the last years that we did. Generally, there was cheer and comfort, knowing that, once again, we would be able to attend Mass and go to confession. While living in Russia, the most atheistic country, where religion was condemned, we now were given the liberty to worship, according to our beliefs, allowing us to observe the rites that were formerly mocked so harshly by the Red government.

The war, once again, seemed to be our ally in releasing the reins on tolerance toward our traditions, bringing us closer to the old lifestyle we once knew.

But as in the past, in Poland, so here again facing my church and its teachings, my old fears were resurfacing. I was deathly afraid of confessions. I could still recall while in elementary school the Saturday evenings, standing by the monster confessional cage of heavy, dark, oak, biting my nails, meditating with gloom, trying strenuously to collect all of my sins from the past month, worrying so as not to conceal any and to save my soul from going to hell.

The pattern of our childhood teachings was emerging with a force again, picking up the vanishing continuity of the past beliefs, to close that last gap, the almost forgotten—religion.

It was Saturday, late in the afternoon, a cold day in Kazakhstan. Our center was crowded with people of all ages and gender, predominately women. A far dark corner was reserved for hearing the confessions. A simple chair, two blankets, thin as a sieve, hanging from the ceiling, weren't very impressive, but the appearance didn't matter. The conception itself of this mission, the cleansing of the soul, almost equaled a psychiatric treatment, to ease the conscience and whatever guilt it dragged behind it. Very noble and effective, I thought, but on my part, bad news and I was hating it!

In front of me, I watched the long line of "sinners," women mostly, a few gray-haired men. My mind was completely empty, with my thoughts somewhere on retreat. I couldn't concentrate very well on either the Ten Commandments or other minor sins, but having plenty of time, waiting my turn, I began to review the last three years since my last confession in Poland.

Suddenly, I felt an oncoming sense of rebellion. Why all this self-abasement and indignity making me feel so guilty? Hadn't we gone through enough? The score of notions kicked up defiance and questions never asked before. At this point I wondered, who had the right to judge our morality? If there was a power directing our lives, why did we have to fight so hard on our own to survive and shape our own destiny? I seemed to have trouble connecting or separating God's will from the affliction of time and the world's unrest. But then my built-up resistance seemed but an excuse and fear thriving way back from the third grade, with a first introduction to this ritual of contrition. I thought of backing away from the long line of people kneeling and meditating in deep silence, but somewhere, back in my mind, I knew I needed support and the strength to go on. I needed a certain control for future blunders, and this forgotten Catholic rite, a humiliating, voiced admission of wrong deeds, was like a leash to keep me and others from running wild.

I was next in line. In front of me, by the thin blanket, a middle-aged, attractive woman was weeping, while whispering her "errors." I had to step back, feeling slightly embarrassed, for her whispers became quite loud and I could clearly hear every word she was saying. She was married, her husband still in the north of Russia; she loved him, yes, yet she made love to someone else close to her here, and not only once. I backed farther away, her voice trailing off. What was love? A temptation? What was a sin?

I was confused, trying to understand the mental and physical evolution taking place in biological functions and changes in the human body. In my serious growing up, it was all up to me to solve the riddles by guessing and avoiding serious repercussions. At those times I missed my grandmother greatly with her wise and helpful advice, which at times, I would laugh at, but now many times ached for, remembering, with mother, there never was a proper time or place.

The silence brought my attention back to the weeping woman with so much guilt. I saw the priest's hand rising with the Latin words of absolution, then a sign of the cross, evidently, the end of her ordeal.

I knelt down, close to the thin blanket, blessed myself: "My last confession was in August-1939." I was never interrupted, but at the end, there was the usual sermon, about the violent changes in the world, the complicated times, being young and to use my head wisely. I expected and understood most of it, except at the end when he came to a cheery part on the subject of stealing, he himself admitting it was unavoidable in order to survive, and it made me giggle at the idea of God's servant, lifting.

Upon hearing "In nomine patrae..." I knew I was forgiven for all my transgressions, my conscience was clean and the words of "in the name of the Father..." gave a comfort and a feeling of being close to God again.

******

During the winter, the influx of once-imprisoned men of all ages, grew in numbers. Most of the transients stayed as guests with local families and were treated as such, according to our Polish motto: "Guest in the house—God in the house"(Gosc w dom—Bug w dom), and at those times we were blessed in abundance.

149

Our young men, surging into freedom from jails and "lagra" camps, were the ones showing the hunger and thirst for life, for happiness and general hell-raising, which was denied to them during the three years of imprisonment. Sometimes there was a humiliating shame for the visible scars of bodily injuries, deficiencies in physical vitality, but now it was secondary, it was behind them. The vivid memories and recollections, no doubt, hurt and stung, but now there was pride in a strength of survival, in enduring abusive treatment and persecution, tales of which were not spoken with ease. The not- so-distant past had to be buried, so as not to interfere with present life, with its hope for the future.

The winter came, our last in Russia. We experienced a most wonderful family togetherness and genuine contentment in many aspects of this simple living. The sub-zero weather and a lack of adequate footwear kept us inside most of the time. I still owned a pair of once-elegant, brown rubber boots from my high-school era, but they were completely lacking the soles as aluminum tape hadn't crossed any inventor's mind yet (what we could have done with that product).

I wore my boots only for short walks, long enough to survive the thick stuffing from the *Izviestia* newspaper, otherwise the worn-out "valenky" served well in the crisp and dry snow, perhaps the last snow we would see for a long time.

Life became easy. None of us except our father had to work. Food was always plentiful, by that I mean we were not hungry at any time, any more. "Kiziak," the very important source of fuel, was stacked the height of the house next to a huge pile of mysteriously imported coal for long-burning fires in the "pietchka." But for the circumstances and the place, we were quite happy.

In a short time we made friends with a family across the hall in the building where we lived, owned by the mill. The space described as a hall, could barely accommodate four people standing close, but it served as a divider between our two families. The other family had four members as did ours-a man named Leo, his wife Esther and two cute little boys with red hair. They were Jewish. Leo worked in the mill with our father, also being a supervisor, and he was an American citizen, with a passport to prove it. In the U.S., where he came from he was quite wealthy, owning a grain mill somewhere in upstate New York. He met his wife, Esther, on one of his visits to Poland, before the war. While arranging to take her back with him to America, hostilities broke out with Germany and the war caught them in the eastern part of Poland, with their fate becoming similar to ours, turning into an unintended destination—Kazakhstan.

Leo was a very likable person and our two families, in no time at all, became the best of friends. His numerous attempts to get out of Russia, proved unsuccessful. The Soviet government was deaf to his pleas, ignoring the fact he was an American citizen, not recognizing his passport, a proof of his country of origin.

We felt sorry for them, but thought that Kazakhstan was a better choice for their survival than western Poland, now under the Nazis. Esther was young, a beautiful redhead and the most gentleperson I had ever met—intelligent, cheerful and smart in many ways. I often turned to her as I would to an older sister and a true friend, for answers that I would never confront my mother about. Through many hours, I told her my "deep, dark secrets," the anxieties and strange discoveries of growing up.

Sometimes we sat on the floor of the two-by-two hall, whispering and giggling, while Leo would light up a stinky Russian cigarette, saying, "Girl talk." Esther was my cool touch of restraint and gave lectures with a sweet smile, whether there was a need or not. I can still see her long and delicate finger, going back and forth in front of my nose, softly repeating a message I have learned by heart now: "Remember, the war will end one day, but your life will go on, with a style of your choice..."

Her preaching must have had some effect on me, for many times on different occasions, I would have that mental image of a long, white finger, wagging as if in warning, reminding me of the war ending one day. Later in my life, it would become a blur and I would confuse her version with poetic lines from Khyam's Rubyat "...the moving finger writes and having writ, moves on, nor all thy piety nor wit, shall lure it back to cancel half a line, nor all thy tears wash out a word of it..." I often thought about the meaning and intent and pondered how right they were, Esther and the Persian poet.

*****

The harsh, icy winter kept us inside, bored and impatient, but there was no complaining, when remembering the first year we came to Russia. I have though of the lost time in education and tried reading books in the Russian language, but deciphering Cyrillic letters itself was a slow process, creating annoyance and a void in my perfect comprehension. Basia supplied the reading material from some bottomless sources, and I guess Alex contributed, he being a teacher.

I never asked about Pietia, as I decided it would be useless and unwise, but I thought about him more than I should have, burying my nose in the poetry of Pushkin and Shevtchenko, struggling even in the Ukrainian language we knew well from school. The two poets became my favorites, yet my mind wandered from time to time without ingesting the themes and the depth of verses, floating out of bounds into areas with unknown and strange names, exotic and foreign sounding. These were places I once had read on the spines of bound books in the libraries back in Poland—Samarkand, Bukhara, Tashkent. They were exciting names of cities, settings in mystery novels, drenched with intrigues of pre-war spy fiction, adventures, now unfolding into realities of a different nature with the added touch of our own fear, transposing once-thrilling pages into a living truth and sobering facts of what may await us there by our own choosing. Destiny seemed to be inching us closer to the land of my favored poet.

Day after day, we sat with the maps spread out, tracing the only route leading to Guzar in Uzbekistan, a town and area where, growing in numbers, the Polish army was training and preparing to leave for Krasnovodsk.

Occasionally now, we saw visitors coming from the south in uniforms, confirming the facts we had envisioned during the long months of waiting, that finally there was rescue and salvation, but to attain it, would take a great effort to pursue this sketchy notion, involving long days of travel into the unknown half-tropical, half-desert territory. Another difficulty was getting the permits from the Soviet authorities, the act itself already being compared to pulling teeth the painful, old style, for their government was not eager to willingly let us go. We would be the first group of foreign prisoners to leave Russia en masse, being also the first freed witnesses to the system of their communist beliefs and principles.

In our large numbers, we could attest to the total failure of its doctrines and what was meant to be a liberation of oppressed people, could turn out to be a harsh punishment for the ones that questioned the effectiveness of their Red rules.

With our mass exodus, the world would learn what was hidden from it through the years, from the time of the Bolshevik revolution. But the world was in turmoil, with war raging on various fronts. The Soviets, after all, in this conflict, were allies, our allies, suffering equally from the Nazi hands, displaying incredible courage and endurance in vicious fights for their land and cities. The major battles for Moscow, Sevastopol, the fierce defense of Stalingrad, had earned the Soviet people the world's respect and admiration. The bloody red star, a symbolic representation of fear and terror in their own system, would remain pallid and harmless in the eyes of the rest of the world, if they were to keep the truth of past crimes done to their own people hidden for now.

*****

In late winter, toward spring, we acquired two house guests, a duo of fast-talking and very good-looking, young guys, who, for two weeks made themselves quite comfortable on our and Leo's premises, until they could continue the remaining long journey south, to join the army. We enjoyed their company and the commotion they created, two of them acting like clowns, with happy dispositions, ready jokes and exaggerated tall tales combined with inflated compliments, sent mostly in mother's direction-the chef in charge of the food. They seemed to be hungry around the clock, inhaling anything edible in sight and we accommodated them, sometimes over our limits, cooking up a storm, using our supplies of grain as if there was no tomorrow.

My fingers got sore from pinching together the scads of pierogi, which I had learned to execute like Chopin's "Nocturne," with my eyes closed. (Sad to say, I can't do either one of them anymore.)

The two weeks disappeared as fast as a crack of a whip. The noise and distraction were gone and so were the young guys, leaving our father in a scramble to make that final decision—it would be now a matter of short weeks, maybe even days.

To eliminate the sadness and anxiety from the anticipation of father's notion of going away, we had spent the evenings discussing what our future might hold for us. The difficulties and obstacles we could encounter seemed formidable, for we were facing a monumental change in our lives again, one putting everything at risk, with father first paving the way, heading south to join the army. We knew from the very first day when he came out of a "lagra," that this would inevitable. Now, since his decision became known, we had only a few weeks together.

During the long, dark nights, when the lamp was turned down and sleep wouldn't come, we stayed up into the late hours, talking about our life in Poland in the happier times, before the war. Whatever was once a wonderful life, we tried to reason, it was in the past and now it was gone.

Sometimes mother would sing little sentimental songs, belonging to her time of growing up, in her lovely soprano. Occasionally wedging in the melodies so popular in the late thirties and those became a throb and a pinch of pain, while we listened to the strange lullabies before the sleep and dreams we could not achieve.

One time, she told us an amusing story about her escapades in Vienna, where in her teens, she was studying singing. Voice lessons and music she loved, but the convent where she stayed and the watchful eye of her great aunt, the nun, she did not. Mother knew her voice needed training and a lot of polishing on her soprano; but she never reached the stage of high gloss. The rigid life of the convent and its discipline, wasn't quite her idea of where to spend her school years. It was "jail," as she called the convent, depressing her spirited personality. The high iron fence didn't seem a serious barrier, so she sold a golden chain watch for a train ticket, with regret, for she had always talked about it, but she was determined to leave "the dark prison" behind. Her independence remained a factor in shaping her future and continued throughout the rest of her life. I often wondered if she ever regretted her madcap adventure in Vienna.

The end of the winter was nearing but the cold, still held the entire country in a strong grip. We were shivering from the penetrating winds and "burians." The high stack of "kiziak" was disappearing rapidly, and we spent hours hugging the warm walls of the "pietchka" and drinking hot soups, waiting till the hours became longer, into the spring.

On some evenings, the young people would gather for occasional causes such as farewells or without any cause at all, just to get out of the house and spend some time together, enjoying each other's company. At this time, I acquired a taste for that seemingly innocent, water looking drink, vodka. Once in a while, during our socials, a smart-ass would bring the bottle and pass it around, mostly a Russian variety, burning the throat as much as the remembered "zhoobrovka." There really never was enough to get smashed on, only enough to make us feel silly and put us in the mood for fun. Our "soirees" lasted into the late evening hours, so by the time I came home, my head would be clear and fortunately vodka didn't leave a strong smell, anyhow.

Our family, at least the older members, were not strangers to alcoholic beverages, with wines being part of normal holiday drinks. As children we were acquainted with various types, except we were not given them as drinks, not even watered down, as the French do.

Most of our wines were homemade, from our own fruits and berries, grown in the orchard. In summer, father and grandmother supervised the process of winemaking with Dorka and few hired people doing most of the work, with us helping, also, for my part with great pleasure. The largest amount of wine came from the dark and tart cherries; others were the minor mixtures from apples, currants and purple plums. The orchard extended through a wide area, tapering off to a clearing of rich, black soil where the vegetable garden was planted, Gran's pride and joy, ours, also, for all through the warm seasons, we enjoyed the great assortment of fresh grown vegetables.

I remember walking between the rectangular plots of red and long white radishes, trying to find the largest of the red ones (the white ones pinched the tongue as sharply as the horseradish). Many times I would pull the half-developed stems then hastily bury them in the potato row, so Dorka wouldn't tear into me for being wasteful. At the very end of the garden, poppies grew in a disorderly clutter, with their delicate, pastel pink blooms. We often inspected the heads, waiting for them to dry and listen for the rattle of seeds inside. At just the right time, we sat down by the water ditch dividing the garden from the meadow and emptied the tiny heads, one by one, into our mouths, sometimes choking on a mouthful, making sure we had saved the dry stems and heads for grandmother, who, while suffering from migraine headaches, would soak them in a hot water, wet the cloth and lay it over the forehead, claiming it did wonders in relieving the pain.

Our orchard was like a small forest, filled with fruit trees, some being quite old, but still bearing an enormous amount, enough to inspire a small wine production for our own use during the holidays or other festive occasions.

In spring, the heavy blooms covered huge areas, resembling snowy pink mountains and when the wind blew, there was a sweet flurry of white petals falling, blanketing the ground underneath, where I would walk carefully, avoiding stepping on the apple blossoms, settled, upturned with pink edges, glistening in the morning sun with drops of dew, feeling so soft to the touch, like the palms of a young child. Picking cherries was an exciting time, for me at least. On those days, I was up early in the morning, walking through the orchard, looking over the trees where cherries were the darkest, the best for eating, sweet and juicy and I could stuff myself all day long, until finally the intestinal outburst would put a stop to that.

The tallest and the oldest trees presented the greatest challenge, being dense, with long, stretching branches (some quite brittle) covered with black bark, leaving dirty, rough scratches on contact, but once reaching the highest point, I felt as if I was sitting on top of the world. I could gaze at the blue and cloudless sky above, a profusion of the darkest fruit around me, with no worries, only a simple pleasure in total contentment, except for the squawking blackbirds, disturbed by my presence.

There were also times when I viewed the blue skies from the lower level, while I crashed a few times. My puffed-up ego and some parts of me suffered a bit when the unsuspected old and dried-up branches wouldn't put up with my stomping around, causing a lot of cuts and bruises, as dark as the fruit I was after.

The month of August was always a very busy time. The cherry picking was just the first phase in father's great hobby of wine making. Poor Dorka was challenged between father's undertaking and mother's putting up the jams and fruit preserves, forever washing the utensils and glass jars.

After the cherries were washed and put into the giant green bottles (the bottles were encased in heavy, two-handled wicker baskets), then the sugar and water were added and the bottles corked. The cork itself was the size of a small cup, with a twisted glass tube in the shape of a letter "S," stuck into it, for fermenting and for us to inspect from time to time the bubbles forming and disappearing. After a few months, the first test was done with a simple red rubber hose and a slurp or two by our father.

When the right time came, there were dark green bottles with long necks, sitting all over the house and quite often, you could hear the slurps coming from the corners where the bulky bottles sat. Father, with Dorka, was at work, filling the bottles with the dark liquid, the sweet cherry wine. I had never seen our mother volunteering for that kind of operation, as she claimed it tasted better from the crystal tumbler.

But while father didn't suffer any ill effects, being already well acclimatized throughout his life with booze, poor Dorka, kept walking close to the walls and towards the evening, would burst out singing the mournful, Ukrainian ballads.

We had a part in that, too, in a way, we were not allowed to do the slurping from the red rubber snake. Grandma always brought to Jez and me, two small bowls filled with the cherries that once sat on the bottom of the giant green bottles, while they were still fermenting. I don't recall if father ever realized or knew about Gran serving us this fruit delight, which was still pretty potent, but it always left us in a happy mood and, soon after, in a sound sleep all through the night.

My taste for vodka had diminished though with the last farewell party we threw in honor of our young friends, leaving south for the army, with whom we worked in the fields during the summer.

That dramatic evening, I turned up my nose for the tasteless vodka and went for a more sophisticated, apricot-flavored drink, resembling a liqueur. God knows where it came from. It was of Russian origin, bearing a colorful label of a fruit I was very fond of with Cyrillic writing on it. I came out from that all right, but not in fine style. This time, I really got crocked. How disgraceful!

Two of my friends practically had to drag me home over the icy road and not until the next day. I knew I was in a heap of trouble, when my father, on the way to the mill, found one of my "valenkys" and asked, "Is it yours?" It made me think, if I could lose so easily my warm footwear on a frozen road, I could lose a lot more…and I hated to think about it.

*****

The weather was changing rapidly; the snows were melting and disappearing into the black, hungry earth. We could feel spring in the air, although there were no visible signs to recognize it, at first glance. In our orchard at home, cherry tree branches would be covered with small pink buds and short-stemmed daisies in the meadow beyond the garden, would start to peek their heads from among the grass.

Gzaroon's air was warm, the breezes from the steppes were gentle, not blowing the sand in every direction, not yet strong enough to inspire a wild "devil's" dance. In spite of the lack of color in the scarce number of trees and shrubs, there was a certain scent in the wind and in the shade of blue in the sky, that made us feel, this was the beginning of a new cycle. It was spring.

This year, when we breathed more freely, everything seemed more intense and vivid. Life took on more meaning and was filled with hope, perhaps, because we knew that each day we lived through, could be a farewell to the surroundings we had lived in for over three long years.

I thought of going into the steppes to see if the tulips were in bloom, take them to grandma's grave, as I might never see any of it again. How melancholy the feeling becomes, no matter in what place one must say goodbye, it may be a day or an hour that you will never see again. Goodbye is a reminder of glancing back, while keeping pace with ever-moving time.

I was almost at the outskirts of the village, walking toward the tulip fields, when faintly, I heard the piano. I turned back. I knew I shouldn't have. I had survived the winter without seeing him, and now with a throb I knew I had lost my unbending will power, entering the sphere I avoided so gallantly all through the last winter's months. I flinched, knowing it would start all over again.

Walking back slowly, in my mind, I saw a map with a red penciled route, weaving through the states of southern Russia, but the sounds of the piano came louder than the frightening pounding of my pulse. I felt lightheaded and the tulips were the last things on my mind.

I stopped by the building, a combination of a public library or a club, a gathering place for Gzaroon's society—walked through the door, following the sounds—then stood listening. His touch was spellbinding, the technique—faultless. I felt envious and bitter, realizing suddenly the loss of years in my studies of music.

I moved slightly and he turned with a surprised look and his disarming smile. He called my name in Russian, it sounding so melodious, then motioned me to sit down: "I haven't seen you all winter, did you sleep through it?" He was laughing of course. I felt annoyed, my foolish age of eighteen, not quite grown up, realizing he was older and treating me now as if I were a pet pupil.

His steady gaze made me nervous, and I avoided looking up for fear he would guess how badly I wanted to see him again.

"Why did you come here?" he asked.

"I heard the piano; I thought it may be you…"

"Then you must remember me," he was teasing again— "come, sit by the piano; once you told me you studied music in Poland—try something, anything"—he moved away, motioning for me to sit down.

Why didn't I go to see my tulips? Stupid girl! I sat embarrassed, trying to find an excuse: "It has been three years, Pietia."

I sat staring at the white keys, yet was so tempted just to touch them, to feel excitement at the sound of a tone and slight curiosity, of how much I remembered.

Back in Poland, the music, the piano, had been my love since I was five years old, when on my own, I signed up for lessons with an instructor who also taught my three cousins next door. My parents weren't aware of my secret, until Madame Szeparowich decided it was time for me to get my own piano and start paying for the lessons. I sailed through the entire year, for my instructor was greatly impressed with my ability, concentration and dedication to practicing exercises without exhaustion or being bored. On the contrary, I loved every minute of it until I was in my high school years and some distraction began to appear, still the piano was my first love.

157

At the end of each school term, in May, my teacher and I, made a trip to Lwow for exams at the music conservatory. Such wonderful memories! There was always a mad scramble and feverish preparations between the instructors and the pupils, short tempers flying, pounding the piano keys to death trying to cram the irritating scales and sonatinas at the last moments into the schedule. I remember the last exam of May 1939, hammering at Chopin's "Nocturne" and the preludes, facing the examining music professor, so handsome in his black tux, a close resemblance to Tyrone Power, a sight enough to make me lose my head and screw up the "Nocturne." Despite uneasiness and anxious waiting for the results, I passed my last exams with flying colors.

But now, between Lwow and today, there was a span of three years, there were oxen, "wabohreikas" and pitchforks. I felt foolish, but summoned up enough nerve to touch the piano keys, my heart pounding as if I was performing at a concert. The once-remembered notes didn't seem to fit in the right places, my fingers were stiff and were slipping, missing the keys with discord in the sound. I shook my head in disgust, but Pietia was very diplomatic as he smiled: "It will come back to you, give it time and a few hours of practice, each day."

Time? It was slipping away. Was it too late? He said I could come here as often as I wished. What a temptation, even for a short spell to enjoy the music and see him again as in the autumn, when I sincerely thought I was falling in love, a risky game for these complicated months and days, at the very end of our stay in Russia. Mother would be ruffled, to say the least, and father, well, he was leaving soon so there was no need even to anticipate his sentiment on this topic.

With my poor performance over, somehow I regained a bit of self-control, enough to carry on a conversation without this strange emotion and restraint that kept drying my throat each time I looked at him. Right then I promised myself, that this should be the last time to see him. Hastily I described my family's plans to leave Russia and now that I had a chance to see him, I would like to say goodbye.

Pietia looked up, his charming smile gone: "I knew you would be going away soon, but we don't have to say good-bye yet, do we?"

We didn't say goodbye that day, or the next day. On the contrary, he helped me improve my rusty piano technique, with great patience and gentle manners, keeping me aware of the passing time and not knowing that, each day, while seeing him, it was so difficult for me to conceal my true feelings and act indifferently. I don't know if he ever sensed it, for I tried my best to control my sentiments, even during tender moments, which I never knew how to interpret. He never tried to cross that line of improper behavior. He was a wonderful human being and I wished then, as I wish now, that I knew him better, but there wasn't time.

All through the spring, my friend and confidante, Esther, watched me going in and out quite often, without being very inquisitive, though she kept giving me those long and serious looks, holding back from preaching. Finally one evening, just before our father's departure for Guzar, she sat me on our door stoop, normally a welcomed place for evening quiet time, except Esther was agitated, not her true sweet and gentle self.

"I haven't had a chance to speak to you lately, my friend, it seems you have been so busy or you are avoiding me." She sounded a little hurt, but she was right, I was avoiding her, as I didn't know how to explain my turmoil of the last few days. Part of me wishing to remain in here, in this deadly place, the hellhole of our past three years, and now softened with strange impulses and unexplained whims. I was confused with the trend of those urges and told her, finally admitting, I thought I was in love. She listened, quietly, without interrupting, then she blew up!

"In love? Are you? With whom? Which one? Mietek? Janusz? Zbyszek? Who else did I miss? Oh yes, the virtuoso, what's his name? Your secret love! How touching, but it's insane! Damn! Listen!" She was seething and hissing without raising her voice: "This time you have a chance to get out of this inferno pit, have you forgotten the last two years? And now you're talking like an idiot! Love? It's infatuation, you're so young, you're in love with the whole world!"

Amazing what I was hearing, perhaps she was right. All through that night, I couldn't sleep, thinking about her anger, Pietia, but the next day when I saw him, I knew she was wrong.

Father left the next day, early in the morning, happy as a lark, promising to send for us as soon as the paperwork would allow for authorized documents. We watched the train disappear against the sun coming up in a pale sky of dawn, listening to the departed, wistful sound of the locomotive, father a blur, waving— leaving behind him an anxious family. I felt as if someone touched my arm, but when I turned around, no one was there.

I must be getting tense, on edge, anticipating the days and months to come. I envisioned myself standing at the top of the train steps, watching the tracks leading to Gzaroon, disappearing from my sight. I felt excitement already! Farewell, dear Russia! Kazakhstan! Yet my excitement was interlaced with sadness. I knew what it was. It hurt.

In the coming weeks, there wasn't much time left for meditating or dreaming. We had to hurry to vacate the living quarters after the termination of father's work, although the mill's officials were nice enough to let us stay for a short while. We began to count the days, as if sitting on pins and needles.

Through the correspondence with our father, we knew he was already in a uniform; he wrote he found a number of our old friends from our hometown in Poland, most of them older and battered like himself, others, the younger ones, now prematurely grown up. He joked a lot about the fact that he outranked his old friend, a wealthy land owner from our area, the prince, who reached only the rank of a corporal. I am not sure, but I think our father's rank was that of either master sergeant or warrant officer, one of them anyhow.

Father was in excellent spirits, notifying us in his last letter, that our documents, a travel permit for a train ride to Guzar, were on the way with a soldier, a friend of his, who was also picking up his family in this area.

Time passed so slowly, while we waited, patiently—but finally, as too many days had gone by, we realized something was wrong.

At the end, when we gave up hope, father's friend did show up, with an apology, claiming, that father gave him the wrong documents! He regretted the loss of time and disappointment on our part, he was very sorry! We never saw him again, but later learned, the son of a bitch did have the right papers, but sold them for a large amount of money, in English pounds! The bastard!

With the slow mail, father didn't have any idea of what was happening. We were devastated, but not for long. Mother's swearing could be heard all the way to the bazaar for half a day, then we all sat down to reassess our grave situation. We explored dozens of wild ideas, but there were obstacles mounting in every direction, without any reasonable solution. We had to act fast, having only a few days left in the free housing in the mill, and that forced mother to a final decision, to go ahead with the journey south, somewhat on the risky side, for it meant to go on an illegal train ride.

Mother screamed, "No more screw-ups!" (Little did she know what would happen.)

Leo and Esther sat with us for hours throughout the rest of the nights, analyzing every step and problem that could emerge on this wild and unpredictable journey south. The first question in our planning came up as to the amount of baggage we could carry with us. With all the wealth we had accumulated for the last three years in the Soviet Union, there wasn't much to worry about. On the other hand, this life we had survived in the "Red paradise," left us with more than our fig leaves to wear and that's where we hit a snag on a major decision in packing.

I had to part with my brown boots, my loyal and silent companions of better and worse ordeals, the reminders of… "Once upon a time."

Now without a happy ending, I actually cried and kissed the soleless tops foolishly goodbye, my tears smudging the yellow mud clinging from the tulip fields, which I finally saw at the end of their blooming cycle. My mind was filled with so many farewells.

Our friends, Leo and Esther, inherited the green bed with a few generations of bedbugs, which had never left, from the time we acquired it on the first day in Gzaroon. The wicker basket, also my personal sleeper, had by now, become quite comfortable with dents and dips to fit my body contours and additional lumpy features, which had developed into lumpier forms, since leaving Poland.

The squeaky top gave me a sharp twinge when I opened it to get my clothing out for packing. It creaked with a whimper, bringing me back again to the summer holidays in the Carpathian Mountains, the view of Czarna Gora we tried to climb, but never did. These images, as with many others, had to go to rest without being disturbed for now, knowing the material things we were parting with were the last links to our past and had to be severed in order to turn our complete attention to a conclusive change in our lives looming ahead, a journey south.

Most of the clothing went into a battered valise, the sentimental photos we decided to keep, after being sorted out by Leo, who also filled the back of a large family photograph with the complete address of his relatives in New York, to contact them and help his family to get out of Russia.

The preparations, making decisions and packing, took on a feverish pace with an anxiety dominating our thoughts and questions of boarding the train without the tickets and permits allowing us to travel so far across the Soviet Union, this was a war time!

I couldn't quite imagine what was going on in mother's busy mind, but her determination was so relentless, giving us great confidence and energy to tie the ends of this last night in Gzaroon.

What was left of the jewelry went into a tight packet, which mother put around her middle, the amount of it I couldn't believe even with my own eyes. The ropes of golden chains and other heavy pieces still jingled and glittered although so much of it went for trade in the past years for bare necessities. The loss of value in weight and karats didn't matter when gauged against starvation and life itself.

Without any sign of sentimental expression, mother sifted through the rings and pins, some belonging to our grandmother, and slipped certain pieces into her old linen purse, the "sacrificial offerings," she said, for bribery, the act not uncommon in the Soviet system and the only solution for us at this time.

Once again, I shuddered a little when I glanced at the red penciled map of the long route, twisting over the deserts, mountains and the mammoth rivers. I didn't need the Gypsy fortuneteller to predict the outcome of this voyage; somehow, I sensed it would be memorable, and it was.

Late that night, before we left, I sneaked away to see Baska to say good-bye. We sat and cried together for a while, making a solemn promise that once out of Russia, we would look for each other at camps now being prepared for the influx of Polish refugees coming out of Soviet Russia, be it in Iran, India or wherever the hell else we would be sent to.

A year later, in a joyful moment I saw Basia again, for only a short time though, as she was in the uniform of the Polish "Pestka," on the way to Kannakin in Iraq. The Polish army was in transit, constantly on the move with the young cadets (my brother Jez included) to "Junak" schools near Palestine. The soldiers, the rest of the fighting forces, were heading first toward Egypt, and from there to the European war theatre, most of them to Italy, where our father took part in the bloody battle of Monte Cassino.

The savage assault and struggle for the ancient Benedictine monastery passed into history without much singling out of the nations taking part in it. But the fields around the mountain, were soaked in blood, so much of it young Polish blood, as red as the dedicated words of the song— "czerwone maki pod Monte Cassino" (the red poppies of Monte Cassino). The noble Poles gave their lives so readily in great numbers, believing it was a justified sacrifice for their country, believing it would help to pave the way to a free Poland...they all had faith and trust, as we all did.

Early at sunrise, we walked to the station with our carefully selected leftover possessions, with Leo and Esther helping us to carry the load. What a sight we were—no dignity, no class! The bulging sacks packed solid with millet and the lightest shade of flour, the bundles of bedding and one pitifully battered valise.

The yellow train station was almost empty, save for a few men in Red Army uniforms. We exchanged teary good-byes and thanks with our dear friends, then they left us to wait.

At a distance, I saw the contours of the wooden bench, the silent confidant of the carefree times in my last months of autumn. I felt glum. I never did go back to say the very last good-bye to Pietia. Perhaps I would write and say everything I could never admit before, the pen and paper forming a shield, this being safer than actual touch.

I heard the faraway sound of a locomotive and mother's shrill voice: "This is it!" interrupting my chain of thoughts. She blessed herself hastily, this giving me a small chill, but with her I knew she could never resist the extra help from above.

The train was nearing the station. I started to walk toward our baggage, but someone picked up the valise I was to carry. I looked up and saw Pietia. The wheels of the train were squealing to a halt. He was so close to me, his eyes always so green and sharp, now dark like a churning sea, while I stood with emotion, heart racing in great confusion. There were only minutes left, between us the last glimpse, that painful, hurried look...the only ever—the last kiss.

"Good-bye, love. I wish you the best in your new life," he said in his soft and hesitant voice. The world spun around and for a mere second, I was deprived of it all - my conscience, the surroundings and my goals.

The whistle blew and he helped me to the steps. The train was picking up speed and there didn't seem to be any more time for thinking, only watching his figure become a blur.

"Good-bye, love," his words blending with the monotonous clicks of train wheels speeding away, toward Tashkent and Samarkand, the exciting and new horizons, toward good luck, in a new life.

*****

Good luck we would need in the extreme, beginning right now, even more-we could use magic with a hat producing tickets, which we didn't have. The train conductor would be here any minute, and mother as much as disappeared. - I felt sweat trickling down my neck, trying to see into the narrow corridor, hoping for a sight of her. Actually we had underestimated our mother, again. She didn't wait for a conductor to appear, she went looking for him. Sure enough, she brought him back where our baggage was still sitting by the entrance of a coach door. He took a long look at the bulging sack of millet and smiled, nodding his head: "Harasho" (Good), he said to our mother, being quite pleased by the offering in an exchange for a free ride a certain distance. The deal was made and we were shown to a compartment with the rest of our baggage, minus the spoken for sack of millet. We were in, and our journey had begun.

The conductor saluted our mother then departed with a grin. We sat quietly, wondering and guessing how far this sack of yellow grain would take us. What town or city would become our temporary destination, before we reached the Polish military area? The train, now at its full speed, was cutting across the desolate land we were now acquainted with for over three long years. The picture of the dull landscape flashed by with recollections of a hot sun, the work and the lazy oxen, without leaving a sadness or a tug of sentiment, except for a fresh image of a young man who came to see me off and wish me well.

Mother took out the map already withered and wrinkled, but with the red penciled route still visible, concentrating on directions of railroad lines and indicators of the changing terrain.

We had reached the city of Ksyl-Orda. Multitudes of people were milling about at the station, among them our conductor, unloading his trophy, the sack of millet. This would be the end of our lucky-so-far line, according to the invisible tickets. It was. Now, we were to face a new inspector who boarded the car with our compartment and in a short time, we were told quietly to get off the train. He was firm and didn't bother with any bribes. Mother was grim. We got off at the opposite side of the station and walked toward the first coach and got back on the train with a hope to cross a few more Kazakhstan miles, before the new conductor caught up with us again. It was a struggle for us, with our belongings and in the summer heat. We boarded the first car and with shock and surprise, found ourselves staring at a lot of faces belonging to the Red Army soldiers. We stood as if affixed to the floor, with our cargo-baggage, realizing we had entered a restricted coach, military, off limits! Their look was also of true astonishment, as if we had fallen through the roof. I keep remembering all those eyes gawking at us, without any words and mother, she caught on immediately but didn't lose her composure. Her next move would have justified receiving an Oscar, today's

Academy Award. It was quite a performance. She started to sob, the instant tears flowing like the Volga river; so convincing, making me almost cry with her, but knowing the truth, I stood listening with a sad face, supporting the story about our predicament. Our father, a Polish soldier in Uzbekistan, being deathly ill, while the Soviet government would not allow us to travel to see him. If we could only reach Tashkent…she didn't finish, her loud sobs, blurring the words. At that time, mother didn't have any inkling of how close she was to the real truth, for father was gravely ill with malaria. The sight of us standing like three sorrowful statues, the pitiful tears and mother like a replica of the ancient Niobe, had its effect, inspiring the sympathy of the entire Russian military corps.

I'll never forget all those stares from the sea of faces—and the silence, until an officer sitting by the window, got up and gesturing with his hand, said "skoro" (quick), offering us a hiding place, pointing to the hanging heavy army coats in the corners of the benches.

I was happy with a refuge directly across from mothers. The window was opened, thank God, for my protector, the jolly Red soldier, began eating his lunch, a smoked herring and some hard-boiled eggs. It wasn't the aroma or the combination of the two that got to me, frankly, I was hungry, my mouth watering heavily and I could see through the crack of the fold in the soldier's coat, the movement of his fingers, shoving the food into his mouth. A few times, I almost stuck my hand out in a begging gesture, but not being able to see the entire area of the coach and unable to predict when the cold-hearted conductor would show up, I decided to exercise patience, since our near future was at risk, more serious than a mere fleeting desire for food.

To ease my hunger pangs, I tried to peek at the view rushing by the open window, and at the same time, inhale some fresher air, which became stale and a little spoiled, from the expelled eggs and herring. The sights running by were still sepia tones for miles and miles of heat-exuding terrain and sandy regions of Kazakhstan. What a boundless territory, would we ever leave it behind us? Our destination was still far away, although we had traveled almost a thousand miles.

The heat was building up quite rapidly in my hideaway behind the woolen blanket Red Army uniform coat. It caused a great deal of sweating, with me feeling as if every pore in my body was opening up like a fountain of sticky perspiration. This was the beginning of summer and we were heading steadily south so the temperature was getting warmer and warmer. Impatiently, I kept wiping the trickling sweat, twisting around until my eyesight caught a view of the entire military group—faces, so many faces, strange and tired looking, some like blank masks. I thought of the vicious fighting taking place on the Russian western front and pictured these young lives thrown into the battles like herds of sacrificial animals. I could clearly see the expressions on the ones sitting close by, most of them looking composed, almost unemotional, all of them wearing rows of medals on their muddy green ("rubashka") shirts.

Would they become the shadows of Stalingrad or Kursk?

For the first time since our arrival in the Soviet Union, the feelings of hostility toward this detested Red Army, seemed to be slipping away, now being replaced by a touch of warm gratitude for their good will and compassion in aiding us on this difficult journey.

With the miles dividing us from the place we had lived for the past three years, it felt as if we were transported to a different era and time filled with hope, that nothing would intervene to take us back to that part of life. Yet, a part of me was still inflamed with Pietia's image, wishing to be there with him just one more day. Would a day, or an hour, turn my whole life around? I didn't dare to answer that question...even to myself.

We were gaining miles, heading south, the speeding train, bringing us closer to Uzbekistan and Guzar, a final safety zone for us. But in between, stood Destiny, a lady of uncertain moods. In the days to come, we would feel her rancor.

While my thoughts were scattered in wild disorder, commuting back and forth to Gzaroon, I heard a slight commotion outside of my confined area. I tried to see all the way to the door of the coach, where one of the soldiers was sending some signals, waving his hand to the rest of the group. Suddenly I heard singing, a beautiful sound of clear and harmonious voices carrying the melodies we were acquainted with so well. There is a certain spirit and character in Russian songs, in the tone and the words, sometimes lifting the listener out of the inner-self, out of reality and surroundings, into an illusion created by the lyrics of the song. Either you were drifting along the Volga river or walking among blooming orchards with Katiusha, or like me sitting at the edge of the world, tossed by the words of the song...

"I'm going far off, far away from the sinful earth.."

I curled up, listening, ignoring the sweat and my grouchy stomach. The series of lively tunes was a pure thrill and a diversion from the nerve-wracking game of hide and go seek with the conductor, throwing me into the blank state of a total vacuum, a momentary relief from complications of the human condition called life.

It seemed an escape from the turmoil of the last few days and the fear of the unknown, yet to come tomorrow. Just one more minute of this luxurious void, I bargained with myself, being quite unaware that only a few paces away from my hideout, our fate was being considered on this very strange and decisive journey. Apparently, the conductor who threw us off in Ksyl-Orda had finally made his way to the military car and now was questioning the members of the Red Army about the stowaways, meaning us.

My sixth sense alerted me to something undefined and threatening taking place. I could hear words now, faintly above the general droning conversations. My woolly peephole revealed the dreaded site. The conductor, the hunter, was

165

describing our features, height and age, while carefully scanning the farthest corners of the coach, including the area camouflaged by the heavy army coats, underneath which we were sweating profusely. The soldier questioned, who had inspired the singing, was shaking his head, with a deadpan face and a negative expression. So were the others, denying any sighting of Polish refugees, on the loose, so they claimed. Bless their atheistic souls!

Then the singing went on! The entire scenario appeared so unreal, yet it was happening, and the train kept moving—clickety-click, cutting the distance, mile after mile, keeping us sweating in fear. The conductor was still standing and talking; either he didn't believe the soldiers, or he just wanted to chat with the men in uniforms.

In a short time, the train was slowing down for a stop at the station, indicating a small town. I caught a glimpse of the conductor getting off with his belongings, a sign of the end of his route. We have squeaked through that one! We thanked God, but there were many prayers yet to say. We began to breathe easier and with caution, like statuary, unveiled ourselves, throwing the heavy coats aside, flushed and glistening with perspiration. We were still a little frightened, though trusting the soldiers, who were cheering and assuring us there was nothing (nitchevo) to worry about, not now.

The Red Army men were great! With good-natured smiles they urged us to share their food and drink, (as if we needed any encouraging). Here, finally, I made real contact with smoked herring and hard boiled eggs, belonging to the young man whose space I had shared. He seemed to have more than enough for himself, so I made quite a dent in his provisions, and from the others there was kvas and borsht, a virtual banquet in its own style, bringing spirit and life to the coach and filling the atmosphere with noisy chatter, the smell of food and strong cigarettes. Now and then, there were rumbles of uncontrolled belching and other less fragrant blusters, combined with the friendly cheers and continuos toasts, but who cared! We felt we were in the best of company!

After the last toast, everybody's wish for the ending of war and objects flying through the air, the celebration quieted down to a restful hush. We had gotten a reprieve for the time being and in our circumstances, without counting hours or minutes, we had thrived on the present moment, nothing further. The nearest future, we felt, would resolve itself with whatever problems arising, as it had been proven in the last few days.

Occasionally, the mournful whistle of the locomotive reminded us that a speeding train was taking us closer to our destination and a rendezvous with the unknown. With so many miles behind us, I knew we should be leaving Kazakhstan soon, finally entering Uzbekistan. At last!

Being in hiding for quite a length of time, still tasting the liters of kvas and borsht, I knew I had to take a walk toward the end of a car. Later, I lingered at the window in the narrow corridor, trying to imagine the train's route on the map, remembering that at a distance away, along the tracks, the great river Syr-Daria was on its course to the Aral Sea. I was hoping the trans-Caspian route running parallel would come close enough, to at least catch a glimpse of this mammoth body of water. Remembering that in my school studies of ancient history, Alexander the Great and his conquests, and now myself, coming in touch and sights with the marks of the past, imprinted in many places on this enormous and savage looking terrain.

Engrossed in my mental geographic explorations, I heard a voice behind me: "Your ticket, please"—he was polite. I turned around to face our third nemesis, the new conductor. Well, the sky had to fall, sooner or later, but now it did because of my stupidity! We were caught, at least I was and now had to face a moment of truth, and the consequences. I knew very well what the aftermath would amount to, but I also knew I had to fabricate a fast lie, this being so difficult for I was overcome by panic and my mind became a complete blank.

"Ticket, please," he repeated, accenting the "please" (pozhalosta). I can still remember his face with the aristocratic features and a pince-nez adding a touch of dignity, except his eyes were so blue and cold, like a whiff of "taiga" forest, even though he grinned, exposing two shiny platinum teeth on one side of his mouth. Feeling scared, I could barely let the words out: "My mother has the tickets."

His grin got wider: "Yes, you and your mother, we have been trying to track you down for the last five hundred miles, where are the rest of you?" I pointed to the car he just came through. "You must have missed her," I said, thinking the crisis had reached its zenith.

He took off his pince-nez and squinted with a scornful look: "I know who you are, what part of Poland do you come from?"

"Lwow," I said without hesitating. It wasn't exactly, but it was close enough. In Poland, we usually defined the distance from a small place to a large city by the "wear and tear" on the footwear; therefore, my hometown being only two pairs of worn-out shoes away from the closest big city, Lwow, wasn't too great of a number in kilometers, pinpointing the vicinity of our living area.

"Lwow?" he echoed, "No, no, you are not from Lwow, you don't lie well enough, people from that city are slippery and sharp! You're giving that city a false image! Where is your family from?" he asked again.

I felt insulted. I loved Lwow, the city with its graceful architecture, an exciting place for our many shopping trips and excursions to historical sites, museums, art exhibits—Lwow was the heartbeat of eastern Poland. On our last visit to that city, also our last shopping spree, one month before the war, I was being rewarded with my first pair of high-heeled shoes, which I decided to wear right out of the store. I remember the stark white linen they were made of and the thin off-white leather straps with a curly bow at the top. I also remember the pain of trotting in them for the rest of the day, with a smile though, for that afternoon we went to view the renowned "Panorama." This was a spectacular painting of life-size figures and the background depicting the battle of Raclavice. Two famous Polish artists, Kossak and Styka created it. The classic masterpiece was done on a canvas suspended from the ceiling, stretching in the great circle of the rotunda, giving the viewer a feeling that she was enclosed in the action of the historical battlefield. A battle in 1774, where the united Polish nobles and peasants fought side by side for Poland's independence against czarist Russia, under the command of Tadeusz Kosciuszko, just returned from America. Even with the large crowds in the rotunda, there was always a respectful hush while viewing this segment of Poland's history, a solemn homage paid to those who gave their lives for the country and its future.

The recollections are rather painful now—Lwow was a part of my growing up, a stepping stone to a finer education aside from the school and variety of cultural traits, ones you could not attain in the daily living of a small town, such as the one we lived in. The visits to my uncle on Czeresniova and his gracious efforts with the introductions to symphony concerts, theatre and my first opera— the unforgettable "Carmen," many of the loveliest moments, I owe to Lwow.

The man who brought all those memories back was still waiting and I, nervous and rattled, was looking through the window, thinking how many miles away was Tashkent? Finally he walked past me, saying, "I'll find them."

Actually, things went quite smoothly, with only a few unrestrained "psiakrew and cholera" from our mother, but the confrontation with the conductor turned out to be civil and calm. Perhaps being so close to our stop, the city of Tashkent, was a factor in a pleasant parting, not to mention the great support from the Red Army guys, who kept up our morale to the very end, noisily saying their final farewells with lots of wishes for good luck in our future and good health for our father.

When the train began to slow down, we guessed Tashkent would be in our sight in a short while. We gathered the bundles, the sacks and the old valise, ready to go down the steps anxiously. At the instant there was no motion, we tumbled down in hurry. The conductor stood watching. We waved the last good-byes to our friends, the army comrades, then walked away, toward the area resembling a small park shaded with a large tree.

For a short spell, we sat in silence, absorbing the view spread out in front of us. We were almost at the end of the road. Listening to the unfamiliar sounds, it dawned on me that we hadn't seen a city of these proportions for over three years. Tashkent, one of the largest and oldest cities in central Asia, lies on the historic trade route, out of Samarkand all the way to China's Peking (now Beijing). Its past dates back to the Seventh century and echoes with names of the Oriental conquerors well known in history—Genghis Khan, Tamerlane, among others. By the choice of God, we were stomping their grounds, but being still alive, we were making our own history.

There were no more decisions to be faced with, but we still had to get back on the trail to reach our final destination, the town of Guzar. I looked around, noticing the streets lined with massive mulberry trees providing relief with their shade from the oppressive daytime heat. Tashkent was hot. I remember the intense color of the sky, azure blue and so clear, without a single cloud. Nearby, the Uzbek vendors were noisily selling produce in their language, new unrecognized sounds, a little guttural, somewhat different than the Kazacks' lingo, so I thought.

The one wonder I shall never forget was the aroma of the native fruit, so rich and sweet, filling the air with a great variety of scents. The whiffs of ripe melons and apricots kept coming in waves, pausing by my nostrils, a small torture to my taste buds. I carried on, sniffing loudly enough, till mother pulled some rubles out of her deteriorating linen purse, saying, "For God's sake, go get some!" I walked across from where we were sitting, toward the fruit wagons visible on the other side of a park. The old Uzbeks were lounging around at the street curbs or squatting, Kazakh style, by their produce.

The sight ahead of me was so picturesque, the subject and colors an artist's dream. Their native garments were different and quite appealing, made out of heavy cotton, with vertical, multicolor stripes on the loose, layered robes. Their heads, like the Kazakh people, were covered with small, pointed skullcaps, richly embroidered over the heavy velvet or silk, giving them a touch of wealth, above the faces rich in character, bronzed by the forever- hot sun.

I approached the cart and lingered, trying to choose the best ripe fruit, which I hadn't seen for the last three years, except maybe in my dreams. I walked around the wagon as if undecided, imagining the taste, which I had forgotten and the aroma itself drove me insane. I wanted to sniff and admire the vibrant contrasts in colors of green and purples on the elongated grapes, the vermilion touches on the round cheeks of peaches and apricots, and the native "Tashkent" pear and melons we used to sniff at Gzaroon station, on the four o'clock afternoon train run. Now I could finally get my hands on the elusive and mysterious produce. My eyes were so hungry and so was my stomach. Once more I glanced at the radiant picture, a composition of a still life worth the brush strokes of Vermeer.

The Uzbeks were chattering, gesticulating to hustle a sale, in Russian indicating the price, but I wasn't in a hurry; patiently, I selected a few of each fruit, not paying any attention to buzzing flies, circling around, probably entranced, like me, with the sweet smell hanging in the air. When it was time to pay for the purchased fruit, I thought, just for the fun of it, I should bargain, which is customary and traditional in the Orient. Accordingly, I suggested my price, but the old Uzbek surprised me, he swore angrily, acting as if I insulted him, mumbling something in his language. But I wanted that fruit! Just when I was ready to hand him the rubles at his price, he surprised me again, nodding his head with a smile and noisily kissing his two first fingers. It was a deal! I didn't argue, just walked away with my fragrant prize wrapped in the Uzbeki newspaper.

The sun and the heat were at their peak. Tension was unraveling itself into a placid state of surprise that we had made it, after all! Now it should be easy, no comparison to our ordeals of the last days and hours, as nothing worse could happen…, but it did.

The still air made me drowsy and not unaware of the surroundings, making me feel as if what was taking place was a long dream—with Gzaroon and the steppes far behind, Basia, Pietia, Esther and Leo almost a blur. I tried to block the memory completely, but the images wouldn't leave.

Mother kept looking into her linen purse, inspecting the bottom where the left over gold chains lay coiled like vipers, maybe another "bribe" for the next and we hoped last train ride, but for now, we remained quiet, refraining from making any plans.

It was peaceful, even with the unfamiliar noise of the city, a sign to us that everything was right with the world. We sat amongst our bundles and sacks, not much to claim as personal wealth, but with a spirit high enough to soar above any perplexities or crisis that could arise with each step we were to take. The park and the greenery were soothing sights, the thick array of entwined branches held the dense layers of dark leaves, giving comfort from the penetrating rays of the hot sun, later finding it an incredibly hot sun. Now just getting acquainted with its greater strength than in Kazakhstan. This was a timeout, a breather to relish our accomplishment of the last few days. In this idle and relaxed state, we noticed at a distance, a group of soldiers walking around the park area, dressed in khaki uniforms, the color we saw before on members of the Polish army.

Mother leaped suddenly, her action typically preceding her reasoning or logic. In a flash, she was shaking soldiers' hands, while talking, with an exalted smile. We watched her from a distance, as the entire group walked away toward the station and disappeared inside. I tried to guess what was taking place and what would be coming next, but with mother's expertise in creating situations for our benefit, we just didn't know; on the contrary, we were almost assured that her dealings, were always done to her advantage.

Time moved slowly. In the heat, we sat waiting, not overly excited. Waiting seemed to be our perpetual game, implanting a good dose of patience, needed constantly for it became a strong base and part of our existence and steady struggle to reach that one goal- exit from the Soviet Union.

The strange and new environment was now more than a diagram, as the short hours interposed the exotic sights of palm trees and majestic mosques, as a normal view, without that impact of a first impression of being in the tropics, recalling the books from the library with their Oriental mysteries. Gazing at the shimmering, overheated air I kept munching on my fragrant apricots, taking small bites and delighting in the long-forgotten taste, savoring each nibble without paying attention to the sticky fingers and buzzing flies circling about.

The heat made me drowsy. I kept closing my eyes, again wondering more than ever, if this entire happening was a long-suspended dream or a delirium that may disappear in a flash. The loud noises of a city, the profusion of greenery and us again without a place, like nomads or tramps, searching for some form of security.

Without measuring time, it was immaterial anyhow, mother's appearance sporting the widest grin on her face, broke up the monotony of waiting. Her hand raised high, she was holding something resembling tickets! Having been freeloaders on the Soviet railways up to now, we didn't know what they really looked like, but mother was aglow and beaming, evidently getting hold of a true fare! That was a reason to boost our morale, it zooming way up there with the degrees of Tashkent heat.

Were some of our troubles over? For now, at least, having been assured of a legit train ride, we could finally sleep without nightmares. Our next departure would be around midnight, taking us as far as Yangi-Yul, where we should get help toward the remaining part of our route. We were close to our goal, and the worst seemed to be behind us. I wanted so much to walk around the busy city, and my brother was eager to join me, but mother said no. At this point, she said, "No more baiting trouble."

However, we took part in what I would call, at that time, a very exciting event. Jez and I went to a public bathing place called "bania." While mother sat by our possessions, the bundles and the sacks in a dusty park, my brother and I walked across the park to a large building, a public bathhouse. Washing our stinky selves was something we needed badly, making it also an ideal occasion for trying out a "bon voyage" gift from Basia, an oval-shaped, highly perfumed cake of Russian soap, which at the last minute, was thrust into the tightly packed valise and did its best, spreading a strong scent into the stale odor of our vintage garments. The elongated chunk got split in half with a vision of seldom-seen suds and a clean smell, instead of foul sweat. Briefly I had recalled mother's home made product in Novaia Zyzn, the suet and the bloody intestines from an unidentified animal—I had a feeling it was a horse, which didn't minimize the awful stench of mother's experiment-and somehow is still a vivid memory.

Inside of the building, the "bania," Jez and I went in opposite directions. The place was dark, steamy and slippery with a few women and children, though with an absence of a noise. The water was hot, yet comfortable in temperature. What a delightful feeling it was, as if we were washing the accumulation of grime and sweat from all the years past.

Women showering around me were not affected by a display of such a large assortment of nude shapes. At first, I felt embarrassed, having never been exposed to so many bare butts and breasts of such various contours. With my reserved, religious upbringing, this exhibit shook the hell out of my timidity and daringly, I sneaked a look at myself. I felt almost grown up. The knowledge of physical maturing through the last years, came at intervals, excerpts picked up here and there, without full lectures on detailed functions of a woman's body. As far as sex was concerned, I didn't have even a slight idea of this strange animal-like instinct, a drive and fascination of making love. Damn, I was dumb, though I remember the few times when being kissed, I had felt the heavy pounding in other areas than the heart and head, but it was so novel to me, I couldn't quite interpret the physical meaning of it, at the time.

"Banias," as I have learned now were quite common in Russian towns and cities of larger proportions and for me, it was a fresh adventure, I would say very enjoyable, for I took my time standing under the water spray and lingered longer than I had intended. Once finished, I felt disinfected and lively, wishing my mind would match the refreshed condition of my body. I hurried back to the park area so mother could experience the same luxury of the "bania" treatment.

We had settled for the night among the trees and powdery dust, spreading the last of our battered bed cover, the once-heavy material now almost threadbare with a faded color and long fringes gone. I lay down, my fingers tracing the pattern of lines that once belonged to a tranquil way of life. Again, the images kept flashing, like a cavalcade of vignettes and in the design of the large leaves above, I saw the bronze ballerina resting at the base of a bed-room lamp, casting a soft light at the picture of daffodils hanging on the wall.

Why were those visions from the past haunting me so persistently now? I thought of nothing else but people and events we had left behind. It was as if the essence of the loveliest moments from our life before was bearing down with a surge, blending into this very hour to confuse the presence of what was real and what was not.

With time elapsing, stretching the distance between places we had called our "home," people we had loved and others we thought of as our friends, they seemed so close, as if we could touch them, yet so silent, the specters we could not get rid of, following like shadows, up to this day.

"Bania" did some wonders for our mother, also, she came back in a great mood, suggesting we all have a good rest and sleep, before the departure of our midnight train.

The clamor and the noise of Tashkent had died down to a quiet murmur and I could see a few brightly shining stars, peeking from among the pattern of dark leaves, twinkling in the stillness of an overheated night. We slept soundly.

I woke up to mother's grumbling, complaining with the worry that we may have overslept and possibly missed the train. It was hard to tell time, for our watches were long gone in trade and never could be replaced. Now they were so greatly missed, in our travels mostly, realizing how a little gadget, a reminder of a civilized world, would have simplified our life and reduced the long streak of "psiakrew and cholera" to less grouching. But this was Russia, the country of backward living, thriving on simple solutions to simple problems, and the only answer for us at this moment was to get our rears off the dust-covered bedding and hurry to the station.

The train was late, a very unusual occurrence in the Soviet system of railways. We boarded it proudly and felt like shouting to the entire Tashkent community that we were traveling legally, being the proud owners of real tickets, but there was hardly anyone at the station, so we settled peacefully on the slick wooden benches with a sigh of relief!

Before dawn, we arrived in Yangi-Yul, a small town, full of greenery surrounding the low-built dwellings with flat rooftops, gleaming in the rising sun and splashes of brightly colored flowers around gardens and orchards. Being in the Uzbek country, I felt like repeating: "Allah Ik Akbar...," but in my own belief I thanked God for this morning, for arriving in Yangi-Yul and the general feeling that life was great! The radiance of an early day seemed to equal the lightness and the optimism of my spirit. Being so close to our goal, the place called Guzar, where our father was, where all our hopes were resting and all the risks and hazards would become the end of the line.

Being told by the Polish information post our permits for the rest of our route would be received shortly, we waited at the station. It became a routine— patience and waiting.

However, early in the afternoon, mother suddenly turned deathly ill, delirious with a high fever, losing consciousness in a matter of minutes. Since we had made the tough decision of leaving Gzaroon on our own, embarking on this difficult journey south, we knew the odds were not exactly in our favor. But as gambling became part of our life, it was the only answer to follow the challenge, turning each day into a struggle of clearing the obstacles to reach that desired point, no matter what. And now, so close to the finish line, we were shattered with a sudden crisis, bewildered and stunned by the impact of this unexpected development.

Perhaps it didn't occur to us or we had chosen to ignore the fact that the area we had arrived at, was swarming with Polish people in great numbers, creating the climate for fast-germinating diseases, being aided by the absence of proper nutrition, medicine and a lack of personal hygiene.

Yangi-Yul, a friendly town as it seemed to us this morning, now changed into a dread. It was filled with our countrymen, the transients creating a death trap in epidemics of bloody dysentery, jaundice and malaria, running in a boundless pattern, striking down old as well as young. Leaving countless bodies lying all over the area in the heat, waiting to be picked up and hauled off to the cemeteries or the closest hastily dug communal graves.

I was spared the gruesome sights, while my brother later recounted to me the horrible details of what went on, as he stood vigil at our mother's side.

173

I caught the first train out of Yangi-Yul, to contact our father, to let him know without the planned surprise we were hoping to spring on him, that we were in the area and needed his help, desperately. Knowing with a slight relief, the distance between the two places wasn't so great, considering the vast stretch we had crossed already.

There was no time for good-byes or meditating on the consequences of leaving my younger brother alone with our seriously ill mother. The pain and distress of the last hours, made me numb with fear, yet somehow, again gave me an inner strength to hold on tight, so as not to abandon faith or deny myself the hope for needed relief.

I sat on the moving train, holding tightly to the wooden seat, staring again at the changing landscape, out of the window. We were crossing the river, that, just hours ago, I wanted to see so badly, the great Syr-Daria. I remember the silvery flecks reflecting from the bright sun on the waves, resembling the sea waves, shimmering and dancing over the green water, hurting my eyes. I tried not to think of what was happening at the place I had left behind.

My mind was filled with worry and I didn't pay attention to the rest of the section of the coach, full of uniformed men, Polish soldiers. With a slight relief I thought, I must be on the right train, heading for Guzar. It gave me comfort, until one of the guys came close and sat by me, his breath reeking of booze, his speech slurred and eyes staring—ugly.

"Where are you heading?" he asked, his face weaving back and forth, trying to get closer to mine.

"My father is waiting for me in Guzar." I made an effort to sound unconcerned, but my fear was growing. The others were watching. This seemed to be a bad dream!

All through our three years of living in Russia, I had never seen this hungry look on a man's face. Never had we encountered problems of this nature (at least not in our circles), and now for the first time, I became frightened, being surrounded by my own people. Another glassy-eyed character staggered in and sat across from me with a stupid smile and a breath like a sewer. Dear God! I thought—what else would happen today?

One of them tried to reach for my arm, but I moved quickly away, pushing myself into a corner of the bench, next to a window. There I huddled, hoping for some intervention, a gesture from other spectators, a bit of help, even sympathy, but for a charged air filled with panic, I counted the seconds till the back door of the coach opened and an old sergeant walked in, noticing the two drunks. All he said was, "Move."

My world came back to motion, from the moments suspended in time of a brief terror and the awareness of my reason for being alone on the train returned, back to my other anguish and hope to be able to bring help, before too late. The rest of my train ride was filled with prayer and a silent urge… "Faster…faster…"

In Guzar, I was given information concerning my father's whereabouts. Night was approaching when I finally located his company in a sea of gray tents covering acres of the Polish army encampment, situated outside the city limits. I walked, running at times, racing the lengthening shadows of the evening.

I could have gathered enough strength to walk through all of Russia, if only I could secure immediate help. I entered the huge area of the military camp, searching for my father's tent, ignoring the curious stares following me while I lifted tent flaps, calling father's name.

The sun had already slid beyond the blurry line of the horizon. The heat was rising out of the dusty gray earth and bone-white round stones scattered among the clumps of dirt, making it difficult to walk as I tried to feel my footing in hurry, avoiding treacherous trenches dug up by army carriers. My eyes darting in every direction, for the darkness was approaching fast.

Finally, I came to the right tent, only to find my father's roommate, who informed me my father was in a field hospital, recovering from a bad case of malaria. I could visit him if I wished to and he would take me to him. My knees were weak, bending down from a need of prayer for a sudden miracle, in quiet despair.

Not since the night of my grandmother's death, had I felt so alone, hurting and helpless. I needed assistance and instant aid for my mother and for my young brother that I had left alone with the grave responsibility of tending to a deathly ill person and making decisions. I knew I had to find some authority to speak to, someone in command to act quickly. People believe in angels, and as I look back, I could have encountered two of them, there in the strange land of Uzbekistan, except my help came from two lovely, older ladies who were employed as cooks in the army field kitchen.

In these very dark moments of my life, they brought advice and cheer I craved so badly while trying to hold myself together. Immediately they got the attention of the camp commander, relating the situation and the problems our family was confronted with. We were assured of mother's safety with the commander's promise of an escort as early as possible, to bring mother and Jez to Guzar, in time also to see our father being released from the hospital.

Marinna and Eliza, my new friends, took me to their "home," a large tent with all the comforts of Gypsy living. After few short accounts on both sides of our personal life stories, I tried to sleep under the flaps of their tent. The dark firmament was overcrowded with a multitude of stars, and their soft glitter had a calming effect. How I hoped my mother was alive.

The next few days were touch and go, with father recovering from the bouts of malaria tremors and mother slowly gaining strength from the ravages of a high fever, most likely caused by the bite of a poisonous scorpion. It was a newly discovered danger we had to guard against, for those critters were bivouacking all over the area, hiding in unexpected places, including the bedding and inside of our shoes. The hard-learned lesson was enough to keep us alert and careful.

Guzar, like the town of Yangi-Yul, was crowded with people of all ages, predominately of Polish nationality, but I suspect other ethnic groups had benefited in joining the army with great hopes and a chance of getting out of the Soviet Union. The massive concentration of troops made Guzar a mammoth transient camp and its peripheries resembling a human carpet made up of civilians, mostly.

Once again it was a time of waiting patiently and anxiously anticipating the great moment of departure, boarding the trains with destination Krasnovodsk, our last outpost in the Soviet Union.

In the meantime, we had to bring our life to a "normal" course, manage the time, to get through each day, stay healthy and out of the hot sun—the very simple formula for survival in a new and strange environment and complicated conditions.

We found a small plot of ground on the outskirts of town, where an Uzbek family cultivated a few acres of cotton fields. The ten-by-ten area we rented, next to a donkey stable, provided us with privacy and shade through most of the day. Being accustomed now to sleeping on the bare soil, this didn't present a problem in preparing our nest, except we missed the soft feathers of the "pierzyna," which we had disposed of in Gzaroon. In due time, the Uzbeks offered us some large wads of cotton, making the rest and sleep easier on our now fatigued bones.

I went to work in the fields, picking cotton, but lasted only a day, as the heat and sun were brutal and my stamina was crumbling anyhow, on the wane since the hard working days in Novaia Zyzn. Another reason it was time to leave Russia!

The days of waiting were so long without clear recollections of time spent on pins and needles, guessing and betting on the length in days or months before we would see the shores of the Caspian Sea.

During the idle days we made brief trips to visit our father at the campsite. I always found an excuse to see my friends Marianna and Eliza, to watch them at work and help sometimes. I became very fond of the two, who seemed to replace my old companion and troubleshooter Esther in sharing my life's joys and miseries, as they came in waves in Guzar.

The nights in the state of Uzbekistan were most beautiful of any place I remember having been. The skies were like an aftermath of a Fourth of July, with a hint of cooler air, bringing relief after the sizzling hours of walking in the hot sun, during the day.

At times when I couldn't sleep, I tried to imagine what our life would be like, after leaving Russia. Scores of ideas would keep crossing my mind, but most persistent of all, was the sensation of breathing free air again. Free of being manipulated as if being owned, against our will, subjugated as senseless puppets by the mighty NKVD with their long-reaching claws and twisted minds. True, at present that importance lost its power over us, but I often shuddered at the thought of the changing world's politics and us detained in Soviet territory.

Iran, being our destination, generated a lot of curiosity and speculation of the unknown conditions, the modified extension to our life, our future, for our goals seemed to be edging closer, with a myth becoming a reality.

The month of June came with a confusion of uncounted days, without notice or special attention to it as being the onset of summer. The "burians" and ice of the Kazakhstan winters were long forgotten with heat dominating each day and night and us patiently waiting for the proper time. From the early sunrises to bloody red sunsets, we breathed heat, a very dry and quivering mirage-like illusion of the air. The blazing sun took our appetite away, it wilted our energy and flattened the ambition in movement, even in a simple act such as walking.

Mother continued with her lunatic habit from the past of drinking hot tea on the hottest of days, sweating buckets and smiling.

Our outdoor premises included a low, mud-shaped "pietchka" with two burners, which were just two holes in the middle of the iron grill for the convenience of cooking, baking or whatever else a demented mind would deem to suggest in the 1OO-plus degree heat. With donkey and camel dung gathered from around the area, mother kept the fire going in the marathon style. Burning red hot, pure manure to keep boiling water for tea and an occasional soup, a sort of liquid mess with a handful of tan-shaded rice or coarse noodles, "lapsha," thrown in for a change. Mother claimed we needed it as a part of our nutrition, besides overripe fruits, already giving us troubling signals of stomach disorders.

At times, disregarding the heat and sweat, she would mix together the leftover flour (a souvenir from Gzaroon's mill) with the watered-down kefir, fashioning it into what she called pompously, "crepes," a facsimile of the French Suzettes, but quite distant in taste and rather heavy in texture. The would-be cakes baked themselves on the fiery-red animal chips, leaving dark burnt edges of which the worst part was blowing off the hot residue from the grimy surface and trying to forget the origin of the ashes.

Not only the heat kept us from communicating with the rest of the world and fast-accumulating crowds. It was the fear of catching the strange and heretofore unknown diseases that held us in isolation, which we didn't mind, knowing it was for our safeguard, during this chaotic and busy preparation to enter the free world.

I doubt there was time and ambition sufficient for thorough research on the instantly sprouting strange tropical illnesses, except for small doses of preventive measures such as keeping your fingers crossed, praying for good luck.

Since the beginning of the war, life had become so cheap! The already neglected health of our people, who had low resistance to infection, was creating a continuos fear of who may be next?

Among the alarming and new diseases, I seem to remember a fever of a short duration, called "papa-tachi," with dreadful symptoms, without causing an epidemic, but of the ones that were stricken, very few had recovered. Luckily, none of us came close to grips with this devastating ailment; however we didn't quite escape the clutches of the other wicked "trio" running loose, raging among the masses without discrimination as to age or sex, the frightful malaria, yellow jaundice and bloody dysentery.

Some of the help to deal with all the problems, came from our father, who, being a member of the military, was getting generous rations of food and medical supplies, generously sharing them with us.

I remember the dark olive green cans with small keys and a lot of swearing attached to them, some bloody fingers during the snorting attempts while trying to open them, without giving up. Each of the dark green or brassy-colored cans of various sizes, represented a novelty in our limited diet and a great treat to our starved stomachs, created a challenge and a thrill of discovering something different and unknown to us before such as peanut butter. I ate it by the spoonful, oil sitting on top and all, subjecting my tongue to a lot of stress when it got stuck to the roof of my mouth (mother's hot tea came in handy). I quickly found out that this novel snack didn't quite mix well with the Australian sardines. However, there was a blessing, we discovered, in the small chubby cans containing round, creamy-white looking cheese, also from down under. The dense and delicious dairy item acted as a "Pepto-Bismol," it stopped the juicy fruits, eaten in large amounts, from passing hastily through our gurgling intestines. It also helped to block the painful maneuvers that eventually turned into bloody dysentery, but at the time kept our meals in a solid state, for a while.

These foreign, somewhat extravagant nibbles, didn't appear on our everyday menu, only at times, whenever father could bring some extra rations or did some other kind of trade-in, something mother excelled in. Unfortunately for us, she was not in uniform and not the immediate recipient of the C-rations.

*****

On June 21st, my name day, I decided to celebrate by visiting my friends, Marinna and Eliza on their army "post." In Poland we didn't celebrate the date of our birth. I guess, time went fast enough, heaping the years upon us, so why be reminded. As we say in Poland, "a country, a habit" (co kraj to obyczaj). Our tradition called for honoring the name day (imieniny) equal to observing a birthday.

178

I was named after the saint whose observance fell on June 21st. Originally, my parents had chosen a different name at my birth, but the church wouldn't allow the pagan name of Ludmilla for me to be baptized in the Catholic faith. On the day of my christening, my parents, realizing the wrong choice, had to hastily decide on a well-established name of a saint, so "bingo," the first letter in the alphabet gave me the name to contend with for the rest of my life. Pity though, I loved the name of Ludmilla.

My baptismal name, went into the documents and school grading reports sent home, and although I was never called by the favored Ludmilla, I took it for granted, puzzled somehow that my nickname, sounded quite different and not very saintly either. My nickname stuck to me for the greater part of my life and it was not until my middle age, after the period of hot flashes and fast accumulating gray hairs that I decided it was time to get dignified, so I reverted to my rightful first name, Alicja, after the saint with the first letter in the alphabet.

My friends were busy, the field kitchen was hot, the large cauldrons steaming, getting ready to boil the noontime meal. I helped in preparing the vegetables, a variety of what was available and also edible—taste and flavor didn't seem to come into the picture.

While we sweated and worked, we kept talking, fantasizing about our journey out of Russia, ignoring the heat and smell, merely secondary nuisances, keeping our heads filled with wild reveries. Talking to Marinna and Eliza was always such a pleasure; before the war the two of them were professors, teaching, and now were gratified to dole out the army chow of burned slushy rice flavored with floating pieces of fat mutton. I believe, anyone living through those times and the places, would never recall eating anything but lamb and rice or, if you preferred, rice and lamb. For miles out of the army camp, one could smell the once-bleating carcass, for the menu seldom changed, with the common assumption that it was healthy, filling and free. Besides, there was no choice in preference and it kept us going.

In the afternoon, when a few hours became leisure, the three of us sat and reminisced about June 21st, being the Eve of St. John. Back home it was a great day, celebrated with a lovely tradition, dating to the pagan era, a colorful ritual, a festival of lovers.

During the warm June night, the roaring bonfires would light up the skies and fields along the riverbanks, there would be singing, dancing and bold jumping by young men over the high shooting flames. The flowing waters would glow and shimmer with thousands of lights from the burning candles placed inside the wreaths braided of summer flowers then thrown upon the river to foretell a fate of lovers and their love. There is an old legend that says during the shortest night of the year, the summer solstice, a flower of fern would bloom at midnight for a brief time, possessing the strange powers that would endow the finder with eternal happiness. Many of the daring ones would venture out into the darkness in search of this mysterious fern. Many of the seekers would look in vain or be deceived by the gleaming light of the elusive flower, guarded jealously by the protective greenery of its leaves, shunning the human touch.

In a midnight quest of it, some bold ones would wander, dazzled by illusions, sometimes led to torment or even death, for as the myth depicts, only a mortal of pure heart and soul could claim the prize, but to this day, the flower of fern, had never been found.

These recollections, left a momentarily sad feeling, with longing for the old days, yet realizing them to be so far away, lost and futile, almost like the legendary search for the flower.

The excitement and the images of the summer festival, the flowing wreaths with burning candles and the scent of wild flowers, would always remain a beautiful memory. Being here in Guzar, such a great distance from Poland, we felt perhaps once out of Russia and at the war's end, freedom would help us find the way back to our country, no matter how far, how long a time, Poland would always wait for us. We never anticipated the political repercussions, the tragic twist of events that would force us to stay away from the land we loved so much.

The heat of Uzbekistan's summer had intensified- the month of July was dragging slowly. Day after day, the sun beat mercilessly on the cotton fields and lush green orchards, laden with their aromatic fruits I coveted so much. Even sitting motionless, leaning against the mud walls of the donkey barn, dozing for hours, kept us exhausted from sweating and breathing the oven-like hot air.

We gave up walks to the army camp, waiting patiently for a break, an interruption, to ease the heat, the monotony and the anxiety of a suspenseful vigil.

Then finally the break came! Father showed up one evening, bringing documents, the small rectangular credentials (still in my possession), printed in Polish, identifying us as his dependents. We were leaving on the transport the next morning! No more waiting!

There would be just hours (well, maybe days), between the free world and us. None of us slept that night from the excitement and fear of some ungodly interference on the morning of our departure. Amidst the heat and sweat, under the inky dark skies, lit brightly with my friendly stars, we had packed and unpacked, then packed again, trying to eliminate unnecessary weight and bulges.

We didn't discard too much of our meager possessions, only tightened the cords and the leather straps on bedding, transferring the fewer garments from the cracked valise to a military knapsack belonging to our father. The leftover flour, the last remnant of Gzaroon, we gave to our "landlords," the Uzbeks with a generous amount of C-rations, a discarded gift, earning us a lot of blessings from their great Allah.

I lay with my eyes open through the whole night. My imagination was swelling like an air balloon. Iran, then Persia, here I come! I envisioned cities, I saw people—did the world change since we left Poland? The visions of my dream world kept flashing like moving pictures without the main characters but friendly crowds of people sitting in cafés, walking into the shops, the cinemas!

In the barn, a donkey brayed, the shrill noise brought me down just when I was trying to recall the taste of chocolate and ice cream, it was just as well to put the brakes on, we were still in Russia and the Persian border was quite a distance away.

Before dawn, we were ready. World travelers, we stood again at the perimeter of another great adventure that would change each of our lives so drastically, splitting our family apart, hurling us into a course to the opposite ends of the globe.

This morning, though, our appearance at first glance, was acceptable, a credit and many thanks to our mom, who labored in the heat with sweaty hands, ripping a pair of army khaki trousers donated by father, who was now parading in English-style Bermuda shorts.

At first, I was a bit skeptical watching mother's enterprise taking shape. Considering her Soviet training as a seamstress, fearing she would botch a garment with a very unflattering cut, where you had to guess the front from the back, but surprisingly, we came out looking like a cover from a *Vogue* magazine well, almost.

The plain and durable khaki, of a simple design, would be able to conceal the travel's dirt, but that was a minimal concern—who cared for looks! We were on our way! We were leaving the Soviet Union!

Again disbelief, and a pinch in the arm, was it really happening? Only three years behind us, yet it seemed like a lifetime. The station I had arrived at a few months ago, while trying to find my father, looked different in the early light, the beginning of a day.

Pietia's face appeared for a second and his last good bye, the emotion I felt then, caught my breath. If only the world was different, if only the horror of war had vanished...

Someone was talking to me, but I couldn't hear. My mind and heart were in Gzaroon for the last time.

The long train, its engine running, was puffing quietly, waiting for the long lines of zigzagging humans to board and fill the cars. Before entering the coach we were checked for our individual identifications, the small insignificant-looking piece of dark paper, now a passport out of Russia.

The boarding went smoothly, women and children were helped with their baggage, older and frail persons were aided or carried. There didn't seem to be much crying or fuss associated with anxiety and this extraordinary type of traveling. The magnitude of the move, the importance of it, was playing itself out calmly, without too much shouting or fanfare.

Perhaps, in most of us, it was difficult to release a deep breath through a clenched mouth, a temporary muscle spasm, waiting for a whistle from the locomotive, announcing a departure that would pierce every raw nerve, a signal of a turning point. A point still quite unconceivable and hard to grasp, but with an ecstatic recognition, that, like the historic Hebrew flight from bondage, this was our 20th century exodus. Our release from the unjust imprisonment, the ruthless denial of human rights—leaving behind the invisible bars, the months of slavery and the suffering, and those unfortunate ones, such as our grandmother, who didn't survive to see this grand moment.

At the first movement of the train, there was a respectful hush, as if everyone was paying a tribute to this hour, only lips indicating the whispers of prayers. The train was picking up speed and someone intoned a song, a religious song of gratitude and thanks. We were on our way.

Looking out through the window, I noticed the train was unusually long in numbers of passenger cars, carrying the families in the front, the rear end being occupied by the army personnel, our father amongst them. In time, the opened and crowded compartments became alive, the nerves, strung tight as a drum, relaxed and all of a sudden, the sounds of small talk broke out among the people. Pleasant sounds of a human buzz of strangers greeting each other with the introduction of their names and places they came from. Most of the civilian occupants originated from the eastern part of Poland, but there were others in great numbers that were caught in the Soviet-occupied territories, fleeing the German bombs from the west, heading for Rumania and Hungary, then unfortunately, ending up, like us, in Kazakhstan.

We had listened to numerous accounts of the last three years in Russia, short sketches of harrowing war experiences mixed with the winsome recollections of a life, "Once upon a time..."

Hours slipped by, while the images of strange and gruesome events were brought back by the ones who were willing to open the wounds of the past. These were only memories, the tales told in stepping back, while destiny already was penciling in red the outlines of our future, closing the last chapter on the longest three years of our lives. The windows were opened in a crowded car on both sides and the hot breeze blew back and forth, almost bringing a comfortable relief from the breathing of the stale air of hundreds of wheezes and exhalations of the young, old and ill.

I found a place at a corner of an opened window, the fierce, hot sun trying to penetrate my deeply tanned skin. The heat was incredible! I didn't mind being exposed to the oven-like blasts, drifting from the fast disappearing countryside of lush green gardens and wide cotton fields.

Each second, each mile gone past, I thought it a widening gap between the present and the accumulated pattern of long stressful years.

A night of April 13, 1940, flashed briefly, our first journey to the Soviet Union, so contrasting to this train ride, because the open window I was standing by, didn't hold the iron bars as the cattle cars we had left Poland in, did. Neither were guards with bayonets pacing along at the stops and stations.

Bukhara, an old city, was one of the longer stops, giving us a chance to walk freely around the park area, look at the universe from a different angle, a world with hopes, offering us possibilities instead of depletion.

At the station's old part of the building, we had assembled for a noon meal in a huge dining area with an impressive interior, a pale reminder of the czarist past. I still remember the sea-foam green painted walls, the tall and narrow windows reaching to the high ceiling and the brightness flooding an enormous hall, filled with sounds of happy people, like a lost family gathered for a long-awaited reunion.

The large tables were loaded with a variety of foods, all originated I am sure from military provisions. It didn't matter which army they represented—the taste was great. Besides, it wasn't time yet to be choosy, not for a while, having the first winter in Gzaroon, still fresh in mind, plus we had learned to tolerate, sometimes an overdose of sardines and lamb with rice.

Leaving Bukhara, we knew that soon we would be saying a farewell to Uzbekistan to cross the border to Turkmenistan. According to the barely visible colors on our steady companion, the old weathered map, ahead of us was a large desert-like terrain to pass through. I felt sorry watching the greenery disappearing, changing into the sullen tans and ochre colors reminders of the Kazakhstan steppes.

When crossing the mighty river Amu-Daria, we finally said so long to Uzbekistan, now we were headed south, then straight west, parallel to the route we took out of Gzaroon, embarking on that hell's journey, so full of risks and grief. But it was behind us now and we knew the direction in which we were going.

When the shadows had lengthened and it became darker over the desert, the slowly descending dusk changed the sharp colors into soft violet hues, the scenery around us turned into a blend of remote and mysterious images, seen once in the exotic movies or read in novels. The wind, blowing gently through the windows, took on a pleasant and a cooler touch, even with a noisy background, the moments were so peaceful, undisturbed, full of eager daydreams and promises of a life that we hadn't known for a long time. Perhaps, there were too many ambitious expectations and craving beyond measure, but it filled our minds with a total serenity and high spirit.

The train was speeding without any challenge from traffic, as if being in a hurry to deposit us at our destination, to get rid of us, the burden and thorn in the Soviet side, the scheme that misfired and went haywire in their strategy, finally resulting in their having to let us go free.

Crossing Turkmenistan, the land of many nomadic tribes, I thought of us now as being nomads also. Although of contrasting Slavic features, light skinned, of a different world and traditions, traveling through their land, observing with amazement their stunning dress and looks, as of another planet, yet close in trends to us, who were still drifting on, without a home or country.

Through the fast descending darkness of the evening, I could make out the outlines of the hovels dug into the sand hills and over the clicking wheels of the train, I could faintly hear the soft sounds of beating drums. In a while, I lost sight of the villages, and it became dark.

Mother handed me a bundle of bedding (Lord, how I missed the feathers of my "pierzyna"), but at this point, complaints were forbidden. I placed the worn-out shams on the car's floor by the window and tried to sleep. A strange lullaby of drums and the sound of a moving train, played for a short time, then I slept without interruption.

The sun was high already, blasting through the window with its potent rays, when I woke up, promising a scorcher, nothing unusual, for we had gotten accustomed to this sickening heat since our arrival in the deep Russian south and following the course on the map, we knew we were traveling close, parallel to the border of Iran.

I don't recall too many stops toward the end of the trip, save for the long waiting at the large city of Aschabad. My memories became rather blurry at times, making me realize I was getting hit with the dreaded malaria bug. We did have a great supper at the station and were given a large amount of canned rations to take with us, making me believe that our next and most important stop, would be the port of Krasnovodsk. Mother also received a bottle of Malaga wine and some quinine tablets, a hint or a premonition of oncoming troubles.

My brother, after surviving a terrifying case of bloody dysentery in Guzar yet, went on a wild binge of devouring everything edible in sight. After eyeing an assortment of various foods mother had stashed away in Aschabad, he grabbed a small can with the funny sounding name of "Spam", eating the entire contents, nonstop in a matter of minutes. I watched him with amazement and a queasy feeling in my stomach. The truth was, his feet got a rest from running and his rear end had finally dried up, but to ingest a hunk of fatty and spicy mixture of meat was really asking for trouble. But Jez was fine, never better.

The prospect of coming closer to the end of our journey and reaching our final destination, the seaport of Krasnovodsk, produced waves of excitement among the crowds. The visions of ships waiting for us, boarding them and crossing the Caspian Sea, kept spinning in our heads without touching the Malaga wine. It was clear there were no obstacles blocking our departure from the Soviet Union. We prayed with atonement, we prayed with thanks.

Still, there were long miles to cut through the rest of Turkmenistan: sands, desert, heat and more of it. In a glaring sun, I could see the groupings of low-slung mud hovels, figures of women appearing busy outdoors and wind blowing their long, dark robes.

Some of them came running close to the moving train, waving hands and uttering sounds in their native tongue, in all probability, greetings, for they smiled and laughed, the sun reflecting with glitter in a display of the gold jewelry. I was amazed at the richness of the dangling large hoop earrings and slightly shocked, upon seeing the rings hanging from their pierced noses. The long, dark necks seemed to be bending from the weight of encircling ornamental metal and then over the arms and ankles. When the train was slowing down, approaching the village, I watched them in fascination, their graceful movements and gestures, and faces quite beautiful, if not covered by chaddors.

As I look back now, the tense time was filled with many bizarre events, discoveries of new worlds and customs, learning the wonders of the places we had once read about or saw in the cinemas. It seems so distant today, as if it happened centuries ago, but it was unavoidable, not of our choosing—a part of our life and to me, being young, it was exciting and daring. With laughter or tears, through turbulence and joys, it was a continuos chain of adventure, some of us living to the present, to reminiscence and think about it with affection and a smile.

We arrived in Krasnovodsk at evening, disembarked from the train with our few possessions and walked a short way into a desert to settle on a beach area, on the coast of the Caspian Sea. We must have looked like an army of seals, crowding around in a semicircle on the hot sandy shores, splashed by the gently ebbing waves, promising relief from the sweaty and long train ride, with a dip in a cool sea.

Although it was nighttime and pitch black, the camping area was abuzz with noise and a flurry of motion. The idle hours spent on the train had boosted everyone's energy, which now was exploding with activity. Children went berserk running all over the beach, shouting, kicking sand and dashing into the water with mothers chasing after, cursing then all of them hitting the water with the loud cries of delight. It was a wild scene, spooky, because we were surrounded by darkness.

I dropped my load and lay down, listening to the happy sounds. I didn't feel well and in spite of the night being very warm, I felt a chill and a shiver, knowing the grisly malaria came at the worst of times.

The next morning, the world appeared in better shape. I looked around me, noticing the calm seawaters fading away into the foggy horizon—the sandy beach barely visible, hidden by the wall-to-wall human carpet, figures dressed and half-dressed, some still quiet and sleeping. There must have been a hell of a

185

celebration during the night, with the visible evidence of empty Malaga bottles sticking out of the sand.

I felt much better, so much better. A disturbing fever, lasting over the night, was gone and even the breakfast of sardines I could tolerate without nausea. Mother kept looking at me with concern, worrying, I suppose, as malaria, although widespread among the masses, was an impediment to our well-being, a stumbling block in this crucial, last phase of our journey, and I was feeling the impact already.

In spite of mother's uneasiness, trying to hide it, her face had a cheerful expression. "Go for a little swim," she said. Was she serious? "I can't swim, you know that!" I reminded her of my life long dilemma, not being able ever to learn to swim. I almost considered it a tragedy and did my best whenever offered free lessons, but always with the same results, I'd the panic and down I would go, like a heavy pebble.

Mother was persistent: "Just go and sit in the water, get cool." I looked at my stiff material of hand-stitched khaki dress, then I noticed mother handing me a garment, resembling a sweater, why yes it was a sweater...once, I recognized the heavy wool yarn, now made into a two-piece bathing suit! I didn't have an idea when she did it, but here it was; I was staring at a fuzzy outfit I was to put on. "Matko Boska!" The top part resembled the armor worn by the legendary Amazon women; the stitches on the cups, running in circles, were large enough to put a fat thumb through, except in the very middle, where mother artistically created a no-see-through zone. The bottom part matched the top, with stitches going in a horizontal direction.

Mother was sounding an alert, not to pull any loose hanging yarn. It took a lot of courage, but I wrestled into the suit and then bravely walked toward the sea. The water was warm, reaching up to my waist, absolutely delightful! I thought, what a great person my mother was!

I walked farther, feeling the gentle ebbing against my elbows and then I saw the black blotches floating around, here, there—allover! Suddenly it dawned on me, Krasnovdsk! The oil! And this greasy stuff was, as the Britishers would say, "petrol"—yuk!

My arms were already glistening with the smelly smudges and I couldn't decide at the moment what to do...so I stood in one place, watching others splashing, diving, having a great time, disregarding the floating oil slicks.

Finally, the heat and blaring sun convinced me it was time to head for the shore and find protection from the potent rays, I turned around and then I felt an obstruction, something heavy and pulling...octopus in the Caspian? ...no, the water was clear, except for the greasy stuff. Damn! I realized it was my bathing suit!

The heavy woolen yarn had become saturated with water and was slipping fast off my oily flesh. My two hands didn't seem strong enough to hold on to the bottom part of a suit sliding off my butt and the upper garment was just impossible to control with one small hand, with water pulling it down, away from my not so small bosoms.

Embarrassed and frustrated, I stood in the water like a caricature of "September Morn" only hoping the kids wouldn't notice me and start clowning around. Gathering all my wits, I made a fast dash for our sanctuary of an old spread stretched over the piece of driftwood and a shaft of the old umbrella that wouldn't open any more. I fell on the heated covers, trying to rub off the stinking oil off my back, swearing off bathing in seas or oceans, unless maybe in a tub (that took another two years).

This being the month of August, the open spaces we lived in were like hot ovens, with skies above all clear and pale, cloudless. The enormous crowds acted almost normally, like one huge extended family bound together with one cause. There was superhuman patience and endurance in the conditions on those last decisive days of waiting.

Many acquaintances were renewed; many friendships instantly made. Here in the Turkmeni desert, not having any beds or tables, we did a lot of (like the hungry native fleas) "sand hopping," to meet new friends, listen to gossip and sometimes, political rumors, solve new problems worth recording in Ripley's "Believe it or not" and check on various symptoms of diseases we didn't know about yet.

We swapped helpful ideas and also canned ration food we had never come across before, giving us the opportunity to taste a new combination of three gulps of sliced peaches and pork and beans from tiny silver cans. At least the large Australian sardines (they grow 'em big, down under) became good mates with the gassy American beans and the peaches relieved the strain on the palate from the sticky peanut butter. Later, there was an additional handout of grape jelly and sweet condensed milk, throwing our taste buds into confusion and a picnic for the nasty flies.

That first morning, after the odious sea venture, I stayed by myself. The heat tended to dull our senses, but we could detect a certain feeling of restlessness touched by the slight fear of unexpected interference, the so-called "last-minute jitters," before the great moment of a departure.

The nakedness of the desert, the sand and dust invading our bodies was another menace to deal with. Water was scarce, rationed. We were constantly on the alert, watching for the announcement of the free distributions and continual briefings, hoping to hear the answer to our "when?"

Once daily we were served a hot meal, no guessing there, the *semper fidelis*, lamb and rice, was still in the program and my job was to tote the white enameled bucket wherever I went, just in case there was a hand out. This large and sentimental relic, the bucket, served as our family vessel for variety of all the given meals.

The spots where the chipped enamel exposed the rough metal kept the flavors pretty well intact, and when we drank the lukewarm rationed water, we could also savor the other pungent ingredients of mutton and petrol. At "dinner" time, three of us would dip our colorful "tcharkas" into the mushy rice, then finish off the solids with our fingers, challenging the germs lurking about in numbers, hoping our Polish red and white corpuscles, would put up a good fight.

After the meal we buried the remains in the sand to prevent spoilage and keep the flies away from feeding and transmitting disease. That part of the Caspian seashore should be quite fertile today, giving a boost to the marine life from our deposits alone.

Walking for food or water almost became recreation, for it gave me a chance to look among the crowd, searching for familiar faces, perhaps from Novaia Zyzn or vicinity, Gzaroon or maybe even Poland.

On many occasions I witnessed persons facing each other with a deep frown, reaching into the memory, trying to place the name, squinting, then breaking into a smile with that fantastic feeling, the joy of recognition, reviving old friendships and catching up on the lost years. Tears and the choking sounds of emotion, so freely released, were the common sights of people, who, up to a short time ago, were only a number in values of labor and grams of bread.

The sand under our feet was hot as we tried to economize on shoes, saving the weak soles for the last and long march we would face in a day or so, but it took an extra caution walking in the areas among the spread-out groups of families. Especially around the outdoor john's sites where a short distance away from them, the trail was full of flies, the evidence and dreadful signs of uncontrolled, stinking bloody stools from the dysentery of the seriously ill, who, oblivious to the heat and food, dropped their waste, wherever they, in their diminished strength, had left them. We shuddered at the sight, but dismissed it from the mind, thinking and caring mostly of our well being.

However, my being was far from well. By late afternoon, the malaria attack came back again in full force, this time with a very high fever, deliriousness and violent shivers. My teeth were rattling and though I couldn't think clearly, I was wishing our "pierzyna" was here instead of Gzaroon. The night was hellish and the sounds of the sea gave me a feeling I was drowning in it (fuzzy bathing suit and all). The dark sky spun around and the stars kept falling, crushing me with their hot rays stabbing like stilettos.

By dawn, I finally slept. Father came next morning to check how we were coping with the heat and became quite concerned about my worsening malaria. His main worry was the possibility that I might not be allowed to board the ship with the rest of the family and, as a result, be forced to stay in a Red Cross field hospital, to await the next transport, till my health would improve.

At the time of an attack I didn't care what was going on, but the next day, when feeling better, I realized the outlook for my leaving Russia could be very bleak.

Alicja R. Edwards

WAITING IN KRASNOVDSK

I remember once reading a book in Poland, entitled "Between the Lips and the Rim of a Chalice..."—the phrase came back to haunt me, for it was my plight, at the end of a long stretch, so close and now in a sudden twist, my chalice was being turned away from me. It was frightening.

We stayed on the beach a few more days, maybe longer, I don't quite remember, but mother, being fearful of the results, didn't dare to report my illness and at the same time, was reluctant to try the quinine tablets, without knowing the right dosage. In the meantime, my bouts with this tropical devil, remained a secret. We all hoped my attacks would subside, but they came back again and again, for a long time after.

On the eve of the march toward the seaport, we were told to eliminate all unnecessary weight and provide head covers. We were to start early, before sunup. At dawn, the next day, the assembly of human bodies formed a long column—no guards, no whips, and only the awareness of this last, tough undertaking on Soviet soil. The continuing endurance was like a silent lash to strengthen our determination to go forward, without giving up. It was a reminder of the Soviet brutality and discipline, imposed on us over the past years, which had become a strong crutch, bringing out in force, our sagging grit.

Fog blanketed the sea and most of the surrounding area, the sun came out, pale yet, rising slowly behind the veil of a mist, not fooling anyone it would stay that way. Without a doubt, it would pick up its strength later to make us believe we were walking through hell.

The fresh morning air put a spring and light feeling to our first step, and a faint breeze blew from the sea, bringing in a slight smell of oil, settling in the stomach on top of the early breakfast of sardines. The unpleasant hint had passed and our attention was turned to people walking alongside of us. Most of us were in great spirits, with a positive attitude, almost assured of seeing the harbor by this evening.

In the back of a column, someone started to sing, a most natural reflex and expression of feelings, particularly with Poles, who, being of a sentimental nature, were in the habit of singing the joys or troubles away. This was one of the greatest occasions, except, unfortunately, the rhythm of a spirited mazurka, didn't quite correspond with hot and tired feet shuffling through the sand, barely in one step! So the singing was put on hold, to conserve energy and pay more attention to the terrain we were to cross, a desert, hot sand, promising an ordeal over the next twelve hours.

The soft sand gave in and we sank with each step, a snag in any gain of time and distance. People, walking briskly at the very beginning, were slowing down and fell back, joining the rest of us at our pace.

I can still recall a feeling of the hot, burning sand sifting through my old open sandals, worrying about one of my two-inch wooden heels, threatening to fall off! Wouldn't you know, the little bastard did fall off. Right in the middle of

191

the broiling desert I lost that part of my shoe! I almost left it lying buried in the sand, but thought better of it and carried it with me. Now, I was not only walking carefully, I hobbled up and down carefully. Taking my shoes off was out of question, as my toes would be fried to a crisp.

The bundle I carried was digging deep already into the flesh of my palm, so I tried to drag it over the sand, then switched to my back, but each effort and maneuver, was painful torture.

The images reappeared, from the other rocky times in Gzaroon and Novaia Zyzn when everything was hopeless, and on this desert, our life was also at stake, being so close to our goal. Minutes became hours, and hours seemed endless.

God, give us the strength to go on, I prayed and between the prayers and sweat, the battle was raging in my head, against the injustice, against the whole world!

Ahead of us, on the blurry horizon, the desert lines faded into the pale, colorless sky, and there was nothing to rest our gaze on. My brother looked fit with a knapsack on his back, carefully carrying the white enameled bucket, which contained precious water. He seemed content and probably thrilled, thinking how lucky he was being over his bloody dysentery. Mother was quiet, a few times when I glanced to the side; I saw her watching me. I guess, like myself, she was dreading the approaching four p.m. hour, the British tea time and my hour of malaria sweats.

There is no way to describe the pain and the anxieties we were all engulfed with, on this horrible stretch of the Turkmeni desert. The moments we stopped for rest didn't bring any relief, except they gave others a chance to get rid off some of their belongings, sentimental burdens.

As once we had watched in a cinema, the American westward-ho sagas, so here in life, I walked by the discarded possessions being pitched to lie in the sand, abandoned—the once-cherished mementos left behind with painful memories of life that never would be the same. I glanced at a wooden box with an edelweiss flower carved on top, perhaps once used for postcards or love letters, farther, a colorful satin pillow lay half-covered by sand and nearby the sun reflecting sharply off a silver "tazza," a family heirloom.

Soon the ever-blowing wind would blanket with dust these remnants of love and sentiments belonging to people who were punished, without cause.

The sun moved ever so slowly—merciless, now and then picking out the victims, already weak and exhausted from earlier illnesses, leaving them lying helplessly in the hot sand, to wait for the Red Cross, while the human column passed by, silently, with pangs of guilt, not daring to glance in their direction…

DESERT MARCH

Such was a denial of feelings in the face of our own survival, for in those trying and profound moments, the human ceased to act as a human, making it difficult to explain to the rest of the world, that this was virtually a "Polish Gehenna."

Except, the world wasn't there to witness and suffer with us. It would never understand the horrors and suffering.

Today, I can't envision any more, how we survived that march under those conditions. Today, I am also a part of this world that weeps and sympathizes with the sorrows and pains of others, but still, doesn't understand the truth of it.

Mother, besides worrying about my malaria attack coming back, was holding up pretty well. I remember her Russian green scarf with huge pink and red roses hugging her head tightly, the ends of the fringes tied just below her mouth. She looked a typical "babushka," but I didn't tell her that, as this time was bad enough without bruising her ego.

She must have had an enormous strength to carry most of our belongings on her back, making sure our weight was lighter for us to make it through the day. And we did make it.

My fear came back when the dreaded fever crept back again at the usual time. My vision got blurry but, in the far distance, all of a sudden, I saw the boats. At first, I wasn't sure if it was an image induced by the hovering fever or a desert mirage. But it wasn't the mirage or an illusion of a semi-conscious mind. We were approaching the harbor and people were crying. It was the climax, a supreme moment for everyone. No words could express the excitement and euphoria upon seeing the docks, the activity around them and the number of ships lined along the wharf, each with a visible red star. Yes, the ships were Russian. To the last, the very last, the Soviets would be our wards, our "charge d'affaires" to this very end.

I tried to fight off the onset of the malaria, suppress the violent shivers and bit my lips to stop my teeth from chattering. I realized clearly, I might not be allowed to go aboard. Mother was following me closely, in case I would need support, however I could still stand on my own, without swaying or getting dizzy. I just felt so miserable.

Soon, there was no sand under my feet; we were walking on a solid surface of wooden planks forming a sidewalk, leading all the way to the pier. All of us were overcome with joy and a sense of gratitude, except for me, there was an added fear. Mother stayed close behind me. Ahead of us, people already were entering the long bridge connecting the ship with the shore, but the line was moving slowly.

The Russian military officials were checking our credentials, the small unimpressive angular documents, frail pieces of paper, yet carrying such a weight! They were our passports to freedom and entry to a civilized and free world.

My convulsive attacks of tremors kept coming frequently now. Mother, standing right behind me, squeezed my shoulder gently and whispered, "When you approach the tables with Russians, smile, make sure you smile." Her words kept spinning in my head while we were moving closer to the checking point.

The wisp of a paper I was holding kept flopping in my hand as if in the wind. I held on to it tightly, afraid of losing awareness with the rising fever and heavy pounding in my head. In only minutes or long seconds—would justice take her blindfold off and let me through?

At last, I remember when mother's hand gave me a slight shove with a hiss: "For God's sake, smile!" I did, a small, tight smile, for it was so hard with teeth sounding like castanets and pulses throbbing, making my eyes cross, almost giving me the appearance of an idiot.

Still trembling and grinning automatically, I handed my flimsy pass for stamping, uttering in Russian a "spasiboh." I wasn't sure, but I thought I heard one of the Red officials say, "Some of the morons are leaving, too."

It didn't matter; nothing mattered now. Three of us were aboard and somewhere father was around. In my incoherent state, I didn't even try to understand what was going on; plus I didn't care.

The irony of it all was that, although we had arrived safely at last, after so many hurdles, the joy of the course became rather fuzzy to me. It was not exactly the grand finale I had imagined our departure from Russia would be.

But today, so many years later, while trying to bring our past into focus—I clearly remember the important moments, the turning points, directing our destiny. I remember them, in every detail.

That evening, when we all had settled on the deck of a ship, mother, on someone's advice, decided to medicate me, to help me with my battle with malaria. She gave me an itsy-bitsy yellow pill, called atebrine. That little yellow devil wasn't coated and when it dissolved on my tongue, before it hit the throat, it exploded with a vile bitterness that wouldn't leave the mouth for hours. Nothing could eliminate the nasty sensation, making me wonder if this is where the phrase originated, "the bitter pill."

During the night, I heard a lot of commotion and a constant talking, as people kept pouring onto a deck we were already settled on and the ones above and below. Every inch of the wooden planks was covered with human bodies, just as on the shore of the Caspian where we had bivouacked until the day before. A tight squeeze already, but the crowds were coming and filling the area wherever one could stretch or sit. It was a long night.

In the morning, to my surprise, we were still anchored, swaying gently, waiting. My health was no longer a threat to me or anybody else; in fact, I was feeling quite hungry and very much alive!

The morning brought hot tea, which removed the atebrine residue from my tongue and the only looming problem, was the bathroom facilities, always a nuisance in this difficult way of living.

The large outdoor johns hung out over the sea on the other side of the ship, hastily slapped together out of wooden boards with gaps in between; without assuring privacy, a word long extinct for us. But even so, the crude toilets made us cringe with hesitation and we had to be alert, taking our life in our hands when we entered them! One slip, and unless one were a circus performer, he was back in Soviet territory, or Soviet waters. Life was still an obstacle course.

Now, our hope was to reach the port of Pahlevi, on the other side, on the Iranian shore, within a short time. On the map it looked very close, a hop and a skip, but it wasn't quite. The voyage turned out to be far from it, a memorable crossing…

The civilians were placed in the middle and upper decks, while the military units were settled below us, our father among them, making us feel safe, having him so close to us.

The ship was definitely not a place for visiting or seeking out old friends. The deck area, where we had settled at the first rush, was packed solid with human flesh, like an oversized can of sardines (ugh! the little fish was finally getting to me). There were masses covering the decks with arms and legs moving constantly about. Sometimes a person was unfortunate to switch positions and cross the legs, only to find someone else's limbs moved into her spot. Body parts were intertwined like vines. The temptation to pinch and ask the question: "Is this yours or mine?" was overwhelming.

The most upsetting sights were ill people, with malaria mostly, yellow jaundice and of course, the ever present-bloody dysentery, whose early symptoms of the two, I was beginning to feel, in addition to malaria. Toward the end of the crossing, things became rather gruesome.

However, on the morning we waited to sail away, everything seemed bright and reassuring. The weather, hot as usual, featured deep blue skies, spreading cheer and high spirits in everyone, including me. My treacherous malaria had vanished without a trace, giving me temporary energy, though not completely eliminating my concern, knowing it would come back to harass me before the evening.

We sat with nervous anticipation, the time lingering. The minutes grew into hours, until, without warning, a loud blast cut through the air, a sound we all were waiting for, bringing suddenly a silence, a brief homage to this great moment.

On the docks, there was the normal activities related to "anchors aweigh," as the boat was preparing to sail. There were shouts and orders, the clanking of metals and other rumbles; but on the ship, the air was emotionally charged from the thunder of the ship stacks, leaving everyone trembling with the slow realization that we were becoming a part of history. We were breaking the Soviet's iron rule, leaving their country without their approval, taking with us the tales and the accounts of their degrading lifestyle and leadership, causing so much suffering to their own people and our three long years of hell, for us, never to forget.

For now, the boat was rocking gently, the sea around us was dipping and the Russian shore seemed to be moving away, becoming a blur. We were finally leaving.

"Do svidania," I whispered once more to the colorful tulips, to Pietia's face, still so close and clear, to the soft tones of balalaikas, Chopin's "Nocturne" I had mangled so badly, all of the moments that had become dear and beautiful to me, left behind, harshly, by choice and circumstances.

There was soft sobbing, changing into loud cries, swearing and tears for the ones that were left to stay in Russia. I closed my eyes in an effort to avoid the pitching hull of the boat and trying to control the nausea racking my stomach, my well being short lived. How strange, I thought, my yellow devil wasn't scheduled at this hour, this being only noontime. I was hoping it wasn't dysentery.

The line of the horizon became straight, void of any shape indicating the harbor we had left. In disbelief, I closed my eyes, knowing if I opened them again, I would see only the clear line of water and the sky. I also knew that just beyond, there was the country we were imprisoned in, and I would always know, there is a Russia.

On the deck, people seemed at ease and to look at them, one would have thought this was an overcrowded cruise. Next to us, a group of men and women were playing cards, quite unconcerned as to the surroundings, concentrating on a banal card game, cussing loudly and rather expressively in Russian.

The sun moved fast, high again, blasting us with heat, without our having any chance at escaping the killer rays, unless we crawled under the bundles of bedding. We were spread all over the open area, the decks, without any shade to hide, I sensed, although our stay on the boat shouldn't be overly long, the old, the ill and the children would suffer the most.

The night was approaching and we were now going full steam ahead on the seas. The Caspian waters were not stormy but were sloshing around, agitated. Time moved slowly. As the hours gave way, I looked toward the west; the low sky was slashed with a crimson streak, a remnant of a sunset. The day was at its end.

I was resting peacefully. My malaria somehow not so fierce this time, being suppressed with quinine and atebrine pills, I was hoping to get through the night, and another day. We should be nearing our destination then.

Before dusk descended, the word was passed around that we were entering foreign waters, truly leaving the Soviet behind. How strange, I thought, watching the sea spray, it was the same—cool, without distinguishing colors. But there was a change, a monumental change in our hearts and minds, a sense of immense relief from the weight of fear and uneasiness, as if a dangerous pursuit had ended, waking from a nightmare.

This tremendous feeling of crossing the watery borderline, gave us a first, small taste of assurance that our lives were taking a novel turn, whatever the unknown future, now, at least we were safe, safe in freedom.

The calm atmosphere gave way slowly to loud and happy shouts, voices cracking with jubilation! The frenzy of the excitement had taken over the crowds, and I was lying down, listening…and at that very moment that's all I wanted to do was rest and sleep. I put my head on the warm planks of the deck, relieved of the final tension, when someone yanked my arm, telling me to stand up. The hosts of people from the decks below and above were singing our pledge to God and country, the "Rota"(nie rzucim ziemi"). The voices rang out with a power and a force of understanding of the true feelings as the words carried over the ruffled waters, the Caspian Sea. The Polish survivors gave their hearts and souls, in an outcry of gratitude to the surroundings and God. "Stand up, stand up" the voice by me was urging, trying to make me get up, to pay respect to our spiritually moving, national song. I struggled to grasp the rail we were settled by, the base of which was leading to the lower deck, with an effort to pull myself up, but somehow, the strength I was usually so blessed with, was gone.

The residue of the afternoon fever and now an additional jaundice attack, combined with the bitterness in my mouth from the yellow pill, was revolting, churning in my stomach, and I knew I was going to vomit. I looked around, over to the side of the deck, thinking if only I could make it to the overboard, but my legs wouldn't quite hold me. I started to crawl over the wooden planks, over the other bodies lying, between the standing legs, trying to postpone the rushing nausea. The overboard was close. I was relieved, till my hand slipped in something slimy, putrid smelling, the sight of it, repulsive! My hand was clutching the waste of someone's bloody dysentery.

I had only a few yards to reach the overboard rail, instead I lay my head on the warm deck, and wretched. The wet vomit floating around my cheeks, my hair…I didn't give a damn! I felt like an animal, without any dignity or human sensibilities left. Someone kicked me— "move on," the voice urged, but I was unable even to lift my head. I just lay there, still. Mother found me later. I didn't want her to see me in this pathetic condition, so I made a motion to leave me alone. I saw her turning away her shoulders twitching as if she was heaving—then she was gone…

Later, I felt my face being rubbed gently; she was back with a torn shred of our old bedspread, wiping the sticky spit and my soiled hands. There was no water and the stench didn't vanish.

Even the word "pryvyknesh" lost its potency and meaning, with an involuntary loss of control in body and spirit, it was a total disgrace, but I was hardly aware of it, I just wanted the night to come quickly, to sleep and forget the smell and the sight.

Another morning on the boat was uneventful, until the nagging thirst gave the signal of an additional problem with a very uneasy feeling of knowing the water was gone. The waiting was the last challenge and the only thing we had to contend with was hoping the Iranian shores were not too far off. Still, the heat was parching the lips and the throat, making it hard to swallow even the syrupy juice from the small can of sliced peaches.

Mother was restless again, always being so full of ideas; this time, she seemed to be drained of any notions, but not of energy. When I watched her, I knew her mind wasn't idle. As tired as we all were, she didn't exactly collapse to stare at the sky; instead, she kept fingering her "thinking cap," the old, battered linen purse, where she kept the leftover trading treasures, the gold.

We never knew how much of the heirloom treasures were left in number or weight, but whatever remained; she guarded it, zealously. If there was any amount of water to be gotten for the price of her gold, I am sure she would have traded it gladly, without any remorse. Up to now, we had learned the hard way of life's values and its essential needs as being pitched against the false and frivolous desires we create ourselves, worshiping the cold metal and stones like pagan idols. But now, during the time of present turmoil the precious ore weighing on the bottom of mother's pouch seemed to have a questionable monetary value in the world's markets. To us, they were not entirely worthless, except the measurements offered a strange balance of principles. Decisions had to be made according to the crises piling upon us one after another. The present lack of water was one of the grave crises and mother was eyeing the white enameled bucket.

Somewhere on this ship, there was water and mother was not going to be a mountain, she would be Mohammed and go find it. Her contemplations usually didn't last long and once she made up her mind, she was raring to act. Now, I sensed she was ready. She got up and reached for the bucket when a young man, dressed in khakis, without any army insignias, approached her saying our father sent him to help us with the water problem. What a streak of good luck!

All he needed, he said, was a large vessel and some money, naturally, and mother had both. She handed him the bucket and whipped out some foreign-looking currency—English pounds, she explained, as our eyes got big, wondering how she came by them, but by now, we should have known better and stop puzzling about anything she did.

The guy eagerly scooped up the money and the bucket and was gone. An hour had passed, maybe more, while mother kept biting her lip and watching, scaling the faces in the crowds as far as her sight could reach in the direction he had disappeared.

199

The heat was becoming intense, but our dispatcher and the priceless water, were nowhere in sight. Mother got up slowly, and without saying a word, she walked out among the entanglement of limbs and other body parts crowding the hot deck. I prayed, dear God, don't let her get into any hassle, not this time. Iran was so close—the port of Pahlevi may be seen by tomorrow! But now, it was today and somewhere mother was going to find the bastard with our pot, money and I hoped, water.

For just one second I felt sorry for the creep and thought, strange how our father had a penchant for trusting con men and kept sending them to us, such as that son of a bitch absconding with our permits in Gzaroon. Jez and I sat waiting, a little jittery, wondering what was taking place, farther away. It helped not to move around, for any motion gave us a feeling as if a dry throat was closing on us, lacking the saliva for swallowing nothing but blistered hot air.

More time elapsed and soon the word was passed around that there was trouble on the other part of a ship. Surprise! Surprise! Our mama had gone that way!

Apparently and unfortunately for the guy, she found the bastard with a pot full of water, selling it by the cup to everyone who was willing to pay. He must have been halfway to making his fortune, when mother caught him unexpectedly. She jerked the white pot from his hands, poured the precious water over his head, then started to beat the hell out of him with my heavy pot. She banged his head on the side, on the top, then aimed at his face and bloodied his nose. The son of a bitch was stunned, trying to shield himself, but mother was fast. "Hell hath no fury…"

She kept her bangs coming in rapid succession while his hands were assuming the six or eight positions like the Hindu goddess, trying to protect himself and staggering to fend off the blows.

It must have been some spectacle—mother attacking and people standing around as if in an arena, watching and cheering our mother. Finally the military personnel intervened and the skirmish was over. Father stayed down below till things cooled down, then the incident was closed but certainly, not forgotten.

Mother came back to our nest, bedraggled, her gray hair flying in a messy halo around her face, which was showing a deep satisfaction and grin like a cat's…

We were relieved to see her unharmed, the white bucket, though was empty and the English pounds not retrieved. It was something about the blind revenge put against the real purpose of her aim. She could have booted him where it hurt and had both, the water, which was paid for and the revenge.

It was tough, but we weathered it. The good news was passed around later that we would be going ashore tomorrow morning, even perhaps during the night, the ship would put into the port of Pahlevi. That was good enough to keep our lifeline going, although, being so hot and thirsty, wasn't very comfortable, not in a physical sense. Morale wise—well, there was no description of the uplift it gave us through the remaining long hours! Occasionally, the loud blasts from the ship's stacks reminded us we were moving forward, closer to the Iranian shores, wondering what lay beyond the line of sky and water.

We had crossed our Rubicon. Still, the high authorities, the Allies were making our life's decisions for us, though we were relieved from fear, under which we had lived for the last three years. The price we paid for the freedom was high and then it didn't come as a total freedom. We had slid with clever manipulation from the forced confinement and slave labor in the Soviet Union, to a subtle bondage of the almighty but already crumbling British Empire.

Our young, many of them once lovely-looking women, now hardened by menial work in Siberian "taigas" and the wild Asiatic steppes, were excellent candidates as future brides and child bearers for the English farmers living in the forlorn lands of Uganda, Kenya, Tanganyika, South Africa and India.

My passport of single sheets of white paper, with the imprints of five fingers, contained visas to most of the British colonies in Africa and India and a few other places I don't quite remember now. There was also Mexico, the most desirable of them all, perhaps because it bordered the United States of America— the dream of heaven on earth for all displaced persons, "D.P.s" as we were called.

All of those places we were possibly being sent to, never materialized as my destination for all of the projected journeys were continuously being canceled, because of the unavailability of spaces for something as unimportant as the throng of D.P.s, utilizing it for more important causes, such as the war.

They scattered us all over the world, into the farthest corners of the earth, dividing families, perhaps meaning well, but mostly placing us to their advantage.

The writing was on the wall! The future of Poland was already predetermined—the devil was cashing in on his deals! The hush-hush bartering was slowly coming out into the open and we, as the ex-prisoners, as exiles, didn't seem to have a choice.

Now, coming close to the ancient land of Persia, there was no reason yet to gaze into the crystal ball, looking so far ahead, challenging a destiny. Time didn't move fast enough, as only the hours mattered to this mass of impatient people staring intently toward the south, eyes glued to the horizon, watching for the faint contours resembling land.

On this last day of our crossing, my unwelcome afternoon hours came without a great impact of shivers and fever. It seemed my young body was winning the tough battle with the yellow monster which caused so much depletion of strength and energy, now and then sneaking a wish, that one were dead.

However, the dreadful moments were "gone with a sea breeze…" leaving me now only with the remnants of jaundice, a very unflattering illness, greatly affecting the appearance in a strange way, unless one's family tree originated on the planet Mars.

The whites of my eyeballs turned an ugly green, my skin a very uncomplimentary tint to my yellow of malaria, creating a revolting facial color scheme. Feeling so ill lately, I hadn't paid too much attention to my outward image; besides, without any normal hygiene, one needed a miracle just to look presentable.

But as we were ready to disembark into an unknown country, I thought I should improve my appearance. In a small bundle of the necessary items I had carried with me through our traveling ordeals, among the mementos I had stashed away, I had a triangular piece of a heavy broken mirror. It was for the occasional glance at my features, but not having done so lately, I did it on an impulse and almost hurled the fragment of glass into the sea!

The reflection staring back at me scared the daylights out of me. I was a walking nightmare! I don't think I ever looked so ghastly. Truly, in a way I was completing a mental picture of a real refugee from Russia. The consolation was, there were many more like me, some even worse looking; though in my opinion, that seemed practically impossible.

The atmosphere of peaceful anxiety was finally giving way to noise and the shouts, becoming louder for a good reason. The horizon to the south was showing the irregular outlines of land, at this moment, a "promised" land. It was Persia, which would one day the new Iran.

The distress of the last few days had vanished, people forgot the heat, the thirst, the sad farewells and future worries; in the face of approaching a new country, we wondered, would we be welcomed?

Another sunset, the last one on the boat. In hours, that same sun would be moving above our orchard, the cherry trees laden with dark berries, drying or picked by the birds, no wine making there, no celebration.

A figure appeared on the captain's bridge, a Polish soldier, an officer, and his voice carried a loud order to disembark, the end of our journey. Our national anthem was intoned, people stood up, I did so, also, with the support of the rail, and sang with the others, through tears and voices choked with emotion: "Poland is not lost, as long as we are alive!"

We were alive, as thousands of others were, some still in Russia waiting to be freed, thousands of others to drift through India, Kenya, Uganda and as far as Mexico, wandering in exile, looking for lost and scattered families, searching for peace and security. Thousands of others were fighting in Europe and North Africa alongside the Allies in bloody battles, with great hopes to see a free

Poland again and the end of a long and bloody trail. At this time, when the ship was pulling into the port of Pahlevi, each of us was full of great expectations and confidence that through the sufferings and heartaches, our perseverance would not be in vain, that at the end of this hard road, there would be a free Poland.

For many of us later, it became a sad disillusion; for many, it ended only a dream. But in each heart, there always will be that eternal flame of love and longing, with which to carry each Pole through life and perhaps the life beyond...

For "Poland is not lost, as long as we are alive!"

"Jeszcze Polska nie zginela, puki my zyjemy!"

THE END

ABOUT THE AUTHOR

I was born in a small town of Eastern Poland. My vivid recollections are of being raised in a comfortable atmosphere of tranquility and culture rich in art, theater, and music. The war brought unforeseen changes and the end of a peaceful era. When destruction from German bombs had ceased, the people in the east of Poland faced another danger, the occupation of the Soviet troops. Our father was arrested immediately as an enemy of the "red regime" and a few months later we followed his fate. I was only sixteen when my family and I were pulled away from our home and country. We were forcibly taken and sent away to the Asiatic state of Kazakhstan in the year of 1940, where we were condemned to slave labor for the next three years, facing mistreatment, sickness, hunger and death till our release from bondage and a flight to freedom across the Caspian Sea to Iran where I met my husband, an American army Lieutenant.

Before meeting my husband, my family and I, lived in refugee camps in Teheran, later after the death of my mother, I was married in 1945. At that time we lived in southern Iran, in Khorromshahr on the Persian Gulf till my husband was shipped back to the U.S., leaving me to wait for a permit to enter the U.S. which came very much later in 1946, letting me arrive in New York. Barely acquainted with a new way of living in the great U.S., I was back on the trail, following my husband to Japan, where my son Chris was born. We spent four glorious years in the land of Rising Sun, then headed back to U.S. to circulate in several army posts finally settling in Washington D.C. where my daughter Tina was born. Next came Germany, a short stint and back to Wisconsin for a while then a stretch of four years in a vacation land, a seaside adventure in La Baule, France.- In 1960 we were back in the States and a time of retirement from the army but still in touch with a government. Our son, Chris, had volunteered for Vietnam and my husband working as a civil service, followed him. One year in Saigon and then back to Chicago long enough to pack again, moving to New England, Ayer MA. New life again, new friends and new interest in antiques. A few years and we were back Chicago with my husband enjoying a new profession, as Auctioneer "Colonel" Edwards.

It has been a glorious life, wonderful children, -no regrets except for the loss of my husband seven years ago. I am back at the keyboard, to bring to life our time in refugee camps in Iran.

Throughout the years of our roaming the world, each return became sentimental greeting with a warm feeling of being back home no matter what state or the corner of the U. S., it always was the safest place, the best, our land of Stars and Stripes and Freedom.

Printed in the United States
21435LVS00001B/158